Dr. Jillian T. Weiss

Transgender Workplace Diversity

ISBN: 978-1-4196-7328-3
Library of Congress Control Number: 2007905925
Publisher: BookSurge Publishing
North Charleston, South Carolina

Cover logo: Diane Goodman-Daniels

For Shayna

TABLE OF CONTENTS

3

Introduction

This book is intended for professionals in human resources, diversity and law who are faced with issues of transgender workplace diversity in the United States. In today's world, if you work for an organization that wishes to be considered an employer of choice, it is essential to understand transgender issues and how these play out in the organizational context. This book addresses transgender basics, gender identity law, policy issues, and gender transition guidelines. It specifically sets forth what steps to take and what issues to consider when confronted with an employee who wishes to transition from one gender to another. Not all transgender employees will wish to transition, but those who do present a major challenge to workplace diversity resources. The goal of this book is to develop cultural competence and knowledge resources so that transgender workplace diversity issues can be addressed successfully for everyone concerned.

This work is only an introduction to the issues that face employers of transgender workers. There is much more that could be said about these issues, and I plan a more comprehensive work for the future. However, it is my hope that this book will get some useful information into the hands of those now confronting these issues. At the same time, it is important to note that successful integration of transgender employees requires the introduction and negotiation of many changes in order to make an organization into a safe place for transgender employees. The issues are complicated by cultural and social mores that frown on transgender identity, and ignorance of the needs of transgender employees. Creating a safe environment for transgender workers requires three areas of action: policy development, training programs and communications planning and strategy. In my experience as a consultant to Fortune 500 companies, full development and implementation generally takes coordination among many departments and managers for a year or two.

This is designed to be a practical book. The main issue faced by HR and legal professionals in the organizational environment is what steps to take when notified of an imminent gender transition in the workplace. What should be done about facilities access, employment records, insurance benefits, and concerns of co-workers and customers? For this reason, the table of contents is issue-oriented, including such topics as medical issues, anti-discrimination statutes, policy tools for gender transition, and sample step-by-step guidelines for HR managers. The book starts with a discussion of transgender basics, moves to a brief analysis of the law of gender identity, gives information on some of the major policy issues, such as bathroom usage, and provides a comprehensive sample policy for gender transition. An Appendix includes the text of relevant regulations issued by OSHA, the EEOC and three major cities, as well as the major court opinions on Title VII, state disability statutes, and bathroom and dressing room usage. There is purposely no discussion of gender theory, legal history, medical controversies or other academic issues of secondary concern to HR and legal professionals. Such discussions are interesting, and I am planning a more academic treatment in the future. This volume, however, remains firmly rooted in the practical question: "What do I do now?"

My treatment of the subject comes from my academic and practical experience with workplace diversity issues over 20 years as a lawyer, professor, consultant and transgender woman. My background includes J.D. and Ph.D. degrees, 20 years in the corporate world, and successful track record in consulting with Fortune 500 companies and public agencies. I am the principal of Jillian T. Weiss & Associates, a consulting firm specifically devoted to transgender workplace diversity. I am also Associate Professor of Law and Society at Ramapo College. My research and consulting has involved hundreds of companies, and there are few situations I have not previously encountered. As a transgender woman, I am also sensitive to the social position occupied by transgender employees.

Updated information on the subjects addressed here may be found in my blog, "Transgender Workplace Diversity." There are monthly updates on transgender workplace topics and a subject index at http://transworkplace.blogspot.com. I hope you find this volume and the blog useful in your work. Feel free to contact me if I can be of any assistance on these issues.

Dr. Jillian T. Weiss
jtwassociates@gmail.com
201-684-7197
Blog: http://transworkplace.blogspot.com

Chapter 1

Transgender basics

A. Terminology

1. Transgender

The Oxford English Dictionary says that "transgender" refers to "identity that does not conform unambiguously to conventional notions of male or female gender, but combines or moves between these." This definition obscures the complexities of transgender identities, but is a useful place to start because it clearly conveys the challenges of the term. "Transgender" refers to a number of related identities, such as transsexuals, transvestites, crossdressers and genderqueers, which are defined and explained below. For this reason, it is often called an "umbrella" term. Each of these identities features ambiguity, combination and movement of gender attributes, though in different ways.

"Transgender" is not a unitary identity, and it includes several different types of people within its scope. For example, it would include both a person who has undergone surgical intervention to live full-time as a member of the opposite sex (sometimes referred to as a "transsexual"), and a person who occasionally cross-dresses in private (sometimes referred to as a "crossdresser"). There are other identities under this umbrella, such as "genderqueer," a formulation used mostly by young persons under 25, and defined by a combination of gender identities and sexual orientations. One example could be a person whose gendered presentation is sometimes perceived as male and sometimes as female but whose gender identity is female, gendered expression is "butch" and sexual orientation is lesbian.

The Oxford definition of transgender is by no means universally accepted, particularly by those who transition from one sex to another and identify only as their new sex. Their concern is that they will not be accepted fully in the new sex because of the idea that they are "ambiguous." They seek to avoid the labels of ambiguity and nonconformity. Another problem with Oxford definition is its implicit reliance on objective standards of binary gender, between which the individual oscillates. Some transgender individuals see gender as a continuum along which all people fall somewhere in the middle. It is also unclear whether the term is referring to an objective phenomenon that is determined by medical evidence, or a subjective self-identification that is decided upon by the individual. The Oxford definition tends to legitimize the idea that transgender people are "trapped" in the body of the opposite sex, requiring medical intervention for pathology, whereas many transgender people understand transgender behavior as matter of self-identification and free choice.

It should be noted that transgender identity is different from the sexual orientation of lesbians, gays, and bisexuals, because "transgender" refers to "gender identity," which is "our own deeply held conviction and deeply felt inner awareness that we belong to one gender or the other" "Transgender" also refers to "gender expression," the expression of behavioral characteristics that are culturally associated with the opposite sex*. The distinguishing characteristic is that transgender self-identification and self-expression as male or female does not correspond to the physical body in the usual way, which is not true of lesbian, gay or bisexual identity.

The term "transgender" was originally created in the 1980s (as "transgender<u>ist</u>") to refer to those who live in the opposite sex role, but

---

* The term "opposite sex" is problematic in discussions of transgender identity because it is unclear whether it refers to reassigned sex, and negates the idea of a gender continuum.

who do not opt for genital surgery, as opposed to the earlier word "transsexual," which refers to those who desire genital surgery. Since then, however, "transgender" has taken on a different usage as an umbrella term to denote transsexuals, transvestites, cross-dressers and anyone else whose "gender identity" or "gender expression" is variant from the binary norm. The most widely known transgender identity is that of post-operative transsexuals, who live in the opposite sex role from that of their birth and have received surgical and medical intervention to change their anatomical configuration to match that of the opposite sex. Many people think of this identity when they hear the word "transgender." There are, however, many different identities that fit within the transgender umbrella.

2. Gender Identity Disorder

The American Psychiatric Association's Diagnostic and Statistical Manual (referred to, in its current version, as "DSM IV") contains a reference to "Gender Identity Disorder" (GID). This is sometimes used to explain gender transition in the workplace. One of the difficulties of using DSM IV's Gender Identity Disorder description is that it is intended as a diagnostic tool for mental health professionals, and is often considered confusing by lay people. It also has a definition that is much more limited than the generally used concepts of "transgender" and "gender identity." This makes it difficult to use in the workplace setting because it may inappropriately limit diversity initiatives. In other words, a transgender worker may not fit the diagnostic criteria for GID at a particular point in time, but a diversity-friendly employer would nonetheless wish to accommodate the employee. In addition, non-discrimination statutes employ the concept of "gender identity," and it is not necessary to find that an employee has GID in order for such statutes to provide protection. Nonetheless, it is important for HR and legal personnel to understand that GID exists and has important consequences. An excerpt from the DSM IV follows, setting forth a description of the types of behaviors and identifications typical of GID:

There are two components of Gender Identity Disorder, both of which must be present to make the diagnosis. There must be evidence of a strong and persistent cross-gender identification, which is the desire to be, or the insistence that one is of the other sex (Criteria A). This cross-gender identification must not merely be a desire for any perceived cultural advantages of being the other sex. There must also be evidence of persistent discomfort about one's assigned sex or a sense of inappropriateness in the gender role of that sex (Criteria B). The diagnosis is not made if the individual has a concurrent physical intersex condition (e.g., androgen insensitivity syndrome or congenital adrenal hyperplasia) (Criteria C). To make the diagnosis, there must be evidence of clinically significant distress or impairment in social, occupational, or other important areas of functioning (Criteria D).

Adults with Gender Identity Disorder are preoccupied with their wish to live as a member of the other sex. This preoccupation may be manifested as an intense desire to adopt the social role of the other sex or to acquire the physical appearance of the other sex through hormonal or surgical manipulation. Adults with this disorder are uncomfortable being regarded by others as, or functioning in society as, a member of their designated sex. To varying degrees, they adopt the behavior, dress, and mannerisms of the other sex. In private, these individuals may spend much time cross-dressed and working on the appearance of being the other sex. Many attempt to pass in public as the other sex. With cross-dressing and hormonal treatment (and for males, electrolysis), many individuals with this disorder may pass convincingly as the other sex.

Differential Diagnosis

Gender Identity disorder can be distinguished from simple nonconformity to stereo-typical sex role behavior by the extent and pervasiveness of the cross-gender wishes, interests, and activities. This disorder is not meant to describe a child's nonconformity to stereotypic sex-role behavior as, for example, in "tomboyishness" in girls or "sissyish" behavior in boys. Rather, it represents a profound disturbance of the individual's sense of identity with regard to maleness or femaleness. Behavior in children that merely does not fit the cultural stereotype of masculinity or femininity should not be given the diagnosis unless the full syndrome is present, including marked distress or impairment.

Diagnostic Criteria for Gender Identity Disorder

A A strong, persistent cross-gender identification (not merely a desire for any perceived cultural advantages of being the other sex).

In adolescents and adults, the disturbance is manifested by symptoms such as a stated desire to be the other sex, frequent passing as the other sex, desire to live or be treated as the other sex, or the conviction that he or she has the typical feelings and reactions of the other sex.

B Persistent discomfort with his or her sex or sense of inappropriateness in the gender role of that sex.

In adolescents and adults, the disturbance is manifested by symptoms such as preoccupation with getting rid of primary and secondary sex characteristics (e.g., request for hormones, surgery, or other procedures to physically alter sexual characteristics to simulate the other sex) or belief that he or she was born the wrong sex.

C. The disturbance is not concurrent with physical intersex condition.

D. The disturbance causes clinically significant distress or impairment in social, occupational, or other important areas of functioning.

While the DSM IV is widely accepted among psychiatrists, some experts have suggested that the DSM IV diagnostic category is too limited in scope and should be expanded to include more non-traditional gender identities. Others contend that it contributes to perceptions of transgender identity as abnormal and should be eliminated. For HR and legal professionals, it is important both to know of its existence, and to be aware of its limitations.

3. Transsexual, Transvestite and Crossdresser

The term "transsexual" is a medical term from the early 20th century often used to refer to someone who identifies as a member of a sex different from that of their birth. It sometimes implies that one lives as a member of the opposite sex full time, and has changed their physical presentation through hormonal and surgical intervention. This presents a difference from the term "transgender," which refers to all people of non-traditional gender identity. While it is somewhat more specific than the term "transgender," the term "transsexual" is, nonetheless, also ambiguous. It is made ambiguous by the fact that those who intend to follow the course listed above, and those who wish to do so but are unable due to medical, financial or social restrictions, are often referred to as "transsexuals."

The term "transvestite" is another medical term, this time from the late 19th century, often used to refer to those who dress in clothing of the opposite sex. In its original usage, it made no distinctions based on motivation for cross-dressing, and applied equally to those we would now call transsexual or transgender. It is currently used by some in contradistinction to the term "crossdresser," which refers to a heterosexual man who enjoys dressing in stereotypically female clothing on a part-time basis, usually in private. As such, the terms transvestite and crossdresser have acquired an element of sexual orientation, in that "crossdresser" refers to a heterosexual man, and "transvestite" to a homosexual or bisexual man. This distinction is not universally acknowledged.

Because the meanings of these words have changed over time, many older books and materials use these terms in senses that are no longer current, making interpretation problematic. This is most difficult in the interpretation of legal texts, because their usage of these terms presume a set of relationships between "sex" and "gender" that are no longer current. Some courts, addressing the issue of employment discrimination, have presumed incorrectly that there is a precise line dividing "transvestite" and "transsexual," and that the line is marked by surgery. This is incorrect. Many of those who are classified as male-to-female "transvestites" have breast augmentation and facial feminization surgery. Many of those who are classified as female-to-male transsexuals can not have phalloplasty. These ontological arguments are beside the point, because all of these identities, crossdresser, transvestite and transsexual, involve gender identity and gender expression. If the principle of respect for identity is followed, then there can be no discrimination based simply on the fact that one identifies as a crossdresser rather than a transsexual.

4. Intersex

Intersex refers to a physical condition present at birth, in which physical attributes generally associated with the opposite sex are mixed. This may include chromosomes, endocrine systems, or gonads. Most "intersex" infants do not have two fully-formed sets of sex organs. The term "hermaphrodite" is an older term that is in occasional use today. It suggests the idea of a person who is both male and female by combining the names of the Greek gods Hermes and Aphrodite. It is considered a term to avoid, both because it is inaccurate and because it has become associated with sensationalism. To the contrary, transgender identity is generally considered to be formed no earlier than age 2, partly because gender expression does not occur prior to that time. However, there is some indication of cross-sex brain structures present at birth in transsexuals, and some expert speculate that there may be pre-birth hormonal influences.

There is controversy among intersex advocates whether intersex is a purely medical condition with no gender identity implications, or whether it should be classified as a social identity related to transgender identity. Those who favor the idea that it is a purely medical condition, and not a social identity, now refer to intersex as "Disorder of Sexual Differentiation" (DSD), a medical condition.

5. Gender identity

"Gender identity" refers to one's self-identification as male or female (or both or neither). It is "our own deeply held conviction and deeply felt inner awareness that we belong to one gender or the other." It may or may not correspond to one's biological sex. Gender identity is usually defined in statutes along these lines: "having or being perceived as having a gender related identity or expression whether or not stereotypically associated with a person's assigned sex at birth." It replaced an older term, "sexual identity," which is no longer used because it mixes elements of sex, gender and sexual orientation together.

6. Gender expression

"Gender expression" refers to the expression of behavioral characteristics that are culturally associated with sex. Gender expression may or may not correspond to gender identity. In other words, there are persons born male whose gender expression is feminine, and persons born female whose gender expression is masculine. This phrase does not refer to a person's identification as male or female. It should not be assumed that because a statute or policy refers only to "gender identity" that there is an implied exclusion of gender expression. Gender identity is often defined to include gender expression, and there is substantial overlap between the two.

7. Gender and sex

Sex is usually understood to include biological characteristics, whereas gender refers to the psychological, behavioral and social aspects of sex. Self-identification as male or female is an important aspect of gender. In addition, "masculine" and "feminine" genders are expressed in many forms, such as manner of speaking, walking, hair styling, clothing and other social cues. Masculinity and femininity come in many versions, variant according to age, place and time, and that which is considered masculine in one society may be considered feminine in another. In this sense, gender is more fluid than sex.

8. Gender transition

"Gender transition" refers to transition from living as a male to living as a female, or from female to male. It does not necessarily imply that one has had any medical or surgical intervention. Transition occurs when one feels strongly and persistently that his or her "gender identity" is different from the sex at birth. It involves a strong and persistent wish to transition from one gender to the other. It often takes a year or more, and usually involves the assistance of medical professionals. This is never undertaken on a whim, and the difficulties, both physical and psychological, cannot be overestimated.

9. Starting and ending points

There are various usages of the word transgender that correspond to different understandings of *when* a person is considered "transgender". Some argue that one is born transgender, although the discovery of this fact is necessarily delayed. In this interpretation, biological differences in the brain and in hormonal influences mark a difference at or before birth in the transgender infant, although the evidence for this is still being gathered. Others argue that one becomes transgender only when one has successful completed surgery to change sexual anatomy to match that of the opposite sex. In this interpretation, being "transgender" is correlated to taking a certain action, that of a change in sexual anatomy by surgical means. Yet others argue that the significant fact is not surgery, but the *decision* to undergo the change, although the surgery itself may be many years away. When one decides to undergo the surgery, one declares oneself "transgender." Still others argue that the significant fact is the perception of difference: one's gender identity differs from social norms, whether or not one does or does not eventually undergo sex reassignment surgery. When one realizes that the internal recognition of being a boy or a girl is at odds with what one is being told by parents and others, at that moment, one becomes "transgender," whether or not any medical or surgical intervention occurs later. It is the life-plot, rather than actual somatic sex change that characterizes the transgender person.

Some, however, use the term "transgender" in such a way as to imply that this status ends permanently when the person unambiguously assumes the opposite sex. In other words, a person prior to surgery is "trans-gender" because there is an incongruity between their physical anatomy and their psychological gender. Once that incongruity is fixed, then the person is no longer "trans," and their sex is congruent with their gender. Thus, the person is now unambiguously female (or male) and not transgender. Others say, however, that transgender status never ends because it marks the fact that a change has taken place. Thus, after surgery, the person is still transgender. Yet others dispute both of these interpretations, and choose to go with self-identification as a marker. In other words, being "transgender" is a self-identification, not a label that others may assign. Thus, if a person identifies as transgender, then they are. If they choose not to do so, then they are not transgender, regardless of any transition.

The different meanings assigned to the word "transgender" are confusing. It is not important for most HR and legal professionals to have an intimate grasp of the different meanings, however. The important thing is to know that different usages exist. For purposes of the workplace, the most significant issue in transgender identity occurs

16

when an employee notifies the company that he or she wishes to transition from one gender to another. At that point, all of these theoretical considerations are irrelevant to the practice issue of what steps to take to accommodate the employee.

B. The Gender Transition Process

There is more than one way to transition, though there are medical standards of care issued by the World Professional Association for Transgender Health (WPATH) that suggest some steps. The full text of the WPATH Standards of Care can be found at the organization's website at WPATH.com. It is important to note that the order of the steps listed in the Standards of Care do not necessarily occur in the order listed there, so there is no single timeline of gender transition that can be applied to all situations. Often, however, gender transition begins with administration of cross-gender hormones. Section VII of the Standards of Care discusses requirements for hormone therapy. There are two sets of criteria: eligibility and readiness. To summarize the eligibility criteria, one must be over 18, understand the benefits and risks of hormones, and have three months of real-life experience in the opposite gender role (or have 3-6 months of psychotherapy). The readiness criteria specify consolidation of gender identity (i.e., clarity around gender identity and expression), stable mental health, and likelihood of taking hormones responsibly.

When transgender health professionals look at whether or not a person's real-life experience is successful, they look at the following:

1. maintaining full or part-time employment;
2. functioning as a student;
3. functioning in community-based volunteer activity;
4. undertaking some combination of items 1-3;
5. acquiring a (legal) gender-identity-appropriate first name;

6. documentation that persons other than the therapist know that the patient functions in the desired gender role.

Some find that the real-life experience confirms their decision; others learn that living the opposite gender role is not what they expected. WPATH notes that the purpose of the real-life experience is to test the person's resolve, the capacity to function in the preferred gender, and the adequacy of social, economic, and psychological supports, helping the patient and the mental health professional in judging how to proceed. When the patient is successful in the real-life experience, both the mental health professional and the patient gain confidence in undertaking further steps.

After the real-life experience is successful, a person may decide to obtain surgery to aid in sex reassignment. It is important to note that "sex reassignment surgery" (SRS) is not a single procedure. For example, female to male transgenders may undergo one or more of the following: hysterectomy (removal of the uterus), salpingo-oophorectomy (removal of the fallopian tubes), vaginectomy (removal of the vagina), metoidioplasty (removal of the skin bridge between clitoris and labia, scrotoplasty (creation of a scrotum), urethroplasty (lengthening of the urethra), placement of testicular prostheses (for simulation of the male testicles and erectile function), and phalloplasty (creation of a penis). Each operation may be considered a form of surgery intended to aid in "sex reassignment". Male to female transgenders may undergo one or more of the following: orchiectomy (removal of the testicles), penectomy (removal of the penis), vaginoplasty (creation of a vagina), clitoroplasty (creation of a clitoris) and labiaplasty (creation of labia). There are also cosmetic surgeries designed to provide a more feminine or masculine appearance to the face. Each of these may be considered a form of surgery intended to aid in "sex reassignment".

The WPATH requirements for eligibility and readiness for genital surgery can be found in Section XII of the WPATH Standards of Care. The eligibility requirements include:

1. Legal age of majority in the patient's nation;
2. Usually 12 months of continuous hormonal therapy for those without a medical contraindication
3. 12 months of successful continuous full time real-life experience. Periods of returning to the original gender may indicate ambivalence about proceeding and generally should not be used to fulfill this criterion;
4. If required by the mental health professional, regular responsible participation in psychotherapy throughout the real life experience at a frequency determined jointly by the patient and the mental health professional. Psychotherapy per se is not an absolute eligibility criterion for surgery;
5. Demonstrable knowledge of the cost, required lengths of hospitalizations, likely complications, and post-surgical rehabilitation requirements of various surgical approaches;
6. Awareness of different competent surgeons.

The two readiness requirements are:

1. Demonstrable progress in consolidating one's gender identity;
2. Demonstrable progress in dealing with work, family, and interpersonal issues resulting in a significantly better state of mental health; this implies satisfactory control of problems such as sociopathy, substance abuse, psychosis, suicidality, for instance).

Those who attempt to define transgender by reference to medical or surgical procedures often fail to appreciate the wide variety of medical and surgical interventions. Such definitions are problematic because not all interventions are available to everyone, whether because of medical conditions, financial issues, or the state of the art. For example, surgeons have not advanced the state of the art for female-to-male transsexuals as far as the better-perfected techniques for male-to-female transsexuals. If genital surgery is the *sine qua non* of transgender status, this means that many female-to-male transsexuals must choose between poor surgical results for phalloplasty (creation of a penis) and the right to live in their chosen sex. For this reason (and many others too numerous to mention here), female-to-male transsexuals are not simply the surgical inverse of male-to-female transsexuals, and these groups have separate and distinct medical issues. "Transgender" cannot be simply defined by reference to surgery.

C. Medical issues impacting the workplace

Because WPATH (the World Professional Association for Transgender Health) recommends one year of living full time in the opposite sex role prior to surgery, an employee who transitions to living in another gender will usually do so prior to sex reassignment surgery, but after hormone administration. Thus, at a certain point, the transitioning employee will come to work dressed as and interacting as another gender. Sometime later, when the employee has received approvals from psychotherapists and surgeons, leave will be needed for various types of surgery in aid of sex reassignment. There are some questions as to whether such leave is covered by the Family and Medical Leave Act (FMLA). Different employers have had different responses to these questions. These issues should be discussed with a transitioning employee so that all concerned are clear about the employer's position.

Various types of surgery require different amounts of leave. Breast augmentation or reduction and facial cosmetic surgeries generally require a week or two of recovery time, depending on the healing time of the individual. Genital surgeries usually require about a month, though some people are able to spring back to work after a week, and others require two months. Complications from genital surgeries are rare, but can be serious, and may require additional leave time. These complications can make cause problems for sitting, walking and lifting, and may constitute short-term disabilities requiring reasonable accommodation in the workplace.

Administration of cross-sex hormones may cause difficulties with health insurance carriers and prescription coverage. It is recommended that contact be made with the insurance carrier to ensure that they will provide appropriate coverage for medications. Some carriers and some employers also cover certain costs for some sex reassignment surgeries. These issues may need to be negotiated by benefits administrators in order to support their transgender employees in the face of confusing and conflicting insurance provisions.

D. Physical changes to expect

The hormonal interventions intended to aid in sex reassignment sometimes precede living in the new gender, and sometimes follow, depending upon decisions made by the psychotherapist and patient. Administration of cross-gender hormones creates major physical changes in a relatively short period of time.

Female to male transgenders usually receive injections of testosterone. Within three months of continuous administration, this causes facial hair to begin growing, hardening and coarsening of the skin, thickening of the vocal cords and consequent extreme deepening of voice, redistribution of fat reserves from the skin, hips, cheeks and breasts to the stomach, chin and arms, and enlargement of the clitoris. The effect seems to be inversely related to age and increases with time of administration, taking full effect within three years. Testosterone does not reduce breast tissue, and chest surgery is necessary to remove the female breasts. Some people report feelings of competitive urges and aggressiveness after administration of testosterone; others do not.

Male to female transgenders may receive oral administration or injections of estrogens. Within six months of continuous administration, this causes softening of the skin, growth of breast tissue (with full effect reputedly being one cup size lower than the average of close female relatives), redistribution of fat reserves from the stomach, chin and arms to the skin, hips, cheeks and breasts, and reduction of the penis and testicles (and eventual loss of erectile function). It does not remove facial hair, for which electrolysis or laser hair removal are required. It also has no effect on the voice, although voice exercises can be extremely effective. Some people report feelings of calmness and peacefulness after administration of estrogen; others do not.

When an employee transitions to living in the opposite gender, one should expect to see clothes and styling of that gender on the start date. These clothes should be in accord with the company dress code, and it is likely that the transgender employee will dress in a manner similar to others at the organization. In other words, if the attire worn by most females in the department is that of a business suit, one should expect to see the transgender employee adopt similar dress. In other words, a male-to-female transgender employee is not likely to come to work in a wedding gown or a miniskirt, nor is a female-to-male transgender employee likely to come to work in cowboy chaps or a muscle tee. If a transgender employee were to wear inappropriate clothing to the job, he or she should be advised of the problem, as with any employee.

Beyond the change in clothes, one may see changes in hair styling, gait, voice tone, facial makeup and jewelry choices. Continued hormone administration will cause further changes over the next two years. Some surgical procedures, such as breast removal or breast augmentation, and facial cosmetic surgeries, will cause sudden

22

changes that co-workers will notice. Genital surgery, however, which often receives much of the attention in thinking about sex reassignment, paradoxically causes no change at all in appearance, as it affects an area that is usually covered in the workplace. For this reason, genital surgery is of relative unimportance for the workplace.

Chapter 2

Gender Identity Law

A. Types of law in the United States

One of the first questions often asked about transgender workplace diversity is whether it is legally required, because transgender identity is not listed as a protected category in the main U.S. federal employment non-discrimination law, Title VII of the Civil Rights Act of 1964. While transgender identity is not listed as a protected category in Title VII, some federal courts have interpreted Title VII's prohibition on sex discrimination to include transgender identity. These include, at the time of this writing, one Circuit Court, the 6th Circuit, and seven federal district courts in Arizona, District of Columbia, New York, Oregon, Pennsylvania, Tennessee, and Washington. The Sixth Circuit's opinion in Smith v. City of Salem, finding legal protection for transgender employees in Title VII, is found in the Appendix. There is also federal legislation pending on the subject, the Employment Non-Discrimination Act. At the time of this writing, it is expected to pass Congress, but the possibility of a veto has not yet been addressed.

In addition to federal law, there are currently twelve states prohibiting gender identity discrimination in employment by state statute, including California, Colorado, Iowa, Illinois, Maine, Minnesota, New Jersey, New Mexico, Oregon, Rhode Island, Vermont and Washington. Ten states have other law, like court rulings or regulations, which prohibits gender identity discrimination in employment, including Connecticut, Florida, Hawaii, Kentucky, Massachusetts, Michigan, New Hampshire, New York, Ohio, and Tennessee. The District of Columbia also has a statute prohibiting gender identity discrimination in employment. There are also about eighty U.S. cities that have such laws.

Cities with ordinances that protect against employment discrimination on the basis of gender identity are, at the time of this writing, as follows:

Tucson, City of	AZ	Lexington-Fayette, County of	KY
West Hollywood, City of	CA	Covington, City of	KY
Los Angeles, City of	CA	New Orleans, City of	LA
San Diego, City of	CA	Northampton, City of	MA
San Francisco, City of	CA	Boston, City of	MA
Santa Cruz, County of	CA	Cambridge, City of	MA
Santa Cruz, City of	CA	Baltimore, City of	MD
Oakland, City of	CA	East Lansing, City of	MI
San Jose, City of	CA	Grand Rapids, City of	MI
Boulder, City of	CO	Ypsilanti, City of	MI
Denver, City of	CO	Ann Arbor, City of	MI
Washington, City of	DC	Huntington Woods, City of	MI
Monroe, County of	FL	St. Paul, City of	MN
Key West, City of	FL	Minneapolis, City of	MN
West Palm Beach, City of	FL	University City, City of	MO
Miami Beach, City of	FL	New York, City of	NY
Decatur, City of	GA	Rochester, City of	NY
Atlanta, City of	GA	Suffolk, County of	NY
Iowa City, City of	IA	Ithaca, City of	NY
Urbana, City of	IL	Albany, City of	NY
Springfield, City of	IL	Buffalo, City of	NY
Peoria, City of	IL	Tompkins, County of	NY
Bloomington, City of	IL	Toledo, City of	OH
Carbondale, City of	IL	Cincinnati, City of	OH
Chicago, City of	IL	Portland, City of	OR
Cook, County of	IL	Salem, City of	OR
Champaign, City of	IL	Beaverton, City of	OR
Evanston, City of	IL	Multnomah, County of	OR
DeKalb, City of	IL	Lake Oswego, City of	OR
Decatur, City of	IL	Hillsboro, City of	OR
Indianapolis, City of and	IN	Bend, City of	OR
Marion County		Benton, County of	OR
Bloomington, City of	IN	Lincoln City	OR
Louisville, City of	KY	Erie, County of	PA
Jefferson, County of	KY	Allentown, City of	PA

25

Swarthmore, City Of	PA	Austin, City of	TX
York, City of	PA	El Paso, City of	TX
Philadelphia, City of	PA	Tacoma, City of	WA
New Hope, Borough of	PA	Seattle, City of	WA
Easton, City of	PA	Burien, City of	WA
Lansdowne, Borough of	PA	King, County of	WA
Pittsburgh, City of	PA	Olympia, City of	WA
Scranton	PA	Dane, County of	WI
Harrisburg, City of	PA	Madison, City of	WI
Dallas, City of	TX		

(Human Rights Campaign 2007)

In terms of pending legislation to create new state statutes that include gender identity, there are six currently pending at the time of this writing: Indiana, Massachusetts, Michigan, Montana, New York and Pennsylvania. (Note that these numbers are subject to change, and will probably have changed by the time you read this.)

Most statutes that seek to protect transgender workers add the terms "gender identity or expression" to their existing civil rights statutes. This phrase is variously defined, as explained in more detail in the next section, but generally refers to an individual's sense of gender, whether traditional or non-traditional. On the state level, the statutes usually provide for a civil penalty, and sometimes a criminal one as well. The criminal penalty would usually be assessed by the state's attorney general. This is fairly rare, and usually requires a widespread pattern or practice of discrimination. More usual is the situation where an employee sues for a recovery of damages in a civil lawsuit, often seeking damages for back pay, future economic loss and punitive or treble damages.

For those who are unclear about the differences between statutes and other types of law protecting gender identity, I note that a statute is a written law passed by a legislative body, such as Congress, which can apply to all persons in the jurisdiction. By contrast, a court ruling or order is an opinion written by a judge, who is part of the judicial branch, in the context of a suit, applicable only to the parties to the suit, though potentially applicable to all persons in the court's jurisdiction in a later lawsuit. Unless one is legally trained, it is hard to find and interpret court opinions.

An administrative regulation is a written policy enacted by the executive branch of government, such as the President or one of his or her agencies, such as the FBI, under a specific grant of authority in a statute. Executive orders are a form of administrative regulation. These are similar to statutes, in that they are written, but they are different in the sense that they may be rewritten by the government agency that promulgated them at any time, so long as the proper procedure is followed.

There also administrative tribunals, which make rulings similar to a court, but which are part of an executive agency, and are subject to approval by the head of the agency. These rulings can be overturned by the courts.

The protection afforded to transgender employees by virtue of these different types of law are dependent on the type of law involved. For example, a ruling by the local Human Rights Commission, which interprets "sex discrimination" to include transgender identity, may not carry as much weight as a state statute that explicitly includes gender identity. To understand the legal protections afforded to an employee in a particular situation, it is best to get an informed legal opinion on the subject.

B. Statutory definitions

Most statutes prohibiting discrimination against transgender persons do not use the term "transgender". Rather, they use the term "gender identity or expression." When a statute uses this term, it refers to protection of both traditional and non-traditional gender identity.

Thus, both transgender employees and non-transgender employees are protected from adverse action based on their gender identity.

Some statutes include "gender expression" in the statutory formulation, and some do not. The purpose of this addition is to make it clear that employees are protected not only on the basis of their identification as male or female (or neither or both), but also on the basis of the way that they express their gender in the workplace. In other words, action may not be taken against a male because he has feminine attire and makeup, or a female who has a masculine haircut, suit and tie. While this additional terminology of "gender expression" is helpful to clarify the intent, it should not be assumed that absence of the phrase means that only "bona fide transsexuals" are protected. One does not need to declare one's intent to change sex or adopt a new sex in order to be protected by the law, as the definition of "gender identity" is usually broad enough to cover gender expression as well.

I note that the phrase is "gender identity OR expression," not "gender identity AND expression." These two alternative formulations have quite different meanings. "OR" might seem an unimportant word, but if you said yes to a hot dog with either ketchup OR mustard, and you got both ketchup AND mustard, you'd know why OR is an important word. The disjunctive "or" makes it clearer that discrimination is prohibited based on "gender identity" alone, regardless of whether a person exhibits particular gendered behaviors or not. Similarly, discrimination based on "gender expression" alone is prohibited, regardless of whether a person identifies as a different sex or not.

While most statutory definitions do not use the term "transgender," the one exception is Cincinnati. By use of the term "transgender", the Cincinnati ordinance only protects the non-traditionally gendered. This is out of sync with most anti-discrimination statutes, which attempt to cover the category generally, not just one group within it. In addition, the term "transgender" is generally considered too imprecise for statutory usage. The Cincinnati definition is:

3

"'Transgendered' shall mean the condition or state wherein a person manifests gender characteristics, behavior, and/or self-identification typical of or commonly associated with persons of another gender, and which may be characterized by assumption of the clothes, hairstyles, cosmetic usage or other appearance qualities commonly associated with another gender and/or by the surgical or medical modification of primary sexual organs in order to assume the gender role of another sex.

A statute prohibiting discrimination based on "transgender status" is rather unusual. It means that someone who was dismissed because they were not transgender would have no protection under that statute. While this situation is unlikely, it could raise the question of whether the law fails to provide equal protection to the traditionally gendered.

The Cincinnati definition is similar to others to the extent that it contains the usual tri-partite reference to gendered identification, self-expression and appearance.

- "Identification" means referring to oneself as male, female or other
- "Expression" means masculine/feminine body language, gait, and communication style, etc.
- "Appearance" covers gendered items like beards, short hair, makeup, heels, etc.

Thus, the statute covers the same territory as most other statutes on the subject, except that it only applies to transgender identity.

As an example of non-discrimination legislation, the New Jersey bill that recently added "gender identity or expression" to the list of classes protected from discrimination is interesting. It amends several statutes, and affects more than just employment actions. It affects public contracts, public accommodations, housing, and credit and lending transactions. These provisions are typical of a comprehensive non-discrimination bill. Not all of the states that have passed legislation prohibiting discrimination based on gender identity have included such comprehensive language. An example of this is Hawaii, which prohibits discrimination based on gender in housing, but not in employment.

The New Jersey law defines "gender identity or expression" as "having or being perceived as having a gender related identity or expression whether or not stereotypically associated with a person's assigned sex at birth." Title 10:5-5(rr). Originally, the statute had a line after this, similar to the Cincinnati formulation, reading 'Gender identity or expression' includes transgender status." The line was deleted after legislation specialists from the National Lesbian and Gay Task Force sent a letter of explanation to the committee overseeing the legislation. A discussion of this issue is found below.

The New Jersey bill contains a number of provisions that preserve traditional understandings of sexual difference in public accommodations and employment. Title 10:5-12 (f)(1) contains an exception that allows for single sex accommodations:

> provided, however, that nothing contained herein shall be construed to bar any place of public accommodation which is in its nature reasonably restricted exclusively to individuals of one sex, and which shall include but not be limited to any summer camp, day camp, or resort camp, bathhouse, dressing room, swimming pool, gymnasium, comfort station, dispensary, clinic or hospital, or school or educational institution which is restricted exclusively to individuals of one sex, provided individuals shall be admitted based on their gender identity or expression, from refusing, withholding from or denying to any individual of the opposite sex any of the accommodations, advantages, facilities or privileges thereof on the basis of sex; provided further, that the foregoing limitation shall not

apply to any restaurant as defined in R.S.33:1-1 or place where alcoholic beverages are served.

When boiled down, this says that the statute doesn't prevent women-only (or men-only) place of public accommodation, such as a summer camp, from serving only one sex, provided that they respect people's gender identity. That's a mite confusing, but after you parse it, you can see that it simply preserves the right to have a single sex facility, and transgender people must be admitted to the facility according to their gender identity or expression.

Title 10:5-12 (g)(3) contains a similar exception for single-sex housing: "that nothing contained in this subsection shall be construed to bar any person from refusing to sell, rent, lease, assign or sublease or from advertising or recording a qualification as to sex for any room, apartment, flat in a dwelling or residential facility which is planned exclusively for and occupied by individuals of one sex to any individual of the exclusively opposite sex on the basis of sex, provided individuals shall be qualified based on their gender identity or expression.

As before, it preserves the right to have a single-sex facility, but nevertheless allows admission to transgender people based on their gender identity.

Title 10:5-12(p) specifically addresses workplace dress codes. "Nothing in the provisions of this section shall affect the ability of an employer to require employees to adhere to reasonable workplace appearance, grooming and dress standards not precluded by other provisions of State or federal law, except that an employer shall allow an employee to appear, groom and dress consistent with the employee's gender identity or expression." The key word here, of course, is "reasonable," which in legalspeak means "socially acceptable." Since differential dress codes for men and women are socially acceptable, this section permits such a dress code. However, as courts have noted, dress codes may not impose an unequal burden on men and women, so there are some limitations.

Looking at the wider picture, advocacy groups have noted that passage of the New Jersey transgender equality law makes New Jersey the third most populous state to outlaw discrimination based on gender identity, and that laws now protect one-third of the US population based on gender identity or expression.

As noted above, the New Jersey statute in an early form included the term "transgender." An excerpt from a letter by Lisa Mottet, legislative lawyer for the Transgender Civil Rights Project of the National Gay and Lesbian Task Force, explained with exceptional clarity why this was inappropriate. In it, she delineates why the language should be removed, and I think she did an excellent job of explaining clearly and comprehensively why the term "transgender" is not useful for legislative drafting or corporate policy.

> The first reason is that the meaning of the term "transgender" is in constantly in flux and is likely to be historically limited. The term "transgenderist" was developed decades ago to refer to people who crossdressed but did not want or could not access sex reassignment surgery. Over the following decades, "transsexual" was reserved for people who had surgery and "transgender" meant those who did not. "Transvestite" was often used as an umbrella term. In the 1990s, transgender started to become an umbrella term that referred to the entire community: transsexuals, crossdressers, androgynous people, and gender-nonconforming people. "Transsexual" came to mean anyone who transitions from one gender to the other socially and/or medically (surgery not required).
>
> Although most LGBT activists still use the term "transgender" as an umbrella term, in my experience, the general public and LGBT people who are not activists tend to believe that transgender and transsexual are precise synonyms. In addition,

there is much current debate within the LGBT community about whether or not the term "transgender" inherently includes "gender non-conforming people." Different LGBT and transgender organizations use these terms differently. For example, the Sylvia Rivera Law Project, a legal services group for transgender people in New York, consistently uses "transgender and gender non-conforming people" instead of just "transgender" as my organization chooses to do.

As another demonstration of how quickly this term is changing meaning, in 2000 my organization published Transgender Equality and in it, we included drag queens, drag kings and intersex people in the transgender umbrella. In our 2003 publication, Transitioning Our Shelters: A Guide to Making Homeless Shelters Safe for Transgender People, we made the decision to remove those identities from the definition of transgender. If history is to be any guide, I expect the definition of transgender within the transgender community, in the LGBT community, and in the larger public arena will continue to be debated. And, I believe the meaning of the term will continue to evolve, and it is possible that it will fall out of use entirely.

Moreover, I am concerned that "transgender" may not retain its positive, non-derogatory meaning. In an example from the transgender context, in the early 1980s, Seattle passed a trans-inclusive nondiscrimination law using the broad term (they thought): transvestite. This term has since taken a negative and more limited connotation, causing the Seattle City Council to need to revise its nondiscrimination law only about twenty years later. Terms from other contexts involving groups of people who experience discrimination that demonstrate my concern about popular terminology acquiring a negative connotation include "colored people" and "handicapped." "Transgender" may not always have a positive connotation and may fall out of favor.

The second concern is that the bill, before the amendment, utilized the best approach for discrimination protections: it used terminology that covers all people, rather than a specific, protected group of people. American non-discrimination laws are generally framed to prohibit discrimination on the basis of certain characteristics, like sex or race, not specific examples of people within those categories, like women or African-Americans. Just as it was unnecessary and would have been inadvisable to add "Race includes black status" to race discrimination laws, this "transgender status" clarifying amendment could unintentionally have a limiting or confusing effect on interpretations of the law. Adding just this one group-based identity to the bill's language makes the bill conceptually incoherent and inconsistent with similar laws; either problem could negatively affect the interpretation of its provisions.

Our third concern is that this language is out-of-step with other laws protecting transgender and gender non-conforming people from discrimination. Eight states have passed similar laws, and none of them use the term "transgender people" or any similar term. No other state legislature, administrative agency or court has found that this type of clarifying amendment was necessary, nor has there been confusion that transgender people are not covered by these laws. Also, in drafting the federal Employment Non-Discrimination Act, which is expected to be introduced this Spring, the LGBT attorneys involved in drafting, including myself, specifically rejected using the term "transgender" for many of the reasons covered in this letter. For consistency throughout the nation, and for New Jersey to be in-step with the federal bill that will eventually become law, it is best that New Jersey use relatively similar language. With similar language throughout the U.S., courts can utilize each other's interpretations to develop a common case law that all jurisdictions can draw upon. For your reference, the definitional language of the eight states is attached as an Appendix.

Our fourth concern is about the term "status." How it would be interpreted in this context is unclear. Would transgender people have to prove that they have achieved "status?" Would someone in the early stages of transition (often when discrimination occurs) qualify as having attained that status? "Status" implies a fixity that does not capture or address the reality of discrimination against transgender people.

Our fifth concern is not about New Jersey's interpretations, but is about future interpretations of other state and federal laws. Including this term in New Jersey's law could cast doubt on what is covered by laws in other jurisdictions that do not include such language. It could beg the question, are transgender people not covered if the law only includes "gender identity or expression?" From a national perspective, the language used in New Jersey could influence other jurisdictions to either adopt the same language (cause for concern by itself for the above-mentioned reasons) and/or could negatively affect the interpretation of similar laws that lack New Jersey's additional sentence.

Thus, in conclusion, nondiscrimination laws should use terminology that is not subject to historical limitations and that is sure to cover everyone exhibiting the protected characteristic, regardless if they are amongst the class or group of people most often discriminated against. Furthermore, New Jersey's statutory scheme is best served by adopting language similar to those eight other states that have already enacted protections based on gender identity and/or expression. No other state has used the term "transgender" or "transgender status" in its discrimination law and doing so opens up the bill to unknown and potentially negative interpretations in the future.

Ms. Mottet's letter makes crystal clear the importance of word choice in drafting statutes and corporate policies that will govern the lives of thousands in many different circumstances. Based on her letter, the sponsors of the New Jersey bill reworked the statute to remove the word "transgender."

Another difficulty in corporate policy is the fact that, if the organization is large and distributed, it will be required to cover many different U.S. jurisdictions with different definitions of "gender identity." These differences should be kept in mind when creating corporate policy, lest the policy unintentionally create conflicts with state or city laws. This is an excellent reason for federal legislation on the subject. Here is a partial list of state statutory definitions. Note the differences among the formulations. It is likely that courts will come up with some distinctions based on these differences in the future.

California (2003)
Cal. Gov't Code § 12926(p):
"Sex" includes, but is not limited to, pregnancy, childbirth, or medical conditions related to pregnancy or childbirth. "Sex" also includes, but is not limited to, a person's gender, as defined in Section 422.56 of the Penal Code.

Cal. Penal Code, § 422.56:"Gender" means sex, and includes a person's gender identity and gender related appearance and behavior whether or not stereotypically associated with the person's assigned sex at birth.

Hawai'i (housing and public accommodations discrimination only) (2005)
HI ST § 515-2:
"Gender identity or expression" includes a person's actual or perceived gender, as well as a person's gender identity, gender-related self-image, gender-related appearance, or gender-related expression, regardless of whether that gender identity, gender-related self-image,

11

gender-related appearance, or gender-related expression is different from that traditionally associated with the person's sex at birth.

Illinois (2005)
775 ILCS 5/1-102:
"Sexual orientation" means actual or perceived heterosexuality, homosexuality, bisexuality, or gender-related identity, whether or not traditionally associated with the person's designated sex at birth. "Sexual orientation" does not include a physical or sexual attraction to a minor by an adult.

Maine (2005)
ME ST T. 5 § 4553(9-C):
"Sexual orientation means a person's actual or perceived heterosexuality, bisexuality, homosexuality or gender identity or expression.

Minnesota (1993)
Minn. Stat. Ann. § 363A.03(44):
"Sexual orientation means having or being perceived as having an emotional, physical, or sexual attachment to another person without regard to the sex of that person or having or being perceived as having an orientation for such attachment, or having or being perceived as having a self-image or identity not traditionally associated with one's biological maleness or femaleness. "Sexual orientation" does not include a physical or sexual attachment to children by an adult.

New Mexico (2003)
N.M. Stat. Ann. § 28-1-2(Q):
"Gender identity" means a person's self-perception, or perception of that person by another, of the person's identity as a male or female based upon the person's appearance, behavior or physical characteristics that are in accord with or opposed to the person's physical anatomy, chromosomal sex or sex at birth.

Rhode Island (2001)

R.I. Gen. Laws § 11-24-2.1(l):
The term "gender identity or expression" includes a person's actual or perceived gender, as well as a person's gender identity, gender-related self image, gender-related appearance, or gender-related expression; whether or not that gender identity, gender-related self image, gender-related appearance, or gender-related expression is different from that traditionally associated with the person's sex at birth.

Washington State (2006)
Wash. Rev. Code § 49.60.040 (15):
"Sexual orientation" means heterosexuality, homosexuality, bisexuality, and gender expression or identity. As used in this definition, "gender expression or identity" means having or being perceived as having a gender identity, self-image, appearance, behavior, or expression, whether or not that gender identity, self-image, appearance, behavior, or expression is different from that traditionally associated with the sex assigned to that person at birth.

Speaking of federal legislation, there is a bill pending in Congress at the time of this writing to eliminate discrimination based on sexual orientation and gender identity. This bill explicitly defines "gender identity" in Section 3 (a):

> (6) GENDER IDENTITY- The term `gender identity' means the gender-related identity, appearance, or mannerisms or other gender-related characteristics of an individual, with or without regard to the individual's designated sex at birth.

This definition is somewhat different from the state statutes, but it makes explicit the tripartite nature of gender identity: self-identification, behavior and dress. Statutory definitions will continue to evolve, as happens in the law, and courts may interpret them differently. There is no way to predict how this will play out in the future, so it promises to be an interesting area of legal and social change.

Chapter 3

Policy Issues and Tools

A. The Gender Transition Plan

There are many foreseeable issues to be addressed in a corporate policy on gender transition. When an employee is about to transition, there are a number of items that should be set down in writing so that expectations can be managed. In this section, I will discuss some of the more difficult issues that need to be arranged before a plan can be created, including bathrooms and dressing rooms, dress codes, identification and records changes, and health benefits. (In the next section, there is a draft gender transition plan that can be adapted for use in your organization.) I have discussed bathrooms and dressing rooms first, because they raise the most difficult issues, though their solution is usually far simpler than first appears. Dress codes raise some issues, but by and large, most dress codes in the U.S. are gender neutral, and occupation-appropriate clothing is required for everyone, so there should be no problem insuring that transgender personnel conform. Identification and records changes pose some problems as well, particularly as corporate records interface with government records. In my experience, however, relatively few cases involve government problems, and those can be worked out fairly simply. Health benefits are tricky because health insurers can create many obstacles, but sympathetic benefit managers can usually help smooth them over. Understanding these issues before the problem arises can help you prevent small problems from blowing up into big problems.

15

B. Bathrooms and Dressing Rooms

1. Legal considerations

Bathrooms and dressing rooms bring up a question that I often get in my consulting practice: what if someone just pretends to be have a female gender identity, but they do so falsely in order to obtain sexual gratification from the presence of females? This is of great concern for many people, who feel that, while they would like to respect a transgender employee's gender identity, to do so would conflict with the rights of female employees.

My answer is that, after a decade of work in this field, I have *never* heard of a situation where a person used a false claim of gender identity for that purpose. I have certainly heard of a few cases where a man dressed as a woman in order to commit a crime and escape detection (though of course, having heard of the cases, the attempts were obviously not successful). I have also heard about men committing crimes in women's bathrooms. But these cases all involved an attempt to escape notice, not to call attention to false claims about gender identity. More significantly, those cases were not spurred by the passage of a gender identity non-discrimination law. Now what if, you think, what if some crafty male, spurred by this new law, were to come up with a lascivious plan to lurk in the women's restroom and then, when confronted by the police about his harassing behavior, claim that he was entitled to commit harassment because of his gender identity? The answer is that harassing behavior is not permitted regardless of one's gender. If I am standing in the women's restroom and the woman next to me puts her hand on my thigh, that's harassment, and it doesn't matter if she claims gender identity issues or not.

Nonetheless, the question still remains as to whether it is legally required to allow a transgender employee to use the restroom of his or her new sex. While many places in the U.S. have laws prohibiting discrimination based on gender identity, this does not necessarily settle the question of which bathrooms and dressing rooms should be used by transgender people. There are two published court cases discussing whether a statute prohibiting gender identity discrimination affects the right of a transgender person to use the bathroom of their new gender identity. In both cases, one in New York and one in Minnesota, the courts denied the right of the plaintiff to use the bathroom of their new gender identity.

In the 2005 New York case, Hispanic AIDS Forum v. Bruno, a NYC building owner allegedly refused to renew a lease of office space because of the use of public bathrooms by transgender clients of the tenant, a social service agency. NYC law prohibits discrimination based on "gender identity." Nonetheless, the majority opinion held that the law did not require the building owner to honor the gender identity of the Forum's transgender clients for purposes of bathroom use.

"Gender" in the City Code was redefined in 2002 as "a person's gender identity, self-image, appearance, behavior or expression, whether or not that gender identity, self-image, appearance, behavior or expression is different from that traditionally associated with the legal sex assigned to that person at birth."

The court threw the case out because the transgender individuals were not selectively excluded from the bathrooms. Rather, they were excluded on the same basis that all biological males and/or females are excluded from certain bathrooms -- their "biological" sex. The landlord's discrimination for purposes of bathroom use, though it denied transgender individuals recognition of their gender identity, did not discriminate on the basis of their gender identity. (There was no evidence in the case regarding the biological status of the transgender clients, so this ruling is a little hard to understand.)

The court referred favorably to the Minnesota Supreme Court's 2001 decision in Goins v. West Group, which can be found in the Appendix. In that case, a transgender employee claimed discrimination based on her employer's exclusion of her from the women's bathroom. The

Minnesota law prohibited employment discrimination based on sexual orientation, defined in part as "having or being perceived as having a self-image or identity not traditionally associated with one's biological maleness or femaleness."

The Minnesota court said that the employer's bathroom rule did not discriminate on the basis of gender identity. The rule contained no reference to gender identity; therefore, there was no discrimination based on gender identity. The Court said that the rule discriminated based on biological sex, not gender identity. Therefore, it did not violate the statute.

Even if the employer's rule were interpreted as gender identity discrimination, the Court questioned whether there was any intent on the part of the Minnesota legislature to change the "cultural preference" for same-sex bathrooms. Since there was no legislative history on this point, the court decided that the words of the statute did not apply to bathroom usage.

The Goins court specifically noted that it did not know whether the plaintiff was "biologically" male or female. Although the statute made no reference to a requirement of proof of sex reassignment surgery in order to be protected from discrimination, the court seemed to decide that such proof is required in bathroom discrimination cases. It indicated that, upon proof that the plaintiff was "biologically" female, the plaintiff should be permitted to use the women's bathroom. The court said that such proof was required because the employee's case made the claim that the rule had a "disparate impact" on a protected class. "Disparate impact" cases, in which employer rules do not contain discriminatory language but have discriminatory impact, have special rules requiring the complainant to show they have the proper qualifications for the job. Here, the court said that proof of sex reassignment surgery is the "qualification" for using the women's bathroom. This point is surprising, because it has nothing to do with Julienne Goins' qualifications for the job, and stretched the law of disparate impact beyond recognition. However, as noted by U.S.

Supreme Court Justice Robert Jackson in another case, "We are not final because we are infallible, but we are infallible only because we are final."

The bottom line on these opinions is that the only two published cases interpreting statutes prohibiting "gender identity" discrimination in the facilities usage context have ruled that these statutes did not prohibit discrimination based on biological sex in the bathroom. The text of the Minnesota Supreme Court opinion can be found in the Appendix.

These cases are not without their criticisms. Most significantly, the courts said that transgender bathroom exclusion is based on biological sex, not "gender identity." The defendants did not impose separate rules on transgender persons because the rules affected all persons, transgender and non-transgender. However, critics question whether it is possible to separate the two so neatly. In the case of a transsexual person, whose psychological gender identity is opposite to that of the biological sex, it may not be possible to discriminate based on biological sex without also discriminating based on gender identity. Arguably, since sex and gender are opposites in such cases, honoring one *ipso facto* means dishonoring the other. Biological sex segregation ignores non-traditional gender identity, and thus discriminates based on gender identity. The court's interpretation is alarmingly similar to the specious reasoning of those courts that allowed separate facilities by race because both White and Black races received similar treatment.

The courts' interpretations of the statute also gave it a narrower interpretation than its plain words indicate. In other words, it protected gender identity only some of the time. This interpretation may have contradicted the legal principle, in effect in both Minnesota and New York, that remedial statutes are to be construed liberally (i.e., more broadly, not more narrowly). In fact, the first section of the Minnesota statute explicitly reiterates the rule: "The provisions of this chapter shall be construed liberally for the accomplishment of the purposes thereof."

19

Critics also complain about the courts' failure to recognize the legal principle, in effect in both Minnesota and New York, that the "plain meaning" of the words of a statute are to be used, not a secret meaning divined by the court. The plain meaning of the words of the Minnesota statute apply to all workplace discrimination, including bathrooms, without exception. Nonetheless, the Minnesota court found an exception for the workplace bathroom. Furthermore, the Court said that the statute requires proof of sex reassignment surgery, though it makes no apparent reference to it. To the contrary, the statute explicitly says that it applies regardless of "one's biological maleness or femaleness."

The Minnesota Supreme Court bolstered its unusual interpretation by reference to the legislative history of the statute, saying that there appeared to be no legislative intent to change the cultural preference for same-sex bathrooms. However, under the usual understanding of the "plain meaning" rule, legislative "intent" is irrelevant unless the words of the statute are ambiguous. The Court pointed to no ambiguity in the words of the statute. Therefore, its reference to legislative intent, aside from the fact that the legislative history is silent on this point, fails to give proper credence to the plain meaning of the statute. This criticism is supported by the recent court opinion by Judge Robertson of the U.S. District Court for the District of Columbia, interpreting Title VII to include transgender identity. Judge Robertson rejected the legislative intent argument in his opinion in Schroer v. Billington, noting that, as Justice Scalia wrote for a unanimous U.S. Supreme Court a few years ago: "it is ultimately the provisions of our laws rather than the principal concerns of our legislators by which we are governed."

The Goins court opinion also has a problem because it ignores the WPATH (World Professional Association for Transgender Health) medical protocols by requiring sex reassignment surgery *prior* to recognition of a new gender identity. The WPATH standards of care for transgender individuals prohibit primary genital sex reassignment until an individual has lived for at least one year in the opposite gender role successfully. In addition, although primary genital surgery to create female genitalia is considered routine at this point, the same is not true for surgery to create male genitalia (phalloplasty). Such surgery does not replicate typical male anatomy reliably, causes disfiguring arm scars, and is much more expensive ($50,000+). As a result, most of those transitioning from female to male never have phalloplasty, and most government agencies do not consider it necessary for gender identity recognition.

The ruling may also conflict with also conflict with the Americans With Disabilities Act. The court said, in effect, that the employer may ask to see a transgender employee's surgical status. The issue of asking about your employee's surgical status is a difficult one. Section 12112(d) (1) of the Americans with Disabilities Act specifically prohibits an employer from requesting post-employment medical examinations and inquiries. I have annexed in the Appendix the EEOC Enforcement Guidance memo on Disability-Related Inquiries and Medical Examinations of Employees. While the memo is clear that medical examinations and inquiries are prohibited unless there is job-related necessity, the ADA specifically states that its definition of disability does not include gender identity disorder. At the same time, however, surgery, regardless of purpose, causes disability and/or perception of disability. While inquiry into gender identity disorder generally may be permitted under the ADA, the inquiry into surgical procedures may not. In addition, all 50 states now have disability laws similar to the ADA, and most of them do not exclude gender identity disorder. Under those state acts, inquiry into the surgical status of an employee, whether referring to sex reassignment surgery or not, is fraught with problems.

In addition, a safe bathroom within a reasonable distance is a requirement of the OSHA bathroom regulations, which can be found in the Appendix. Failure to arrange for this could result in a finding of unsafe working conditions.

21

I note that I have heard a number of people claim that the ruling is also in violation of HIPAA, the federal Health Insurance Portability and Accountability Act. HIPAA prevents an employer from obtaining or using information provided to health insurers under threat of stiff penalties. In my understanding, this would not prevent employers from asking a transgender employee directly for information about his or her surgical status. Thus, HIPAA appears to be a statute that has little play in regard to bathroom usage issues of transgender employees.

Ultimately, the existence of genital surgery that no one will see (at work, anyway) is a red herring issue in regard to transgender bathroom usage. The real issues here are comfort with heterosexual norms and homophobia. Visible androgyny -- blurring of sex roles -- raises the specter of homosexuality, which makes old-fashioned judges and businessmen uncomfortable, and they retain the privilege to ignore statutory commands against discrimination.

A number of cities have legal guidelines on the bathroom issue. In the Appendix, you will find the regulations of New York City, San Francisco and the District of Columbia. In the New York City regulations, see section IV(C). In the DC Regulations, see sections 802 and 805. In the San Francisco Compliance Rules and Regulations, see sections A and F. Whether or not your organization conducts business in these cities, the regulations are a helpful guide to the types of protocols your organization should be considering.

These regulations are designed to implement the statutory gender identity to the non-discrimination ordinances. Specifically, the regulations provide guidance to employers, housing, and commercial space providers, public accommodations, educational institutions, and others on the specific requirements of the law. These regulations are an attempt to ensure that transgender individuals are treated in a manner that is consistent with their identity or expression, rather than according to their presumed or assigned sex or gender. The regulations direct entities to allow transgender individuals the right to use restrooms, dressing rooms, and other facilities that are consistent with their gender identity or expression.

There are some important differences in the way these policies are written. The most comprehensive regulations are those in DC -- remarkably comprehensive, specific and progressive, even more so than the San Francisco regulations or New York guidelines. There are a lot of similarities -- for example, all three prohibit gender identity discrimination and specifically address the foreseeable issues, such as access to restrooms. However, only DC requires by regulation that employers permit access to the restrooms that are "consistent with" the employee's gender identity or gender expression. That means if I identify as a woman, or if I express my gender as a female (regardless of whether I identify as a man or woman), I must be allowed access to the women's restroom the same as other women.

By contrast, SF's regulations say only that employers must provide transgender employees with a bathroom "appropriate" to their gender identity, omitting the term "consistent with" (although that phrase is used elsewhere in the document) . "Consistent with" seems to imply assigning one who identifies as a male to the men's restroom and one who identifies as a female to the women's restroom. On the other hand, "appropriate" seems to imply that one who identifies as male can be barred from the men's restroom even though it is consistent with his gender identity, and required to use a single-use bathroom in the basement because it is "appropriate." I'm not sure, but it's not terribly clear, either. Even less clear, New York City's guidelines merely say that failure to allow use of a restroom consistent with gender identity or gender expression is one of the "factors that *suggest* that discriminatory conduct related to gender identity has occurred." Since NYC's rules are not regulations, but guidelines, they don't have the force of law. Though it is likely that the NYC Human Rights Commission will take them seriously, it's not clear whether a court would do so. Its status is also slightly in doubt because NYC has court precedent saying that bathrooms may be segregated on the basis of "biological sex", though only in the NY Supreme Court (the lowest of New York State's court system and not binding on any other courts).

When it comes to locker rooms, SF and NYC get positively vague. SF says employers only need to make "reasonable accommodations" in this regard and only for "gender identity which is publicly and exclusively asserted" and for which they have ID or a doctor's note. That last part contradicts another part of the document, which states that asking for proof of gender, before a transgender person is permitted access, is prohibitAs to what's "reasonable" -- lawyers have long known that "reasonable" is a synonym for "what 12 people who couldn't get out of jury duty think is normal." NYC says that not allowing use of a locker room consistent with gender identity or gender expression is a factor "*suggesting*" discrimination. DC, however, comes right out and says that employers "shall allow" employees the use of dressing rooms "consistent with" not only their "gender identity" but also their "gender expression" and regardless of whether they have ID or a doctor's note (and requiring one is prohibited).

SF's regulatory scheme "strongly urges" that all single-use bathrooms be designated gender neutral. NYC's guideline "recommends" it. Only DC says that employers "shall" use gender-neutral signage for single occupancy restrooms.

SF and NYC have some language prohibiting harassment, but only DC spells out specific foreseeable scenarios that protect transgender employee privacy:

> (a) Deliberately misusing an individual's preferred name form of address or gender-related pronoun;
> (b) Asking personal questions about an individual's body, gender identity or expression, or gender transition;
> (c) Causing distress to an individual by disclosing to others that the individual is transgender; and

(d) Posting offensive pictures, or sending offensive electronic or other communications.

This type of specific guidance is very useful for employers. However, since mistakes in pronoun usage, improper personal questions and whispers behind the back are part of American culture, training is very important for litigation control. A couple of incidents may not meet the threshold requirement that the conduct is so pervasive that it "alters the terms of employment," However, a workplace environment can quickly get ugly unless a tone is set early.

Interestingly, the DC regulations use and define the term "transgender," which very few statutes do because the term is so ambiguous. The regulations give a definition that indicates that anyone whose identity or behavior differs from gender stereotypes is transgender. Under this broad standard, a man in the office who likes to cook and go to romantic comedies could be called transgender. As noted above in the case of Cincinnati, which also uses the term "transgender" in its statute, the definition there was similarly overinclusive, referring to gender characteristics, behavior, and/or self-identification typical of or commonly associated with persons of another gender.

While I realize that the word "transgender" is intentionally inclusive, and is considered an "umbrella term" for all sorts of gender variance, I disagree with those who would define transgender to include every person who engages in some atypical behavior, which includes every last one of us on earth. I would return to the Oxford English Dictionary, which defines it as "a person whose identity does not conform unambiguously to conventional notions of male or female gender, but combines or moves between these." There is an identity component, which means that the person identifies themselves as transgender, as well as exhibiting certain behavior.

2. Bathroom Usage Criteria

Bathroom usage is one of the most complex areas of decision-making with regard to transgender employees who are transitioning on the job. I recommend consideration of five criteria for making these decisions on a case-by-case basis, rather than a bright-line rule. A bright-line rule is inappropriate for the delicate issues involved, and will undoubtedly raise questions in a distributed organization that has locations in both conservative and liberal political environments. It is, however, important to have criteria set forth in the policy, lest the "case-by-case basis" turn into what the lawyers call "arbitrary and capricious decision-making." My sample gender transition policy for large organizations, which sets forth a policy for bathroom usage, is set forth in the next chapter.

Here are five criteria that can be explicitly spelled out, and yet are flexible enough to allow case by case tailoring.

1. Number of bathrooms within reasonable walking distance

If there is only one, then options are limited. If there is more than one set of multi-use bathrooms (multi-use = more than one person at a time) within reasonable walking distance, then one of these may be designated as the bathroom to be used by the employee in gender transition. The reasoning here is that co-workers, if they feel uncomfortable using that bathroom, may use others. Reasonable walking distance is important because of the OSHA regulations, which require it. The OSHA regulations are set forth in the Appendix.

2. Availability of single use or lockable bathrooms

If there is a single use bathroom, or a multi-use bathroom that is lockable, that may be designated as the bathroom to be used by the employee in gender transition. However, this should not be assumed to be the best permanent option for all concerned. The employee in gender transition may feel that his/her new gender is not being recognized if they are not permitted to use the multi-use facilities. In my experience, most employees going through gender transition are happy to compromise, at least in the beginning, because they understand that facilities usage is a sensitive issue. If, however, the employee is forced to use such facilities against his/her will for a long period of time, particularly if it involves an additional burden on their time, they may view this requirement as discriminatory.

3. Length of employee's transition

Over time, most co-workers tend to become more comfortable with the employee in gender transition, and the bathroom becomes much less of an issue than it is at the beginning of the process. If the employee is transitioning to living in the new gender within a few weeks, more time may be needed for co-workers to become comfortable. If the employee transition will take place over a few months, there is time to allow co-workers to become sufficiently comfortable to reduce concerns about bathroom usage to a manageable level. It also depends on the local area in which the transition is taking place. The local culture in some areas are extremely tolerant of differences, and gender transition is in the workplace is accepted more quickly. In other areas, the local culture is more traditional in regard to deviations from accepted social norms, and comfort level with gender transition will progress more slowly.

4. Employee's comfort level

Some employees in gender transition feel more comfortable using a private single-use bathroom. Others feel comfortable using a multi-use public bathroom, and have successfully done so consistently over a period of time. An employee in transition who is hesitant in using the bathroom may convey anxiety to co-workers, causing objections to arise. This comfort level should be taken into account.

5. Co-worker comfort level

In some work environments, all co-workers are comfortable with sharing a bathroom with an employee in gender transition. In other work environments, an objection will be raised by co-workers. The work environment should be assessed to determine the likely scenario. This should not, however, be the sole consideration used in deciding on facilities usage, because there will always be varying levels of comfort and discomfort. HR should work to achieve a reasonable comfort level over time, but it should not be assumed that every co-worker must be delighted with the idea before permitting a transgender employee to use the opposite-sex bathroom. Rather, the importance of this factor is that it allows HR to prepare appropriate resources to provide guidance to employees who have concerns about the decision. In some environments, conflict over the issue may continue for months after the employee has transitioned. If it appears, after several attempts at mediation over several months, that there is an irreconcilable conflict between the employee's position on facilities usage and that of management or co-workers, I recommend that the HR group in charge of transition issues make contact with the legal department for their input on an appropriate solution.

I have not included sex reassignment surgery (SRS) as a factor in the bathroom use determination. There are several important reasons for this. There are numerous types of SRS, some of which alter the genitalia only slightly and others of which vary in their effectiveness and appearance. An SRS requirement requires the Company to obtain and assess proof regarding specific details of the employee's medical history and treatment. This is problematic because such questions may impact medical privacy laws, which differ by jurisdiction. Furthermore, the use of SRS as a factor may create the perception that the Company endorses, condones or regulates its employees' decision to undergo gender transition. This is undesirable for reasons including employee relations, public relations, insurance coverage and potential litigation. It is best for the Company to stay out of the employee's medical decision-making.

Most problematic is the fact that the standards of care of the primary medical organization in this area (www.hbigda.org) require successfully living as the opposite sex for a year or more prior to medical approval for surgery. Therefore, it is likely that an employee in transition will not complete his/her medical treatment for a substantial period of time. Requiring an employee who appears female to the general public to use a men's facility, or vice versa, will likely cause more workplace distraction than necessary. The criteria adopted in these guidelines better addresses these issues than a surgical requirement. Frankly, although the use of SRS as a factor is intended to avoid objections to facilities usage, it fails to accomplish this goal because SRS does not address all objections to facilities usage. SRS affects only a small portion of the body not usually disrobed in a workplace restroom. SRS does not remove visible androgyny, nor does it remove the knowledge of co-workers that a transgender employee was born in the opposite sex. The source of the concern among co-workers, if any, lies here, and will not be removed by an SRS requirement. Rather, the issue is the comfort level of reasonable co-workers with sharing that particular space with that employee. The set of five Facilities Usage Criteria better achieves the Company's goals of maximizing workplace harmony and minimizing distractions.

One way to address objections from co-workers about sharing a bathroom with a transgender employee is to set aside a separate restroom for employees who feel strongly that they are unwilling to share a restroom with a transgender employee. If, as is sometimes done, the transgender employee is required to use a separate restroom, this tacitly approves the attitudes of those who object to the presence of transgender employees altogether, encouraging a discriminatory attitude and possibly condoning future harassment.

It should be noted that, at some point, the comfort level of the employee in transition and the co-workers usually increases. In addition, the appearance of employees in transition tends to conform more to the expected norms of their new gender with time, increasing co-worker comfort. The initial decision about facilities usage should be put in place for 30 to 90 days, to be reassessed at the end of that time. Often, by this time, positions have softened in the light of experience, and the fear of the unknown diminishes.

As an interesting comparison, the Human Rights Campaign Workplace Gender Transition Guidelines, which may be found at hrc.org, handle the issue differently, stating that "Transgender employees will be permitted to use the facilities that correspond to their gender identity. However, usage of reasonable single-occupancy or unisex facilities may be considered for a temporary period during the employee's transition process or on an ongoing basis. A transitioning employee will not be required to use the restroom of his or her designated sex at birth after he or she has begun transitioning." This could be confusing to some, as it says first that the employee definitively can use multi-use public restrooms, but then says the employee can be restricted to "single-occupancy or unisex facilities."

An important issue that must also be considered is employees who work outside the employer's facilities. It is an issue that should be considered when creating a transition plan. The plan should call for a procedure to be followed when the employee works outside the employer's facilities. This issue is highlighted by the story of Helena Stone, transgender woman and Verizon telephone technician, who was arrested three times after using the women's restrooms at Grand Central Terminal in New York City, where she was assigned to repair pay phones. Her office in the building has no bathroom, so she was required to use the public restroom.

Stone had been transitioning to become a woman over the previous 10 years and wore female clothing and make-up. She was charged with disorderly conduct each time. According to news reports, an MTA cop called her 'a freak, a weirdo and the ugliest woman in the world.' During the last arrest, three male MTA cops entered the women's restroom, searched her in front of gawking onlookers, told her she didn't belong there, handcuffed her and dragged her away.

The MTA subsequently dropped all criminal charges against Stone, and reached a settlement on her civil suit, in which the MTA agreed to allow people to use the restroom for whichever gender they consider themselves. The agreement also called for the MTA to sponsor a transgender sensitivity training program for its employees. This story underscores the importance of ensuring that part of the transition plan should include interfacing with those offsite facilities to locate appropriate bathrooms for your personnel.

The popular press has begun to discuss the bathroom issue. Dear Abby recently weighed in on the "bathroom question."

> DEAR ABBY: I visited a city larger than the one in which I reside and encountered a problem. I was in a women's restroom when a man wearing a wig walked in. It was obvious that this 6-footer, dressed in a floral print dress and high heels, was a man. Should transvestites or transsexuals be allowed to use the ladies' restroom? -- Bewildered in Adam, Okla.
>
> Dear Bewildered: There is a difference between a transvestite and a transsexual. A transsexual is a person who feels trapped in the body of the wrong sex. Before a transsexual is allowed to have gender reassignment surgery, he or she must live for one year in the role of someone of the opposite sex. This includes using the restroom facilities of the opposite gender. It is not against the law, and it was no threat to you.

Dear Abby is an important cultural icon, so her opinion becomes important, regardless of her expertise on the subject. The "trapped in the wrong body" analogy is not, in fact, a distinguishing characteristic of all transsexuals. It does, however, neatly make the point that this is no mere ogler attempting to get a look at the ladies. As discussed in the opening section on definitions, Abby is incorrect in implying that "transvestites" are attempting to do so. "Transvestite" does not mean "heterosexual man," just as "transsexual" doesn't mean "attracted to men." There is confusion here between "gender identity" and "sexual orientation" that makes her response less than accurate, despite its well-meaning intent.

Newsday also recently addressed the issue, publishing a question in the business column (October 22, 2006) about the discomfort of a male colleague with sharing a bathroom with a "Karen," a male-to-female transgender co-worker. The questioner intimates that Karen has transitioned to the female gender role on a full-time basis. He also notes that she engages in "disruptive" antics in meetings and that he tries to ignore her. Lastly, he notes that he saw her coming out of the men's room, which made him very uncomfortable. He asks about the legal regulations regarding the colleague's bathroom use.

The column's writer, Carrie Mason-Draffen, is clearly sympathetic to transgender employees. There are a few points, however, in her answer with which I would quibble. She begins by noting that companies have some legal obligations toward transgender employees, and that some judges have interpreted New York State's Sexual Orientation Nondiscrimination Act (SONDA), even though it does not specifically mention transgender persons, as extending protections to transgender employees.

This is not quite correct, as it is not SONDA that has been so interpreted, but rather the New York Human Rights Law (section 296(1)(a)). This is a minor point, but Ms. Mason-Draffen's words might be misinterpreted by some as meaning that New York judges have found that transgender employees are the same as gay employees because both are issues of sexual orientation. Being transgender is an issue of "gender identity," the internal gender identification as male and/or female, whereas being gay is an issue of "sexual orientation," the romantic desire for a partner of a certain sex.

She then quotes Sharon McGowan, staff attorney at the American Civil Liberties Union's Lesbian Gay Bisexual Transgender Project in

Manhattan, as saying that New York's laws banning disability discrimination have been interpreted as applying to transgender people. This is not correct as far as I am aware, and I checked Westlaw quite carefully. (It is, however, true of New Jersey, a neighboring state.) She also notes that the state's sexual orientation law specifically prohibits discrimination against gays and lesbians in employment and other areas. She does not note any differentiation between gays and lesbians on the one hand, and transgenders on the other. It's not clear what these references to sexual orientation are doing in a column regarding transgender employees.

She mentions that the employer may have rebuffed Karen's request to use the women's room, and quotes McGowan as saying that the employer has the option of giving Karen access to a single-occupancy rest room or a bathroom connected to someone's office. I find this response problematic. First of all, there is no mention of the impropriety of requiring a transwoman to use the men's room. Second, it suggests that the co-worker's discomfort should require segregation of Karen. Rather, it would be more appropriate to set aside a separate restroom for employees who feel strongly that they are unwilling to share a restroom with a transgender employee. By requiring Karen to use a separate restroom, the employer tacitly approves the attitudes of those who object to the Karen's presence altogether, encouraging a discriminatory attitude and possibly condoning future harassment.

I do, however, applaud the next suggestion given in the article. She suggests that the company use the situation to educate the staff: to explain what Karen is undergoing and give people the information they need. Personally, it is surprising, in this day and age of diversity training as a common occurrence, that such a step was not taken.

3. Dressing Rooms and Shower Rooms

These issues are even more difficult than the bathroom issue because of the increased level of public nudity involved. This is one of the bugaboos that one must deal with in creating transgender policy -- the idea that transgender employees will enter the bathroom, the locker room or the shower in order to leer at other employees.

The idea that such would be a common occurrence because of the employee's gender confuses gender identity with sexual orientation. Gender identity is a strong and persistent identification with being male or female, and is not the same as sexual orientation, which is the romantic desire to be with a partner of a specific sex. Thus, transgender women (i.e., those who transition from male-to-female) may be of any sexual orientation (straight, gay or bisexual). The idea that they will be sexually attracted to people of the same sex is incorrect. In addition, just as straight men and women understand that appropriate behavior in the workplace precludes propositioning other members of the workforce at random, the same is true of gay and bisexual workers. Companies that allow gay, bisexual or transgender workers to use the bathroom or locker room are not engaging in sexual harassment.

In creating a policy on locker rooms and similar spaces, the same five criteria as set forth for bathroom usage above should be used, with the addition of a sixth: "The presence of private stalls within the locker room where employees can shower and change clothes."

Some locker room facilities have private stalls within the locker room where employees can shower and change clothes. This reduces the impact of public nudity, though it does not eliminate it. In very tolerant environments, this may reduce the impact sufficiently to make this locker room appropriate for use by the employee in transition at some point. A recent case shows that the New Jersey courts agree with this assessment.

In the recently decided case of Opilla v. Lucent Technologies (2006 WL 2787047, Sept. 29, 2006), an employee sued for sexual harassment based on the presence of a transgender woman in the locker room of an on-premises health center provided by her employer, Lucent Technologies (though operated by a separate corporate entity). According to the plaintiff, one of her co-workers, a transgendered female entered, the women's locker room and stared at the plaintiff, who was then dressed only in her underwear. When asked how long the incident lasted, plaintiff testified that "[i]t could have been a minute. It felt like a long time." The transgendered co-worker left after another employee entered the locker room and told her to go change on the "other side."

The plaintiff immediately complained to the manager of the Health Center, who told her that he "didn't know what to do about the situation. He didn't know how to direct which locker room [the co-worker] should go into." But he promised her that he would check with Human Resources and "ask them what he should do." It appears, however, that no further inquiry on this matter, however, was made by either the plaintiff or the manager.

The plaintiff claimed that Lucent was liable for sexual harassment because it permitted transgender women to use the locker room, and in addition, that it was responsible for the alleged actions of the transgender woman in this incident. However, the motion judge referenced the legal requirement that the alleged harassment must "alter the conditions of employment" or "create a hostile working environment. She concluded that the one incident in the Health Center was not "severe or ... pervasive enough to make a reasonable female believe that the conditions of employment were altered and the working environment was hostile or abusive." Hence, she dismissed the discrimination complaint against Lucent.

The judge concluded that since the transgendered employee was not a supervisor, the plaintiff could not maintain a hostile work environment claim against her under the New Jersey Law Against Discrimination. The judge also concluded that the plaintiff's common law tort claims, against her employer Lucent and against her co-worker, were barred by the Worker's Compensation AThe appellate court agreed with the motion judge's conclusions, and the case was dismissed. The text of the opinion is very instructive about how courts will view claims of

35

company liability for sexual harassment based on the presence of a transgender employee, and it is attached in the Appendix. It puts to rest the fear that merely allowing transgender personnel access to restrooms and dressing rooms will subject organizations to sexual harassment claims. In my decade of work on this subject, only once have I heard of a similar case. I was told that it involved IBM some years ago, and that it was dismissed in favor of IBM. Even people from IBM who I have asked had not heard of the case, so it apparently had little impact on the company.

One caveat: While the opinion seems to specifically validate a corporate policy permitting locker room access, the appellate court specifically noted that it was not addressing that question. (I note, however, that I think such a policy is unquestionably legal in most states.)

Another lesson to be learned from this case is: talk to all involved parties when you create policies inclusive of transgender employees. Talk to the vendor providing health club services. Talk to the manager of the health club. Talk to the corporate liaison with the vendor.

In regard to company dressing room policy, it is important to keep in mind that inappropriate behavior in a locker room (or bathroom) is inappropriate regardless of the gender of the actor. Sexual harassment should be regulated by sexual harassment policy, not by barring transgender workers. This is especially true after Oncale v. Sundowner, the US Supreme Court case in which it is noted that same-sex sexual harassment is actionable. If such behavior is demonstrated by anyone, regardless of gender, the actor should be subject to the appropriate corrective action.

I was recently involved in training 300 shelter staff of the New York City Department of Homeless Services in 2006 and 2007, and the issue of showering in a residential facility was one of the most difficult addressed. The problem was compounded by the fact that the shelter system for men is separate from that of the women. The Department's managers were clear that transgender women – those who transitioned from male to female – should be permitted to reside in female shelters and to use the same bathrooms and shower rooms as the other residents. There was hardly any choice, as all the facilities in the women's facilities are combined women's bathrooms and shower rooms.

The New York City regulations (annexed in the Appendix) made it clear that transgender persons should be allowed to use shower rooms based on their gender identity:

> **D. Public Accommodations Where Nudity is Unavoidable** (e.g., health clubs, dressing or changing rooms, etc.)
>
> Public accommodations should provide access to appropriate facilities for all individuals. The Human Rights Commission recommends that public accommodation facilities, such as locker rooms which are designated for use based on sex, take steps to create private spaces within them (for example, by installing curtains or cubicles). Factors that suggest discriminatory conduct has occurred will include not allowing individuals to use a dressing or changing room consistent with their gender identity or gender expression.

My inspection of several facilities showed that each shower stall was separate and that there were usually curtains on the stalls, allowing them to also be used for the purpose of changing clothes. The Department made it clear to me that transgender persons were to be allowed to use these shower stalls, and that, although one facility still had a large multi-use shower room, it was no longer in use. In working with the shelter staff from various shelters, it became increasingly clear that, even in shower rooms, there was no need for public nudity. Those who want more privacy can use stalls or cubicles.

Interestingly, in the current version of the Employment Non-Discrimination Act, a federal bill to prohibit discrimination based on sexual orientation and gender identity, there is a section specifically designed to address this issue, and it follows this logic.

> Section 8(a)(3) CERTAIN SHARED FACILITIES- Nothing in this Act shall be construed to establish an unlawful employment practice based on actual or perceived gender identity due to the denial of access to shared shower or dressing facilities in which being seen fully unclothed is unavoidable, provided that the employer provides reasonable access to adequate facilities that are not inconsistent with the employee's gender identity as established with the employer at the time of employment or upon notification to the employer that the employee has undergone or is undergoing gender transition, whichever is later.

I understand that the bill has enough votes to pass, though the question of a veto has not yet been addressed. If Congress can agree on such language, it is surely not inappropriate for company policy.

C. Dress Codes

The gender transition process requires violating gender-normative dress codes. Courts have long upheld an employer's right to regulate employee dress and grooming. Some courts have even gone so far as to say that an employer has a right to demand that employees with customer contact be not only well-groomed, but attractive. Other courts have held that a dress and grooming policy based on sex stereotypes violates sex discrimination laws. Does that mean that a man can come to work wearing eyeliner and a tasteful lipstick? The answer is that it may mean exactly that, although it would likely require litigation to decide the issue either way because the legal standards are still evolving.

Your organization should avoid dress codes that place managers in the position of "fashion police." Trying to restrict a transgender employee's clothing can create an unreasonable situation. In one case, the company, upon being notified of the employee's intention to transition from male to female, informed her that, while she was an "anatomical male," she could not dress in "feminine" attire. The company permitted her to wear either male clothing or unisex clothing. Unisex clothing included "blouses, sweaters, slacks, flat shoes, nylon stockings, earrings, lipstick, foundation, and clear nail polish." The employee was instructed not to wear "obviously feminine" clothing, such as "dresses, skirts, or frilly blouses." While psychologists indicated that what she was allowed to wear at work was "sufficiently feminine" to allow her to satisfy the prerequisite of living as a female full-time for one year prior to sex reassignment surgery, the situation satisfied no one. Management began to receive anonymous complaints regarding the employee's attire, and a written warning was issued. Corrective action was taken, requiring the employee to have her compliance with the company's dress code monitored each day by her direct supervisor. One day, she came to work wearing, as part of her outfit, a strand of pearls, which she refused to remove. The employee was terminated and litigation ensued. While the company won the lawsuit, it required the attention of several courts, eventually winding up in State Supreme Court, and took several years. It also resulted in a finding that the employee could be considered disabled under state law, and had the facts been slightly different, the company would have lost the case.

Many companies have gender neutral dress codes, asking all employees to: (1) dress neatly; (2) have clean fingernails; (3) not wear sandals; (4) not wear fragrances; and (5) not wear jewelry on their faces except for earrings. You may include a rule that only certain kinds of clothing may be worn, or that employees project a polished look. This rule should be applied even-handedly to both male and female employees. Putting an unequal burden on one sex or one group of employees could be considered sex discrimination.

When an employee transitions to living in the opposite gender, one should expect to see clothes and styling of that gender on the start date. These clothes should be in accord with the company dress code, and it is likely that the transgender employee will dress in a manner similar to others at the organization. In other words, if the attire worn by most females in the department is that of a business suit, one should expect to see the transgender employee adopt similar dress. A male-to-female transgender employee is not likely to come to work in a wedding gown or a miniskirt, nor is a female-to-male transgender employee likely to come to work in cowboy chaps or a muscle tee. If a transgender employee were to wear inappropriate clothing to the job, he or she should be advised of the problem, as with any employee.

D. Identification and Records Changes

The organization should arrange for changes to be made to the transitioning employee's name and gender in the Human Resources information system, including databases such as PeopleSoft. A new email address should be created with the new name. New ID badges, uniforms, business cards, name plates should be issued. Phone directory, website and facebook listings should be changed.

These changes should not await a court-ordered name change. From a legal standpoint, a person has a right to use any name without a court order, so long as they do not do so for purposes of fraud. In addition, many jurisdictions will not issue a name change to a transgender person. A recent story from the Rochester (NY) Democrat and Chronicle illustrates this problem. "A transgender Rochester man must provide medical evidence to justify his request to change his first name from Sarah to Evan, a local judge has ruled."

While it is unclear exactly what State Supreme Court Justice William P. Polito meant by this, since the opinion was not made public, it seems reasonable, in the context of the story, to assume that it imposes a legal requirement that a transgender person first undergo sex reassignment surgery before being allowed to change their name to one stereotypically associated with that of the opposite sex. This was not such a big deal in the past, because the common law permitted one to use any name without judicial approval, and to place that name on any identifying document, so long as there was no intent to defraud creditors. Today, however, many institutions, such as the Social Security Administration, banks and libraries, increasingly assume the need for judicial approval before one's name can be changed on identifying documents. The advent of Real ID Act regulations, requiring formal judicial approval for a name change on driver licenses, further solidifies judicial control of identity.

This requirement of judicial approval for name changes creates a catch-22. Medical standards require that one must live in the opposite gender role for at least *one year before medical permission is granted* to have sex reassignment surgery. This obviously requires that one choose a name associated with the opposite gender role. However, if Judge Polito and Real ID Act regulators get their way, the use of such a name would not be permitted unless and until there is evidence of sex reassignment surgery. Thus, the government is requiring this man Evan to carry and show identification saying "Sarah," and to represent himself as a female, perhaps at the risk of a fraud charge (related story). As I discussed at length in a law review article in 2001, there are serious privacy implications to Polito's position on this, and it would not surprise me if Evan's lawyers raised a constitutional challenge.

It is important to note that there are a number of different types of sex reassignment surgery, so a simple requirement of sex reassignment surgery is not clear. Nor is a requirement of "full" reassignment surgery clear, as that simply switches the ambiguity to the question of what constitutes "full." The state of the art for sex reassignment surgery for those moving from female to male lags sadly behind, and most of those moving from female to male forego the hideously expensive (like $30,000-$50,000) phalloplasty, which is widely considered to produce results that do not provide adequate sensation or function. Many consider mastectomy and metoidioplasty "full" sex reassignment for FTMs. And if you're left wondering what those are, and want a fuller explanation before you agree or disagree, it simply points up why administrators and judges ought to get educated before they start creating rules.

It is important for corporate record-keepers to recognize that it may be difficult for transgender employees to receive a court-ordered name change, thus making it impossible to obtain a social security card in the new name. To make life easier for transgender employees in this situation, corporate rules requiring a new social security card or a court order before changing names on corporate records should be relaxed, allowing the substitution of other documentation.

The Human Rights Campaign's Transgender Issues Manual, available at hrc.org, suggests the following: "Upon an employee's request, change the employee's name and sex in all personnel and administrative records, including internal and external e-mail and business cards. While this stance is admirably accommodating, it may not be possible to change "all personnel and administrative records." If the employee has been with the organization for a long time, there are years of previous records, which would be burdensome to change. A less onerous suggestion is to change the company database to reflect the new name and gender prospectively for the future only. This could, however, result in a discrepancy in the future, causing inquiry and some distress to a transgender employee. Some thought should be given by the organization to which records in its particular system are most likely to pop up later on.

A change of gender is much more problematic administratively than a change of name. Only one US state (Texas, interestingly enough) will give a court order recognizing a change of sex, albeit for limited purposes. The gender change on the company's database will cause a discrepancy when it does not match the database gender marker on other systems. For example, unless and until the employee changes the gender identity marker on the Social Security account, insurance plans, pension plans, security classification, and professional licenses, the discrepancies may trigger an inquiry. In addition, there is no universal document that will satisfy all organizations to change the gender marker.

For example, Social Security Administration rules recently changed to require sex reassignment surgery for change of gender marker on the SSA account. This is a problem for some transgender employees, because the medical standards of care call for living in the opposite gender for at least a year prior to receiving permission for sex reassignment surgery. There are stories about SSA contacting employers about the gender mismatch, causing some distress for transgender employees. However, when I queried SSA about this, I received the following reply:

> "SSA may inform employers of discrepancies through a No-Match letter, Basic Pilot (Employment Eligibility Verification) or Social Security Number Verification Service (SSNVS)....SSA only matches the name and SSN reported against its records (not gender). The Basic Pilot assists participating employers in confirming employment eligibility of newly-hired employees. Employers participating in the Basic Pilot electronically match the newly hired employee's data against SSA and Department of Homeland Security electronic records such as SSN, name, date of birth, and citizenship/work authorized status. Basic Pilot does not match the gender."

One legal department raised the concern that changing the gender marker before SSA approval could cause a loss or interruption of benefit accrual to the individual's social security account. I spoke to Christopher Daley, an attorney and former director of the Transgender Law Center (TLC), which provides legal services to hundreds of transgender people and their families each year. TLC has worked with many transgender people whose birth-identified gender marker on their SSA account conflicts with the corrected gender marker on their employers' records. To his knowledge, this particular inconsistency has never resulted in loss of benefits for any of the Center's clients.

E. Health Benefits

Although many companies have included "gender identity" as a protected category, the relationship between such a policy change and health benefits are poorly understood. Most benefit plans contain an exclusion for "transsexualism." This means that mental health counseling, hormone replacement therapies and surgical procedures will not be covered if they are associated with transsexualism.

The exclusion for "transsexualism" began appearing in insurance contracts in the 1960s, after media publicity about new treatments for transsexuality. There were generally three reasons for the blanket exclusion for transsexualism: the experimental nature of medical treatments, the lack of evidence of medical necessity, and the onerous costs. This reasoning may no longer be as persuasive. Most physicians no longer consider them experimental, there have been medical studies demonstrating medical necessity, and the cost per insured is low. This is not to say that health benefits should in every case be changed to cover any and all treatments for transgender employees, but rather that health benefits should be reviewed to determine whether the organization considers its current coverage appropriate.

A research study undertaken from 2001 through 2006 measured the frequency and cost of sex reassignment surgeries, and the total cost of Transgender Health Benefits for the employees of large companies was projected. The study, performed by Dr. Mary Ann Horton, found that the annual cost per insured US resident was $.06. Combined with the cost for hormones, doctor's office visits, and therapy, the total annual cost per insured for all transgender health benefits was $.39. The added cost to an employer to cover all four transgender health benefits was projected at $.11/year/insured or less. There are now a dozen major organizations in the United States that cover sex reassignment surgery, and their loss experience has been less than anticipated.

Since employers negotiate insurance benefits for their employees, the inclusion of "gender identity" as a protected category may make it appropriate to revisit this issue with the insurer. For example, Microsoft not only recently added "gender identity" to its EEO policy, but also announced increased coverage of transgender-specific health benefits.

This issue is of increased relevance for all companies because the Human Rights Campaign, which issues the Corporate Equality Index (CEI), a measure of corporate diversity, is now reviewing health benefits for transgender employees for its rankings. A company cannot get 100% on the CEI unless there is "parity in at least one transgender wellness benefit." The new standards are set out below. The original point scoring system is on the left, the new scoring system is on the right.

1. a. Non-discrimination policy includes sexual orientation   14   15

    b. Sexual orientation diversity training offered   7** 5

2. a. Non-discrimination policy includes gender identity and/or   14   15
      expression

    b. Gender identity diversity training offered OR supportive gender   7** 5
      transition guidelines in place*

    c. Parity in *at least one* transgender wellness benefit*   5
      Counseling by a mental health professional, pharmacy benefits
      covering hormone therapy, medical visits to monitor the effects of
      hormone therapy and other associated lab procedures, medically
      necessary surgical procedures such as hysterectomy, or short-term
      disability leave for surgical procedures.

3. a. Company-provided domestic partner health insurance   14   15

b. Parity in COBRA, dental, vision and domestic partners legal 5
dependent coverage*

c. Parity in *at least three* other domestic partner benefits* 5
FMLA-like leave†, bereavement leave†, employer-provided
supplemental life insurance for a partner, relocation/travel
assistance, adoption assistance, qualified joint and survivor
annuity for domestic partners, qualified pre-retirement survivor
annuity for domestic partners, retiree health care benefits, or
employee discounts.

4. Company-supported GLBT employee resource group or firm-wide 14 15
diversity council that includes GLBT issues, or:

(half credit) Company would support a GLBT employee resource
group with company resources if employees expressed an interest

5. Engages in appropriate and respectful advertising and marketing 14 15
or sponsors GLBT community events or organizations

6. Engages in action that would undermine the goal of GLBT 14 -15
equality**
In the original scoring system, companies that *did not* engage in
such activity received 14 points for this category.
*In 2006, companies that do engage in such activity will lose 15
points, with a minimum possible total score of 0.*

Total 100 100

* Additional criteria for 2006.

** Prior to 2006, companies earned 14 points for offering diversity training
covering *either* sexual orientation *or* gender identity and expression.

† Benefit provided to the employee *on behalf of* the employee's same-sex
domestic partner.

(©Human Rights Campaign)

IV. Sample Gender Transition Guidelines

We have previously discussed some of the policy tools and criteria that present major issues. It is important, however, to put these into the context of a policy that can be adopted and used in the organizational context. To that end, here is a sample gender transition policy. Because many organizations reserve the term "policy" for Board-level documents, however, I use the term "guidelines," as this is thought to introduce a desirable level of flexibility. It should be tailored to the individual organization, and not used "as is." This document is most definitely not "one size fits all."

These guidelines are intended for large U.S. organizations with 500 employees or more, multiple locations, and operating within a moderately conservative business environment. Other types of organizations may find them instructive, but the embedded cultural assumptions may interfere with effective functioning, and they should be tailored accordingly. In sections A and B below, you will find a sample policy, and a draft transition plan for use in creating a plan tailored to a specific employee. This is followed in Section C by a detailed guidance memo for HR professionals regarding how to implement the policy, how to communicate gender transition issues effectively, and how to negotiate a transition plan. Section D discusses co-worker training, and Section E sets out frequently asked questions about gender transition in the workplace.

A. Sample Gender Transition Policy

1. Purpose/Summary

These guidelines specify the steps to be followed in cases of gender transition of Company employees. For ease of use, the steps to be taken are listed separately for different personnel, including Global Diversity, Gender Transition Leaders,

48

Employees in Transition, Supervisory Management and Co-workers.

While all Company employees should, of course, receive respect for their personal identity, the case of Company employees who undergo gender transition presents unique challenges and opportunities for the workforce. These guidelines are intended to create an environment that fosters workplace harmony in cases of gender transition. Their working principle is a four step mediation process implemented by a Gender Transition Leader (GTL). The GLT function requires advanced skills in employee relations and workplace diversity, and should consist of a minimum of 20% FTE for 3 months. The guidelines are designed to provide information and communicate expectations while at the same time providing respect and privacy to employees in transition, supervisory management, and co-workers in the diverse sites and environments contained within the Company.

These guidelines do not constitute a contract or contractual obligation or a promise of specific treatment in a specific situation, and the Company reserves the right, in its sole discretion, to amend, modify, or discontinue its use without prior notice, notwithstanding any person's acts, omissions or statements to the contrary.

2. Company Commitment and Objectives

The Company is committed to fostering a work environment where everyone is treated fairly with trust and respect, including employees in gender transition and their co-workers. The Company is, therefore, committed to creating a work environment that maximizes the opportunity for successful gender transition with minimum workplace distraction. There are three objectives

A.   Communicate guidelines in cases of gender transition

B.   Define norms of appropriate conduct by Company
        employees

C.   Provide a list of resources for Company employees

3. Definitions

A.   "Gender identity" is defined by the Company for purposes of
        these guidelines as "gendered identification, self-expression
        and appearance," corresponding to a person's deeply-felt
        psychological identification as male or female. Gender identity
        may or may not correspond to a person's sex assigned at birth.

B.   "Gender transition" refers to transition from male to female, or
        from female to male. Those who transition feel strongly and
        persistently that their gender identity is different from their sex
        at birth, and wish to transition from one gender to the other.
        Thus, a person born female may decide to transition to living as
        a male. Conversely, a person born male may decide to
        transition to living as a female.

C.   "Gender transition plan" refers to a plan that governs the
        employee's transition. It is agreed to by the Gender Transition
        Leader and the employee's supervisory management, in
        collaboration with the employee. It addresses issues such as
        timeline, dress, facilities usage, and appropriate norms of
        conduct for Company employees.

D.   "Gender Transition Leader" (GTL) refers to the local liaison
        officer responsible and accountable to ensure that these
        guidelines are properly implemented in a particular case of
        gender transition by a Company employee.

E.   "Employee in transition" refers to an employee who is undergoing gender transition.

4. Steps to be taken by Gender Transition Leader ("GTL") upon notification of gender transition

A.   Local Liaison as Gender Transition Leader

1. Certain local offices will be the local liaison for gender transition.   These may be the local Human Resources offices, local Diversity offices, or other offices responsible for employee relations. When the local liaison is notified of a gender transition, an employee trained in these procedures will be designated as Gender Transition Leader (GTL) to be accountable and responsible to ensure that these guidelines are appropriately implemented at the site.

2. The GTL will notify Global Diversity and local HR

3. In keeping with Company policy, the local Diversity Manager will take steps to keep information regarding gender transition confidential except as noted herein.

B.   Four step mediation process

Step 1: The GTL will immediately schedule a meeting with the employee in transition to begin creation of a transition plan and provide information about the Company's guidelines, expectations and resources

Step 2: Meet separately with supervisory management to discuss creation of transition plan and provide information about the Company's guidelines, expectations and resources.

This should be scheduled to occur after the initial employee meeting in order to be able to present complete facts to management.

Step 3: Meet with employee in transition and supervisory management together to complete transition plan.

Step 4: Set up guidelines review session for co-workers in frequent workplace contact with employee in transition to explain Company policies and expectations with regard to gender transition on the job. The scheduling and notification of this meeting should not take place until the transition plan is signed by the employee and management.

C.   Monitoring and follow up

- Monitor the transition plan to maximize successful completion and to allow provision of appropriate guidance for employees in transition, managers and co-workers to ensure a harmonious work environment.

- Follow up requests for guidance and complaints to ensure timely and appropriate resolution.

5. Responsibilities of Employee in Transition, Supervisory Management and Co-workers

D.   Employee in Transition

- Be present for meetings scheduled by the Gender Transition Leader (GTL).

- Cooperate with the GTL and management in creating a successful gender transition plan

- Follow the gender transition plan without deviation. If changes are required, follow the procedure for amendments contained in the plan.

- Respond appropriately to co-workers who make mistakes in references to name or pronoun of the new gender, or who ask inappropriate questions or make inappropriate comments, particularly during the initial phases of the gender transition plan.

- Avoid making inappropriate disclosures of private medical or surgical information in the workplace.

- Immediately report discriminatory or harassing conduct to the GTL, so that the GTL may provide appropriate guidance to employees.

E.   Supervisory Management

- If supervisory management receives notice from an employee of his or her plans for gender transition, notify the local Diversity Manager if not already notified.

- Be present for meetings scheduled by the Gender Transition Leader (GTL).

- Cooperate with the GTL and the employee in transition in creating a successful gender transition plan

- Follow the gender transition plan without deviation. If changes are required, follow the procedure for amendments contained in the plan.

- Model appropriate norms of conduct by treating the employee with respect, using correct references to name or pronoun of the new gender, refraining from asking inappropriate questions or making inappropriate comments, and respecting employee confidentiality.

- Cooperate with the GTL in the investigation of discriminatory or harassing conduct and any employee guidance or corrective action determined by the GTL to be appropriate.

F.   Co-workers

- Be present for meetings scheduled by the Gender Transition Leader (GTL).

- Treat the employee in transition with respect, using correct references to name or pronoun of the new gender, refraining from asking inappropriate questions or making inappropriate comments, and respecting employee confidentiality.

- Particularly at the beginning of gender transition, it is normal for co-workers to make some mistakes regarding these matters. Do not take offense at respectful corrections offered by the employee in transition. Requests for guidance may also be made to the GTL.

- Bring complaints to the GTL. Do not approach the employee in transition to address your complaints about gender transition.

6. Resources

- The GTL can assist employees in transition, management and co-workers who have questions or concerns about the Company's Gender Transition Guidelines.

- The local EAP has counselors who can assist employees in transition, supervisory management and co-workers who have concerns about gender transition in the workplace.

- Questions about medical leave can be answered by calling the Leave Administrator at ____.

- Questions about insurance coverage can be answered by contacting your local benefits administrator.

- The following publicly available information may be helpful. The Company does not endorse the opinions expressed in these publications.

  - The Human Rights Campaign, the world's largest gay, lesbian, bisexual and transgender advocacy organization, has a section on transgender issues in the workplace at http://hrc.org/worklife

  - This book, written by psychologists in the field, uses real life stories, actual letters and other examples to give an understanding of what it means to be transsexual and offers practical suggestions for compassionate dealing. Brown and Rounsley, True Selves: Understanding Transsexualism--For Families, Friends, Coworkers, and Helping Professionals (Jossey-Bass 2003) 288 pages

- This book, written by a counselor/activist, gives information on the basics of transsexualism, the process of gender transition at work and management issues. Walworth, Transsexual Workers: An Employer's Guide (Center for Gender Sanity 2003) 135 pages

- The standards of care of the primary medical organization in this field (World Professional Association for Transgender Health) can be found at http://wpath.org

<u>Customization Questions</u>
The guidelines above should be customized to fit the circumstances of the particular organization, particularly with regard to pre-existing HR policies and procedures. Here are some questions that should be considered in customizing the policy.

What is the reach of the policy?
> US only
> US and Canada
> North America
> Global

What is the company name to be referenced in the policy or guidelines?

What, if any, legal disclaimers are desired, to avoid contractual obligations?

Do the guidelines make appropriate references to existing EEO, diversity and anti-harassment policies?

How will these guidelines fits with policies now in place?
> Dress code
> Company records
> Facilities usage
> Insurance coverage
> Leave
> Job change
> EEO
> EEO policy statements and displays
> Harassment
> Records change
> PeopleSoft
> I-9
> SSN
> Facilities

Health club
Insurance
Leave
FMLA
Short-term disability

Are definitions of words in the guidelines appropriate to the environment? For example, if the word "transgender" is used, is it defined to include crossdressers?

Should there be different criteria in regard to gender change or documentation?

Is there a particular step-by-step process envisioned?

What should be included in training materials? Should transgender issues be included in periodic diversity trainings?

Do the guidelines appropriately address co-worker trainings? Here are some issues to consider:
Meeting attendance
Transitioning employee presence at meeting
Meeting length
Topics to avoid
Letter from transitioning employee
Letter of management support

Are specific guidelines envisioned for communications with customers/clients? What should the transgender employee and co-workers say in response to questions or comments?

Who are the vendor interfaces?
EAP
Insurance company/TPA
Health club
Security

B. Draft Gender Transition Plan

This section is to be used to create a plan that alerts both the transitioning employee and his or her managers to the steps that will be taken, expected behavioral norms, available resources and contemplated training. In this way, all foreseeable precautions are taken to ensure the success of the transition for all concerned. Without it, managers may mistakenly engage in discriminatory actions and transgender employees may engage in behavior considered inappropriate by a manager. I have seen very difficult situations arise out of the fact that expectations were not managed.

The employee known as _____ ("the employee") has notified the Company of his/her intention to transition from one gender to another. This plan will govern the actions of the Company and the employee in regard to this gender transition, including:

- timeline
- dress
- Company resources
- ID changes
- security clearance issues
- facilities usage
- appropriate norms of conduct for Company employees
- gender transition guidelines review session
- complaint procedures
- deviations from plan
- amendment of plan
- change of location
- ending date

[Legal professionals may with to consider whether to include a disclaimer that the written Transition Plan is not a contract and is not binding. At the same time, such a disclaimer may have the counterproductive effect of allowing an employee to deviate from the plan without consequences. Section 11, covering plan amendments, gives sufficient flexibility to the Company such that a disclaimer would seem unnecessary and counterproductive.]

1. Timeline

The employee has notified the Company that he or she will begin living in a different gender role on or about _____.

2. Dress Code

It is expected that the employee in transition will adhere to the dress code of his/her new gender, and that appropriate work attire will be worn.

The applicable dress code for the employee is as follows:

3. Company Resources (Note: It is important to place this information here because many employees do not know how to find these contacts, and it helps to have them gathered in one location.)

> GTL – contact info:
> EAP – contact person:
> Affinity Group – contact person:
> Diversity Council – contact person:
> Leave administration – contact person:
> Insurance benefits – contact person:

4. ID Changes

> The name and gender on all employment records created on or after _____ will be listed as
> _____.

The name in the HR database will be changed on or about _____ as follows: _____

A new email address will be issued to the employee on or about _____.

5. Security Clearance Issues

If the employee has a security clearance, Company industrial security will be notified by the employee in writing no later than _____.

6. Facilities Usage

After discussion with the employee and Company management, and based on consideration of the criteria listed in the Company guidelines, the following arrangements have been made for facilities usage:

Bathrooms

Locker Rooms, if any

Other Gender-Specific Spaces, if any

If the employee is notified that he or she or she will be reassigned to another Company location, permanently or temporarily, the employee should notify the GTL as soon as possible.

7. Appropriate Norms of Conduct for Company Employees

- Form of address – The employee shall be known by the name of _____ as of _____. The proper pronouns to use shall be _____ (he/him or she/her).

Because most people have not been exposed to gender transition, it is likely that co-workers will make mistakes, such as referring to the employee in gender transition by the wrong name or pronoun, or asking inappropriate questions. Employees in transition should gently correct a co-worker who makes a mistake. It is assumed that mistakes will be less frequent after a reasonable period of time.

If, after a reasonable period of time, a particular employee continually addresses the employee by the wrong name or gender identity, the GTL should be notified. The employee should not attempt to correct the situation by inappropriate conduct in return.

If a Company employee, contractor, vendor or customer requests not to work with the employee because of his/her gender identity, such a request cannot be honored. Company cannot subject employees to adverse employment actions based on his/her personal identity. Therefore, Company cannot honor a request to isolate the employee from certain contacts. Those who choose to work with Company must respect The Company's policies. However, the GTL may be able to provide some guidance to the requester that will help make the transition easier.

Medical information – Other than the fact of gender transition, the employee should not discuss medical condition or procedures with other Company employees. Employees should keep medical information confidential. Discussion of such information at the workplace is a breach of confidentiality, and in such a situation the Company may take action to amend the transition plan and/or take corrective action based on such information. Further, it is likely that public disclosure of sensitive medical information regarding gender transition will lower the comfort level of co-workers and require changes to the facilities usage plan.

Media contacts - All media contacts should be referred to the media office.

8. Guidelines Review Session

A Gender Transition Guidelines Review Session will be held with those in frequent workplace contact, including co-workers, vendors and customers who are in direct contact with the employee. This meeting will be held on or about _____. The purpose of the meeting is to inform them of changes in dress and proper forms of address, The Company's guidelines, and expected norms of conduct. Except for the fact of transition, medical privacy will be maintained.

The employee will not be present at the session in order to give attendees the opportunity to ask questions with less discomfiture. However, if the employee desires, he/she may write a short letter to be given to those attending the meeting. The employee should give the letter to the GTL no later than _____ to ensure its inclusion in the meeting. The letter should introduce the new name, express the employee's commitment to a good working environment, and if desired, include a short personal message about his/her transition. A letter expressing management support may also be given to those attending the meeting, if appropriate. The management letter should be given to the GTL no later than _____ to ensure its inclusion in the meeting.

9. Complaint Procedures

Any employee concerns or complaints about gender transition, including those of the employee in transition, co-workers, managers, vendors, customers or others, are to be referred to the GTL, not to the employee in transition. If complaints or concerns are voiced to the employee in transition, the employee should refer the person to the GTL, and notify the GTL.

When concerns or complaints about gender transition are raised to the GTL, the GTL will speak to those concerned to provide guidance regarding the Company's policy. The matter may also be referred through the usual Company grievance procedures.

10. Deviations from Plan

Deviation from the terms of this transition plan may constitute grounds for corrective action by Company to ensure that the plan is adhered to in the future.

11. Amendment of Plan

If the employee or the manager feels that the transition plan needs to be changed in order to constitute a reasonable accommodation, the request is to be made to the GTL. The request should be in writing, and specifically state the change requested and evidence supporting a significant need for the change. Within a reasonable period of time, the GTL will contact the employee and supervisory management to discuss the change, and issue a written decision granting or denying the request.

12. Change of Location

If the employee is notified that he or she or she will be reassigned to another Company location, permanently or temporarily, the employee should notify the GTL as soon as possible.

12. Ending Date

This plan will be terminate one year from the date listed in section 1, unless the GTL determines, in his or her sole discretion, that circumstances require continuing it for a specific period of time to address problems or concerns that have arisen. The employee and supervisory management shall be notified in writing of the time of extension and the reason.

C. Gender Transition Guidance Memo for HR Professionals

1. Introduction

This memorandum provides in-depth guidance on the creation and implementation of a gender transition plan. It is designed to assist in training of Gender Transition Leaders who will be in charge of gender transition plans. Because this document is written on an advanced level for those with expertise in the issues of gender transition in the workplace, it is anticipated that this document will not be circulated outside of HR. In the absence of such expertise, it is easy to misconstrue this document, thwarting the Company's intention of maximizing workplace harmony.

Steps to be taken in case of gender transition

When an employee notifies Company of a gender transition, the following steps should be taken by the Gender Transition Leader (GTL):

A.   Schedule an initial meeting with the employee (without supervisory management) to discuss the transition plan.

B.   Schedule a meeting with the employee's immediate supervisor (without the employee present) to discuss the transition plan. If the GTL considers it appropriate, the supervisor's manager may be invited to the meeting. This should be scheduled to occur after the initial employee meeting is completed in order to be able to present complete facts to management.

C.   Schedule a meeting with both the employee and supervisory management present to discuss the transition plan. This should be scheduled to occur after the other two meetings are completed, in order to understand and facilitate the issues of importance to both employee and management.

D. If deemed appropriate, schedule a meeting with co-workers and others in workplace contact. The scheduling and notification of this meeting should not take place until the transition plan is signed by the employee and management.

The following explanations are designed to provide an understanding of the intention of each of these four steps and to provide suggestions for smooth implementation.

2A. Initial Employee Meeting

This is an initial meeting with the employee (without supervisory management) to discuss the transition plan. It is important that this meeting take place very soon after assignment of the GTL to ensure that the employee does not take precipitous action that may cause workplace disruption.

Some information should be prepared for this initial employee meeting, if possible.

Items prior to initial employee meeting if possible:

▪ Identify and contact local resources below without divulging confidential information. The employee may be given a contact with a person at the resource provider who is ready to provide assistance on the issue of gender transition in the workplace. It would be wise to contact the resource provider to determine who specifically has training or experience with gender transition.

- o The local EAP may have counselors with expertise or resources useful to employees undergoing gender transition.
- o Local diversity council
- o Local affinity group
- o Other HR professionals who have been involved in gender transition at Company

- Identify co-workers, customers, vendors and others who are in frequent contact with the employee at the workplace.

  - o These are the people who will be invited to the optional policy review session that may be scheduled after the transition plan is agreed to by the employee in transition and supervisory management.
  - o The employee in transition will not attend this meeting in order to give attendees the opportunity to ask questions with less discomfiture.
  - o It is a good idea to have a sense of how big such a meeting would be. 20-25 people is probably the natural limit in order to give people a chance to share questions and concerns. If there are more, perhaps there should be more than one meeting.
  - o The list of people is also useful to determine if there are concerns about potential overreaction by certain employees.

- Do independent research on gender identity issues until you are satisfied with your level of knowledge.

  - o Some additional information may make you more comfortable with addressing employees' questions.

- o It is not necessary to become an expert on gender issues in order to facilitate gender transition in the workplace.
- o Resources for such research are set forth at the end of this memo.

- Assess the considerations for facilities usage.

  - o Facilities usage is determined on a case-by-case basis.
  - o The decision is based on the Facilities Usage Criteria set forth in 3 below.
  - o The GTL, in collaboration with supervisory management and the employee in transition, is authorized to make the decision as to the most appropriate plan for facilities usage.

- Determine if the employee has a security classification.

  - o Employees with a security classification who plan to undergo gender transition have an obligation to notify industrial security.
  - o Psychological counseling for "Gender Identity Disorder" (as it is referred to in the Diagnostic and Statistical Manual of the American Psychiatric Association) is a Reportable Event.
  - o Living in a different gender role from that of sex at birth represents a change in major life circumstances that is a Reportable Event.
  - o A gender transition, with no additional diagnosis code, has not been known to automatically result in disqualification.
  - o Failure to report Reportable Events will almost certainly result in revocation of security clearance.

Agenda of initial employee meeting

- Company's commitment to a nurturing work environment

- Ask about gender transition plans
- Introduce idea of a plan to manage workplace transition successfully
    o Discuss 4 step process
    o Briefly review Company Gender Transition Guidelines
    o Briefly review Draft Transition Plan
    o Leave copies and request comments (no cc)
- Ask about questions/concerns

2B. Initial Management Meeting

Schedule a meeting, to take place after the initial employee meeting, with the employee's supervisory management (without the employee present) to discuss the transition plan. Remind the manager that notes of the meeting should not be given to secretaries or other personnel until the information is made public to avoid leakage of confidential information.

Agenda of management meeting (without employee):

- Present employee's plans regarding gender transition
    o note need for confidentiality until co-worker meeting
- Explain basic steps of gender transition
- Introduce idea of a plan to manage workplace transition successfully
    o Discuss 4 step process
    o Briefly review Company Gender Transition Guidelines
    o Briefly review Draft Transition Plan
    o Leave copies and request comments (no cc)
- Discuss budget for site education
- Ask about questions/concerns

2C. Follow-up meeting with employee and management

- When you receive comments from employee and management, determine the issues of potential conflict, and sound out the employee and manager to see how much flexibility they have on these points.
- Fill in the draft transition plan to the best of your ability and forward to both employee and management. Give them time to make further comments, which should be forwarded to you (GTL) only. Let them know to send their comments without a cc. Your mediation will reduce the time, effort and energy required to finalize the plan. Direct negotiation between employee and managers on this sensitive subject may result in unintended conflict and hardening of positions.

- Schedule a meeting, with both the employee and supervisory management present, to discuss the transition plan. At the meeting, hand out a list of points of agreement and points of disagreement. Suggest appropriate compromises and mediate the discussion. Make notes of the items agreed at the meeting and send a follow up email to each of the participants afterwards to ensure these were correctly noted. Make sure to ask if there are any questions or concerns other than those discussed regarding the transition plan.

- If agreement cannot be reached on all points after a reasonable time in this meeting, schedule a later meeting and request participants to think about possible resolutions.

- Ultimately, if agreement cannot be reached after reasonable attempts, you (GTL) will make the decision.

- The GTL has the authority to decide points upon which there is not agreement of the employee and manager after a reasonable time for negotiation.
- If the employee or manager ultimately refuses to sign or abide by a reasonable transition plan, as determined by the GTL, that employee or manager will be subject to corrective action, up to and including termination. This is permissible because the Company retains the legal right to set terms and conditions of employment.

- Employee and manager receive a copy of the completed and signed transition agreement. The manager has a duty to keep the information contained therein confidential.

2D. Guidelines Review Session

This is an information session with those in frequent workplace contact, including co-workers and, if appropriate, vendors and customers. Media relations should also be invited to the meeting. This session may be conducted by the GTL or an outside expert, if warranted. The purpose of this session is threefold: 1) to introduce them to gender transition and to advise them of what to expect, 2) explain The Company's guidelines and appropriate norms of employee conduct, and 3) where to go to obtain guidance or make a complaint. The scheduling and notification of this meeting should not take place until the transition plan is signed by management and the GTL, in collaboration with the employee in transition, so that information given to the employees is correct and not subject to change without warning.

Depending upon the circumstances, it may be more appropriate to have a separate meeting for vendors, individual meetings with customers, or notification of these groups by the GTL in a brief letter noting the new name and pronoun. The GTL should get input from the employee in transition and management when making this decision. It may also be appropriate to consider the input of others who have a primary relationship with these vendors or customers, such as purchasing officers and sales representatives.

Some employees in transition may be concerned about the Guidelines Review Session. The GTL should consider the concerns of the employee in transition in the set-up and conduct of the meeting, and assure the employee in transition that it is not a referendum on the employee's personal choices. However, it is important for the session to be held. To the extent that the employee in transition is appearing in public in a different gender role, his/her transition is a public event. Company employees must be apprised of the Company's guidelines and expected norms and have a forum to express questions. All other aspects of the employee's private life will remain private. However, if an employee in transition insists that a policy review session not be held because of concerns about safety or privacy, the GTL may decide that a policy review session is inadvisable. In that case, private meetings with select co-workers may be appropriate.

3. Facilities Usage Criteria

Some facilities, such as bathrooms and locker rooms, are segregated on the basis of sex. This section sets forth the factors to be considered in regard to bathrooms, locker rooms and other gender-specific spaces.

Because of the cultural preference for sex segregated facilities, a great deal of sensitivity is required in regard to facilities usage. The employee in gender transition may feel that his/her new gender is not being recognized if they are not permitted to use facilities reserved for that gender. On the other hand, co-workers may differ as to the

73

employee's gender, raising objections to the usage of any facilities whatsoever.

Company, as the employer, is permitted by law to set the terms and conditions of employment, as long as it does not contravene the law. Company has an interest in minimal workplace disruption during gender transition. Therefore, facilities usage will be determined on a case-by-case basis. This is not to say, however, that the decision is to be arbitrary or capricious. Rather, after considering the relevant factors, the GTL must make a decision as to the most appropriate plan for facilities usage.

1. Bathrooms – factors to be considered

- Number of bathrooms within reasonable walking distance

  If there is more than one multi-use bathroom within reasonable walking distance, then one of these may be designated as the bathroom to be used by the employee in gender transition. The reasoning here is that co-workers, if they feel uncomfortable using that bathroom, may use others.

- Availability of single use or lockable bathrooms

  If there is a single use bathroom, or a multi-use bathroom that is lockable, that may be designated as the bathroom to be used by the employee in gender transition.

- Length of employee's transition

  Over time, most co-workers tend to become more comfortable with the employee in gender transition, and the bathroom becomes much less of an issue than it is at the beginning of the process. If the employee is transitioning to living in the new gender within a few weeks, more time may be needed for co-workers to become comfortable. If the employee transition will take place over a few months, co-workers probably will become sufficiently comfortable to reduce concerns about bathroom usage to a manageable level.

It also depends on the local area in which the transition is taking place. The local culture in some areas are extremely tolerant of differences, and gender transition is in the workplace is accepted more quickly. In other areas, the local culture is more traditional in regard to deviations from accepted social norms, and comfort level with gender transition will progress more slowly.

- Employee's comfort level

   Some employees in gender transition feel more comfortable using a private single-use bathroom. Others feel comfortable using a multi-use public bathroom, and have successfully done so consistently over a period of time. An employee in transition who is hesitant in using the bathroom may convey anxiety to co-workers, causing objections to arise. This comfort level should be taken into account.

- Co-worker comfort level

   In some work environments, all co-workers are comfortable with sharing a bathroom with an employee in gender transition. In other work environments, a reasonable objection will be raised. The work environment should be assessed to determine the likely scenario. This should not, however, be the sole consideration used in deciding on facilities usage. There is always a possibility that someone might object, however unreasonably. Rather, its importance is that it allows human resources to prepare appropriate resources to provide guidance to employees who have concerns about the decision.

If it appears, after several attempts at mediation, that there is an irreconcilable conflict between the employee's position on facilities usage and that of management or co-workers, the GTL should make contact with the legal department for their input on an appropriate solution.

2. Locker rooms and other gender-specific spaces (e.g. shower rooms) – factors to be considered

Some sites have locker rooms for changing into work clothing and showering. Even more than bathrooms, locker room facilities raise cultural concerns about public nudity.

- the availability of single use or lockable facilities for showering (if appropriate) and changing clothes

If there is a single use locker room or shower room, bathroom with shower, or a multi-use locker room/shower room that is lockable, that may be designated as the facility to be used by the employee in gender transition.

- The presence of private stalls within the locker room where employees can shower and change clothes

Some locker room facilities have private stalls within the locker room where employees can shower and change clothes. This reduces the impact of public nudity, though it does not eliminate it. In very tolerant environments, this may reduce the impact sufficiently to make this locker room appropriate for use by the employee in transition at some point. In more traditional environments, the presence of private stalls may not create sufficient comfort to make the use of this locker room appropriate for use by the employee in transition.

- Length of employee's transition

Over time, most co-workers tend to become more comfortable with the employee in gender transition, and the locker room may become less of an issue than it is at the beginning of the process. If the employee is transitioning to living in the new gender within a few weeks, more time may be needed for co-workers to become comfortable. If the employee transition will take place over a few months, co-workers may become sufficiently comfortable to reduce concerns about locker room usage to a manageable level.

It also depends on the local area in which the transition is taking place. The local culture in some areas are extremely tolerant of differences, and gender transition is in the workplace is accepted more quickly. In other areas, the local culture is more traditional in regard to deviations from accepted social norms, and comfort level with gender transition will progress more slowly.

- Employee's comfort level

Some employees in gender transition feel more comfortable using a private single-use locker room. Others feel comfortable using a multi-use public locker room, and have successfully done so consistently over a period of time. An employee in transition who is hesitant in using the locker room may convey anxiety to co-workers, causing objections to arise. This comfort level should be taken into account.

- Co-worker comfort level

In some work environments, all co-workers are comfortable with sharing a locker room with an employee in gender transition. In other work environments, a reasonable objection will be raised. The work environment should be assessed to determine the likely scenario. This should not, however, be the sole consideration used in deciding on facilities usage. There is always the possibility of some objection being raised, however unreasonably. Rather, its importance is that it allows human resources to prepare appropriate resources to provide guidance to employees who have concerns about the decision.

If it appears, after several attempts at mediation, that there is an irreconcilable conflict between the employee's position on facilities usage and that of management or co-workers, the GTL should make contact with the legal department for their input on an appropriate solution.

3. Changes in Circumstances

    When gender transition has been in place for a few months, the comfort level of the employee in transition and the co-workers usually increases. In addition, the appearance of employees in transition tends to conform more to the expected norms of their new gender with time, increasing co-worker comfort. Lastly, there may be changes to the site that change the considerations for facilities usage. The initial decision about facilities usage may be put in place for 30 to 90 days, to be reassessed at the end of that time. Of course, changes in circumstances may be brought up at any time if such changes necessitate modification of the transition plan.

4. Sex Reassignment Surgery (SRS) as a factor in facilities usage determinations

    Sex reassignment surgery refers to surgical procedures intended to assist in transition from one sex to another. The guidelines do not base decisions about facilities usage upon SRS. The Company has based this determination on the following reasons.

• The use of SRS as a factor is inappropriate because there are numerous types of SRS, which vary in their effectiveness and appearance. Such a requirement requires the Company to assess proof regarding specific details of the employee's medical history and treatment. This is problematic because such questions may impact medical privacy laws, which differ by jurisdiction.

- The use of SRS as a factor is inappropriate because it may create the perception that the Company endorses, condones or regulates its employees' decision to undergo gender transition. This is undesirable for reasons including employee relations, public relations, insurance coverage and potential litigation. It is best for the Company to stay out of the employee's medical decision-making.

- The use of SRS as a factor is inappropriate because SRS does not address all objections to facilities usage. The set of five Facilities Usage Criteria better achieves the Company's goals of maximizing workplace harmony and minimizing distractions.

- The use of SRS as a factor is inappropriate because the standards of care of the primary medical organization in this area (www.hbigda.org) require successfully living as the opposite sex for a year or more prior to medical approval for surgery. Therefore, it is likely that an employee in transition will not complete his/her medical treatment for a substantial period of time. Requiring an employee who appears female to the general public to use a men's facility, or vice versa, will likely cause more workplace distraction than necessary. The criteria adopted in these guidelines better addresses these issues than a surgical requirement.

- The use of SRS as a factor is inappropriate because bathroom usage does not generally involve public viewing of nudity. Therefore genital surgery is irrelevant to the facilities usage determination. Locker room usage sometimes involves public viewing of nudity, and therefore the particulars of SRS could be relevant, through the Company will not seek this information from the employee. Rather, the issue is the comfort level of reasonable co-workers with sharing that particular locker room with that employee. This may depend, in part, on the availability of private changing facilities within the locker room.

4. Legal Aspects

Legal protections in the workplace for gender identity are constantly evolving. In the last ten years, there has been a rapid increase in protection on the international, federal, state and local levels.

Some of the countries in which Company does business have prohibited discrimination on the basis of gender identity, including Canada, Britain and Australia. The European Union also prohibits such discrimination. U.S. Federal statutes, however, such as the Americans with Disabilities Act and the Rehabilitation Act of 1973, exclude "transsexualism" and "gender disorders not resulting from physical impairments" from protection. Title VII of the Civil Rights Act prohibits discrimination because of sex, though it does not mention gender identity. However, several states and about one hundred local U.S. communities have passed laws protecting employees from discrimination based on gender identity. Minneapolis passed the first such law in 1975. On the state level, Minnesota passed the first such law in 1993, followed by Rhode Island (2001) New Mexico (2003) California (2004), Illinois (2005) and Maine (2005).

In the last five years, several federal courts have ruled that discrimination on the basis of gender identity is prohibited "sex" discrimination. This means that one may not discriminate against a person because they do not conform to stereotypes about how men and women should appear and behave. For example, a federal Appeals Court held that a transgender bank customer, born male but living as a female and dressing in traditionally female attire, stated a claim for sex discrimination under the Equal Credit Opportunity Act based on a bank loan officer's refusal to serve that customer because of non-traditional gender identity.

State courts and administrative agencies have also been active in extending protection to transgender employees. In 1993, the Washington Supreme Court held that transsexuality is protected disability under that state's disability law. Courts in Massachusetts and New Jersey, and administrative agencies in Florida, Illinois, and Oregon have also so ruled. Some have ruled that state sex discrimination laws include transgender people, including courts in New York, Massachusetts, and New Jersey, and administrative agencies in Connecticut, Hawaii and Vermont. Courts in Washington, D.C. have interpreted the D.C. statute prohibiting "personal appearance" discrimination to include transgender people.

While many jurisdictions do not have laws against gender identity discrimination, it is likely that more and more jurisdictions will adopt such laws in the future. It is in the best interests of the Company not to make employment decisions based on personal identity or other grounds not affecting job performance.

D. Training Co-workers - Guidelines Review Session

Purpose/Summary

In most cases, it is appropriate to hold a meeting for those in frequent workplace contact with an employee in gender transition to review The Company's Gender Transition Guidelines. Due to the sensitive balance between information and privacy, special sensitivity must be shown in the scheduling and conduct of this meeting. This memorandum sets forth guidelines for such meetings. Reference should also be made to the Guidelines for Gender Transition that explain the other steps to be taken in cases of gender transition. This is not to be called a "training session," which may imply to some that the Company advocates and seeks to train employees to accept transgender lifestyles. The purpose of this session is to introduce co-workers to Company policy regarding expected norms of behavior in the workplace regarding an employee who has chosen to transition from one sex to another.

These guidelines do not constitute a contract or contractual obligation or a promise of specific treatment in a specific situation, and the Company reserves the right, in its sole discretion, to amend, modify, or discontinue its use without prior notice, notwithstanding any person's acts, omissions or statements to the contrary.

1. Company Commitment and Objectives

The Company is committed to fostering a work environment where everyone is treated fairly with trust and respect, including employees in gender transition and their co-workers. Company is committed to maintaining a harmonious work environment in cases of gender transition. The objective is to provide guidance for GTLs responsible for conducting a Gender Transition Guidelines Review Session.

2. Requirements for Session

A. Actions to be taken: When an employee notifies the Company of a planned gender transition, there are a series of steps to be taken, contained in the Global Diversity Guidelines for Gender Transition. One of these is to schedule a meeting for those in frequent workplace contact, if appropriate.

This session is conducted by the GTL or, if warranted, by an outside expert with training and experience in speaking about gender transition in the workplace. The employee in transition is not present at the session. If there is an expert, s/he should be provided with these guidelines on a confidential basis to ensure that s/he is aware of The Company's requirements.

The GTL should determine the names and contact info of co-workers in frequent workplace contact with the employee in transition, to determine who should attend the meeting. Media relations should also be invited to the meeting. If there are vendors or customers with whom the employee in transition has frequent workplace contact, these may be invited to the meeting as well. Depending upon the circumstances, it may be more appropriate to have a separate meeting for vendors, individual meetings with customers, or notification of these groups by the GTL in a brief letter noting the new name and pronoun. The GTL should get input from the employee in transition and management when making this decision. It may also be appropriate to consider the input of others who have a primary relationship with these vendors or customers, such as purchasing officers and sales representatives.

The GTL should consult the employee in transition to decide if he/she would like to write a short letter to be handed out at the meeting. The text of the letter should be reviewed by the GTL to ensure that there are no typographical errors or other content distracting to the intent of the letter. The letter should be short, introduce the employee's new name, state his/her commitment to good working environment, and if desired, include a short personal message about his/her transition. A model of an employee letter is provided below.

The GTL should solicit a short letter from management expressing management support. The letter should reference The Company's Equal Opportunity Policy, express management's commitment to non-discrimination and harassment-free work environment for all, commitment to maximizing workplace harmony, express support of employee in transition and encourage co-workers to seek out the GTL for guidance. A model of a management letter is provided below.

The GTL should attend the meeting and be available to speak with employees afterwards.

The GTL should advise the employee in transition of how the meeting went. The GTL should not discuss the names of co-workers or others at the meeting who voiced particular questions or concerns.

B. Purpose of the session and considerations: The purpose of the session is threefold: 1) explain the Company's Gender Transition Guidelines and appropriate norms of employee conduct, 2) to introduce attendees to the concept of gender transition and to advise them of what to expect, and 3) advise where to obtain guidance or voice a complaint.

Some employees in transition may be concerned about the requirement of a Guidelines Review Session, particularly since they will not be present. The GTL and session leader should consider the concerns of the employee in transition in the set-up and conduct of the session. However, it is important that the session be held. To the extent that the employee in transition is appearing in public in a different gender role, his/her transition is a public event. Company employees must be apprised of The Company's guidelines and expected norms and have a forum to express questions and concerns. All other aspects of the employee's private life will remain private. However, in some cases an employee may insist that a Guidelines Review Session not be held because of concerns about

This session requires a balance between information and privacy. While the old and new name of the employee will be revealed, the session is not a referendum on this employee or his/her personal choices, nor is Company taking any position on the employee's personal choices. The intent is strictly as stated above. At the same time, questions and concerns of the employees must be encouraged, because if not addressed directly at this meeting, they will surface in suboptimal ways. This is the reason the meeting is held without the employee in transition. The presence of that employee will make it more difficult for co-workers to voice their questions and concerns for fear of appearing ungracious or critical.

The session leader should be prepared for questions that seem ungracious or critical. Such questions should be answered with sensitivity, even if the meeting leader believes that the question is malicious or mean-spirited. The purpose is not to convince everyone of the morality or propriety of gender transition, and employees are not being asked to change their personal opinions. They are being asked only to follow The Company's guidelines in order to create a harmonious and productive work environment.

If an invitee cannot attend, the GTL should speak to them to review the basics and see if they have any questions or concerns.

3. Draft Agenda

There are certain topics that Company would like to see covered during the policy review session. The session leader's judgment should be used to decide if changes in content, order or style are appropriate given the particular circumstances.

Agenda of Guidelines Review Session (without presence of employee in transition)

- Statement of purpose of the meeting
    - Review Company Gender Transition policies and appropriate norms of employee conduct
    - Introduce gender transition and advise what to expect
    - Advise where to obtain guidance or voice a complaint

- Explanation of gender transition
    - Early feelings of different gender, intensifying into maturity
    - Unclear whether biological or social, possibly both
    - Medical treatment requires concurrence of mental health professionals and physicians
    - Transition often occurs years later because of shame and prejudice
    - There are three main prejudices against non-traditional gender identity: serious mental illness, sign of criminal tendencies, and indicator of promiscuity. These stereotypes should be put away.

- Company nondiscrimination policy
  - Company's Policy states commitment to non-discrimination and harassment-free work environment
  - Company's Gender Transition Guidelines states commitment to maximizing workplace productivity in cases of gender transition
  - Company's guidelines are a response to gender transition in the workplace, not an endorsement or position of any kind.

- Employee in gender transition
  - Include name and job title (reference to title reframes context from personal to business)

- Changes co-workers can expect to see
  - Name
  - Dress
  - Gendered behavior
  - Appearance
  - Not much else

- Facilities usage
  - As set forth in transition plan

- Appropriate norms of conduct for co-workers
  - The new name of the employee, if any, and the proper pronoun to use (he or she).
  - It is likely that co-workers will make mistakes with name and pronoun, especially at the beginning
  - An appropriate response to making a mistake is to mention the correct name or pronoun. Extended apologies are not necessary.

- If, after a reasonable period of time (i.e., a month or two), a particular employee continually uses the wrong name or pronoun, and such usage appears to be intentionally designed to harass, the GTL will provide guidance to the offending employee.
- It is appropriate for those with a personal relationship to inquire about personal matters generally.
- If you ask a question you think is appropriate, and the co-worker indicates that the question seems inappropriate, it would probably be best to refrain from pursuing it.
- It is The Company's policy that medical privacy be retained by the employee in transition; employees in transition should not be asked to discuss his/her anatomy with co-workers.

- Procedures for guidance or complaints
    - The Company recognizes that this is new for most people, and that employees will have questions and concerns
    - The Company encourages seeking guidance from the GTL
    - Give contact information for GTL
    - Concerns or complaints about gender transition should be directed to the GTL, not to the employee in transition
    - The usual Company grievance procedures apply.
[NOTE TO GTL: While co-workers should bring complaints or concerns to the GTL, the GTL should keep in mind that some matters may fall under other policies, such as sexual harassment.]

- Letter from employee in transition (if any)
- Letter expressing management support

- [when previewing this agenda, make a note to ensure there are sufficient copies of these letters at the meeting]
- Q&A

4. Model Employee and Management Letter

For use at the Gender Transition Guidelines Review Session, , the GTL should consult the employee in transition to decide if he/she would like to write a short letter to be handed out at the meeting. The text of the letter should be reviewed by the GTL to ensure that there are no typographical errors or other content distracting to the intent of the letter. The letter should be short, introduce the employee's new name, state his/her commitment to good working environment, and if desired, include a short personal message about his/her transition. A model of an employee letter is provided below. The content of the letter should be changed as appropriate to fit the particular situation and the writer's individual style.

Dear Friends and Colleagues,

I must share some news about a major personal decision that will affect my appearance at work. In consultation with management, it is now appropriate to discuss this matter in more detail.

My doctors have diagnosed me with *gender dysphoria*, a medical condition in which psychological gender is not in alignment with biological sex. For many, this condition ultimately results in sex reassignment.

During the past few years, I have worked intensively with a therapist having expertise in gender issues. I have finally come to understand the need for a final answer. With this revelation, a huge weight was lifted from my shoulders. After much consideration, I now know what I must do to make my life whole. Though this was a difficult decision, I have decided to begin living my life as a man/woman.

My name has been changed legally to _____.
Additionally, on or about _____, I will be on medical leave. Upon my return I will begin living my life fully as (new name). I will not look very much different than I do now, other than some different clothes. For some of you, this may be difficult to understand or accept. I do not ask that you change your personal opinion. I only ask that you continue to accept me as a valued member of the workplace. It is my hope that this process will be completed with the least amount of disruption to the workplace.

I emphasize that this will not negatively impact my job performance in any way. In fact, having this issue behind me, I will be more at peace. It is my expectation that I will maintain the good working relationships that I currently have with you all. Some of you might feel apprehensive initially, but please remember that I am still the same person that you have always known.

Thank all of you for your consideration, patience and understanding.

Sincerely,

Model Management Letter

For use at the Gender Transition Guidelines Review Session, the GTL should solicit a short letter from management expressing management support. The letter should reference The Company's Equal Opportunity Policy, express management's commitment to non-discrimination and harassment-free work environment for all, commitment to maximizing workplace harmony, express support of employee in transition and encourage co-workers to seek out the GTL for guidance. A model of a management letter is provided below. The content of the letter should be changed as appropriate to fit the particular situation and the writer's individual style.

To Our Team:

We are writing this to notify you of a change regarding one of our team members in the _____ department. Although this change is of a personal nature, it is one that will be visible to you. Consequently, we feel that it is important to let you know about the change and any possible impact it may have.

One of our valued team members, _____, will be continuing a personal transition that began some years ago. Beginning on _____, he/she will be taking a major step in a gender transition and will begin living full-time as a man/woman. He/She _____ has adopted the name _____.

We realize that this may come as a surprise to some people and anticipate that a variety of personal reactions may surface as this change occurs. For that reason, we felt that it would be beneficial to our employees to have an opportunity to learn about The Company's guidelines regarding gender transition and ask any questions they may have.

We reiterate The Company's support for all our employees and their diverse personal lives, as well as The Company's commitment to employee diversity. As always, our responsibility is to ensure a safe and healthy working environment where employees of diverse backgrounds and beliefs can work free of harassment, intimidation, or discrimination.

Please treat _____, with respect, using correct references to name or pronoun of the new gender, refraining from asking inappropriate questions or making inappropriate comments, and respecting employee confidentiality. Particularly at the beginning of gender transition, it is common for co-workers to make some mistakes regarding these matters. Do not take offense at respectful corrections offered by the employee in transition.

If you are interested in learning more about the issues involved in gender transition in the workplace, here are some resources for your consideration. These are provided for informational purposes only, and the Company does not endorse the opinions expresses therein.

1. The Human Rights Campaign has a section on transgender issues in the workplace at http://hrc.org/worklife

2. Brown and Rounsley, True Selves: Understanding Transsexualism -- For Families, Friends, Coworkers, and Helping Professionals (Jossey-Bass 2003) 288 pages. This book, written by psychologists in the field, uses real life stories, actual letters and other examples to give an understanding of what it means to be transgender and offers practical suggestions for compassionate dealing.

3. This book, written by a counselor/activist, gives information on the basics of transgender issues, the process of gender transition at work and co-worker issues. Walworth, Working with a Transsexual: A

Guide for Coworkers (Center for Gender Sanity 2003) 135 pages

Your Company management along with Human Resources is working to support _____ during this transition period and in the performance of her job and ask that you do the same. To minimize disruption to our colleague, we ask that you address any questions or concerns about this subject to _____, our local Diversity Manager.

Thank you for your understanding and consideration in keeping Company a productive and safe working environment for employees of diverse personal backgrounds.

E. Gender Transition: Frequently Asked Questions

This document is for the guidance of HR and legal professionals. It is for their use in being prepared for questions from employees in transition, managers and co-workers. It is not intended to be generally distributed as those without a background understanding of the issues may misconstrue its meaning and intent.

- *What does "gender identity" mean?*
- *What does "gender transition" mean?*
- *How is this related to "sexual orientation"?*
- *Are there medical standards of care for gender transition?*
- *How much accommodation is to be made for employees in gender transition?*
- *How will the employee in transition dress?*

- *What is a "gender transition plan"?*
- *What if the employee in gender transition wishes to deviate from the transition plan?*
- *Isn't this solely a private matter?*
- *What if I or others have a religious or moral objection to gender transition?*
- *What is appropriate or inappropriate to ask a co-worker about his/her gender transition, or for an employee in gender transition to disclose?*
- *What if I make a mistake?*
- *What if I prefer not to recognize the employee's "new identity"?*
- *What about bathrooms?*
- *What about locker rooms?*
- *Is this required by law?*
- *How will this be explained to co-workers, customers and vendors?*
- *What if co-workers, customers or vendors ask not to work with the employee?*
- *How should I respond to media contacts on this issue?*

What does "gender identity" mean?

"Gender identity" is broadly defined as "gendered identification, self-expression and appearance" corresponding to a deeply-felt psychological identification as male or female. Gender identity may or may not correspond to a person's sex assigned at birth. "Gendered identification" refers to the employee's self-determination of his/her gender as male, female, or other, "gendered self-expression" refers to the employee's expression of gender, such as clothing, and "gendered appearance" refers to the employee's appearance that may be interpreted by others as masculine or feminine. Employees may not be subject to discrimination or harassment based on gender identity.

What does "gender transition" mean?

"Gender transition" refers to transition from male to female, or from female to male. Those who transition feel strongly and persistently that their gender identity is different from their sex at birth, and wish to transition from one gender to the other. Thus, a person born female may decide to transition to living as a male. Conversely, a person born male may decide to transition to living as a female.

This transition often takes a year or more. You may have heard the term "transsexual," a term popularized by the medical community in the 1960s, referring to one who undergoes sex reassignment surgery (sometimes called gender confirmation surgery). The term "transgender," of more recent origin, is a broader term encompassing all gender variance, including those in which surgical reassignment is contraindicated.

The Company's guidelines do not use the terms transsexual or transgender. Their meanings are currently subject to debate, making them inappropriate for The Company's purpose. The Company's guidelines are designed to provide for a harmonious workplace in cases of gender transition, and to minimize workplace distractions. Instead, the guidelines use the terms gender identity and employee in transition.

How is this related to "sexual orientation"?

"Sexual orientation" refers to one's orientation towards male and/or female partners. The terms for "sexual orientation" include straight, gay, lesbian and bisexual. Unlike "gender identity," "sexual orientation" does not refer to one's self-identification as male or female. Those who undergo gender transition may consider themselves heterosexual, that is, they prefer partners of the opposite sex (though "opposite sex" can be ambiguous in this context). Thus, everyone has both a sexual orientation (e.g., heterosexual) and a gender identity (e.g., male).

Are there medical standards of care for gender transition?

> The Harry Benjamin International Gender Dysphoria Association (HBIGDA) is considered the leading medical association regarding gender transition. They maintain standards of care regarding gender transition that are observed by most physicians and psychologists who have patients in gender transition. In general, these standards indicate that, in order to qualify for surgical intervention, clients must live for 12 months in the new gender, though there are exceptions. (www.hbigda.org)

> The Company's guidelines are designed to leave medical management to the employee's health providers. The Company does not monitor the employee's medical treatment. The employee's medical treatment is considered a private matter.

How much accommodation is to be made for employees in gender transition?

> When Company becomes aware of gender transition, a gender transition plan is created. That plan sets out reasonable accommodations that the employee is to receive in light of the specific circumstances at the work site.

How will the employee in transition dress?

> It is expected that the employee in transition will adhere to the dress code of his/her new gender, and that appropriate work attire will be worn.

What is a "gender transition plan"?

> This is a plan that will govern the employee's transition. It is agreed to by the Gender Transition Leader (GTL) and the employee's supervisory management. It will address issues such as timeline, dress and facilities usage.

What is the Gender Transition Leader (GTL)?

> This is the local Diversity Manager in charge of the gender transition plan. The GTL has had extensive training in creating and implementing a gender transition plan.

What if the employee in transition wishes to deviate from the gender transition plan?

> The purpose of the transition plan is to ensure that gender transition does not unduly disrupt the work environment, both for the employee in transition and for others in the workplace. Deviation from the transition plan without management approval may constitute grounds for corrective action by Company to ensure that the plan is adhered to in the future. However, if an employee feels that the transition plan needs to be changed in order to constitute a reasonable accommodation, a request should be made to the GTL. The request should specifically state the change requested and evidence supporting a significant need for the change. Within a reasonable period of time, the GTL will contact the employee's manager to discuss the change, and issue a decision.

Isn't this solely a private matter?

> Because of the nature of gender transition on the job, it cannot be kept from those at the workplace. Company deems it best to address the needs of managers and co-workers by providing information on The Company's guidelines in cases of gender

transition. Beyond the fact of gender transition, however, it is a private matter.

What if I or others have a religious or moral objection to gender transition?

Company is not asking employees to change their religious or moral opinions. Employees are entitled to their private opinions regarding these guidelines. The Company's policy only prohibits discrimination and harassment, that is, adverse employment actions or hostile working environments.

What is appropriate or inappropriate to ask a co-worker about his/her gender transition, or for an employee in gender transition to disclose?

Because most people have not been exposed to gender transition, it is often unclear what is appropriate to ask. Here are some guidelines. There are three levels of information.

1. Form of address – if a co-worker is in contact with an employee in gender transition, and is unsure how to address them, it is appropriate to ask how they preferred to be addressed by name (should I call you Susan rather than George?) and what pronoun to use in reference to them (should I refer to you as "she"?).

2. Personal questions – if a co-worker is in frequent contact with an employee in gender transition, and there has been a personal relationship involving sharing about other personal matters, it may be appropriate to ask general personal questions about his/her life. General questions such as "how is it going?" and "are things going well?" are both appropriate and comforting. If you ask a question you think is appropriate, and the co-worker indicates that the question seems inappropriate, it would probably be best to refrain from pursuing it.

3. Medical information – it is not appropriate to ask co-workers questions about medical condition or procedures. Employees in gender transition have a right to keep medical information confidential. Discussion of medical information at the workplace is a waiver of workplace confidentiality, and Company may take action based on such information. Further, it is likely that public disclosure of medical information regarding gender transition will lower the comfort level of co-workers and raise objections to facilities usage.

What if I make a mistake?

Because most people have not been exposed to gender transition, it is likely that co-workers will make mistakes, such as referring to the employee in gender transition by the wrong name or pronoun, or asking inappropriate questions. Employees in transition should gently correct a co-worker who makes a mistake. It is assumed that mistakes will be less frequent after a reasonable period of time.

What if I prefer not to recognize the employee's "new identity"?

Company is not asking employees to change their religious or moral opinions. Employees are entitled to their private opinions regarding the provisions of these guidelines. However, continually addressing the employee by his/her former name or gender identity after a reasonable period of time may constitute a hostile working environment. If brought to The Company's attention, the matter will have to be addressed to ensure that the work environment is not hostile to the employee.

What about bathrooms?

Bathroom accommodations will be based on the specific circumstances at the work site. There are five criteria: number

99

of bathrooms within reasonable walking distance, availability of single use or lockable bathrooms, length of employee's transition, employee's comfort level and co-worker comfort level. At some point, an employee in transition will begin to use public bathrooms of the opposite sex. Co-workers who may be uncomfortable with such arrangements should speak with the GTL to receive guidance.

What about locker rooms?

Locker room accommodations will be based on the specific circumstances at the work site. There are five considerations: the availability of single use or lockable facilities for showering (if appropriate) and changing clothes, the presence of private stalls within the locker room where employees can shower and change clothes, length of employee's transition, employee's comfort level and co-worker comfort level. At some point, it is likely that an employee in transition will begin to use public locker rooms of the opposite sex. Co-workers who may be uncomfortable with such arrangements should speak with the GTL to receive guidance.

Is this required by law?

Legal protections in the workplace for gender identity are constantly evolving. There has been a rapid increase in protection on the international, federal, state and local levels, and the law is in a state of flux. These guidelines are based on Company policy rather than specific legal requirements.

How will this be explained to co-workers, customers and vendors?

A Gender Transition Guidelines Review Session will be held with those in frequent workplace contact with the employee in transition to give guidance on The Company's guidelines.

What if co-workers, customers or vendors ask not to work with the employee?

> The Company does not subject protected employees to adverse employment actions based on his/her personal identity. Therefore, Company cannot honor a request to isolate the employee from certain contacts. Those who choose to work with the Company must respect the Company's policies.

How should I respond to media contacts on this issue?

All media contacts should be referred to the media relations office.

Appendix

Regulatory Issues

OSHA Bathroom Regulations

This excerpt is provided because it is a federal regulation that affects the provision of bathroom facilities for all workers, including transgender workers. While transgender workers are not specifically referenced, the regulation is important to an understanding of their rights to request bathroom facilities within reasonable walking distance.

Code of Federal Regulations, Title 29, Part 1910, Sec. 1910.141 (2006) Sanitation.

Authority: Secs. 4, 6, and 8, Occupational Safety and Health Act of 1970 (29 U.S.C. 653, 655, 657); Secretary of Labor's Order No. 12-71 (36 FR 8754), 8-76 (41 FR 25059), 9-83 (48 FR 35736), 1-90 (55 FR 9033), 6-96 (62 FR 111), 3-2000 (65 FR 50017), or 5-2002 (67 FR 65008), as applicable.
Sections 1910.141, 1910.142, 1910.145, 1910.146, and 1910.147 also issued under 29 CFR part 1911.

(a) General--(1) Scope. This section applies to permanent places of employment.
(2) Definitions applicable to this section.
Nonwater carriage toilet facility, means a toilet facility not connected to a sewer.
Number of employees means, unless otherwise specified, the maximum number of employees present at any one time on a regular shift.

Personal service room, means a room used for activities not directly connected with the production or service function performed by the establishment. Such activities include, but are not limited to, first-aid, medical services, dressing, showering, toilet use, washing, and eating.

Potable water means water which meets the quality standards prescribed in the U.S. Public Health Service Drinking Water Standards, published in 42 CFR part 72, or water which is approved for drinking purposes by the State or local authority having jurisdiction.

Toilet facility, means a fixture maintained within a toilet room for the purpose of defecation or urination, or both.

Toilet room, means a room maintained within or on the premises of any place of employment, containing toilet facilities for use by employees.

Toxic material means a material in concentration or amount which exceeds the applicable limit established by a standard, such as Sec. Sec. 1910.1000 and 1910.1001 or, in the absence of an applicable standard, which is of such toxicity so as to constitute a recognized hazard that is causing or is likely to cause death or serious physical harm.

Urinal means a toilet facility maintained within a toilet room for the sole purpose of urination.

Water closet means a toilet facility maintained within a toilet room for the purpose of both defecation and urination and which is flushed with water.

Wet process means any process or operation in a workroom which normally results in surfaces upon which employees may walk or stand becoming wet.

[[Page 453]]

(3) Housekeeping. (i) All places of employment shall be kept clean to the extent that the nature of the work allows.

(ii) The floor of every workroom shall be maintained, so far as practicable, in a dry condition. Where wet processes are used, drainage shall be maintained and false floors, platforms, mats, or other dry standing places shall be provided, where practicable, or appropriate waterproof footgear shall be provided.

(iii) To facilitate cleaning, every floor, working place, and passageway shall be kept free from protruding nails, splinters, loose boards, and unnecessary holes and openings.

(4) Waste disposal. (i) Any receptacle used for putrescible solid or liquid waste or refuse shall be so constructed that it does not leak and may be thoroughly cleaned and maintained in a sanitary condition. Such a receptacle shall be equipped with a solid tight-fitting cover, unless it can be maintained in a sanitary condition without a cover. This requirement does not prohibit the use of receptacles which are designed to permit the maintenance of a sanitary condition without regard to the aforementioned requirements.

(ii) All sweepings, solid or liquid wastes, refuse, and garbage shall be removed in such a manner as to avoid creating a menace to health and as often as necessary or appropriate to maintain the place of employment in a sanitary condition.

(5) Vermin control. Every enclosed workplace shall be so constructed, equipped, and maintained, so far as reasonably practicable, as to prevent the entrance or harborage of rodents, insects, and other vermin. A continuing and effective extermination program shall be instituted where their presence is detected.

(b) Water supply--(1) Potable water. (i) Potable water shall be provided in all places of employment, for drinking, washing of the person, cooking, washing of foods, washing of cooking or eating utensils, washing of food preparation or processing premises, and personal service rooms.

(ii) [Reserved]

(iii) Portable drinking water dispensers shall be designed, constructed, and serviced so that sanitary conditions are maintained, shall be capable of being closed, and shall be equipped with a tap.

(iv) [Reserved]

(v) Open containers such as barrels, pails, or tanks for drinking water from which the water must be dipped or poured, whether or not they are fitted with a cover, are prohibited.

(vi) A common drinking cup and other common utensils are prohibited.

(2) Nonpotable water. (i) Outlets for nonpotable water, such as water for industrial or firefighting purposes, shall be posted or otherwise marked in a manner that will indicate clearly that the water is unsafe and is not to be used for drinking, washing of the person, cooking, washing of food, washing of cooking or eating utensils, washing of food preparation or processing premises, or personal service rooms, or for washing clothes.

(ii) Construction of nonpotable water systems or systems carrying any other nonpotable substance shall be such as to prevent backflow or backsiphonage into a potable water system.

(iii) Nonpotable water shall not be used for washing any portion of the person, cooking or eating utensils, or clothing. Nonpotable water may be used for cleaning work premises, other than food processing and preparation premises and personal service rooms: Provided, That this nonpotable water does not contain concentrations of chemicals, fecal coliform, or other substances which could create insanitary conditions or be harmful to employees.

(c) Toilet facilities--(1) General. (i) Except as otherwise indicated in this paragraph (c)(1)(i), toilet facilities, in toilet rooms separate for each sex, shall be provided in all places of employment in accordance with table J-1 of this section. The number of facilities to be provided for each sex shall be based on the number of employees of that sex for whom the facilities are furnished. Where toilet rooms will be occupied by no more than one person at a time, can be locked from the inside, and contain at least one water closet, separate toilet rooms for each sex need not be provided. Where such single-occupancy rooms have more than one toilet facility, only one such facility in
[[Page 454]]

each toilet room shall be counted for the purpose of table J-1.

106

Table J-1

Number of employees	Minimum number of water closets \1\
1 to 15....................................	1
16 to 35..................................	2
36 to 55..................................	3
56 to 80..................................	4
81 to 110.................................	5.
111 to 150...............................	6
Over 150.................................	(\2\)

\1\ Where toilet facilities will not be used by women, urinals may be provided instead of water closets, except that the number of water closets in such cases shall not be reduced to less than \2/3\ of the minimum specified.
\2\ 1 additional fixture for each additional 40 employees.

   (ii) The requirements of paragraph (c)(1)(i) of this section do not apply to mobile crews or to normally unattended work locations so long as employees working at these locations have transportation immediately available to nearby toilet facilities which meet the other requirements of this subparagraph.
   (iii) The sewage disposal method shall not endanger the health of employees.
   (2) Construction of toilet rooms. (i) Each water closet shall occupy a separate compartment with a door and walls or partitions between fixtures sufficiently high to assure privacy.
   (ii) [Reserved]
   (d) Washing facilities--(1) General. Washing facilities shall be maintained in a sanitary condition.

(2) Lavatories. (i) Lavatories shall be made available in all places of employment. The requirements of this subdivision do not apply to mobile crews or to normally unattended work locations if employees working at these locations have transportation readily available to nearby washing facilities which meet the other requirements of this paragraph.

(ii) Each lavatory shall be provided with hot and cold running water, or tepid running water.

(iii) Hand soap or similar cleansing agents shall be provided.

(iv) Individual hand towels or sections thereof, of cloth or paper, warm air blowers or clean individual sections of continuous cloth toweling, convenient to the lavatories, shall be provided.

(3) Showers. (i) Whenever showers are required by a particular standard, the showers shall be provided in accordance with paragraphs (d)(3) (ii) through (v) of this section.

(ii) One shower shall be provided for each 10 employees of each sex, or numerical fraction thereof, who are required to shower during the same shift.

(iii) Body soap or other appropriate cleansing agents convenient to the showers shall be provided as specified in paragraph (d)(2)(iii) of this section.

(iv) Showers shall be provided with hot and cold water feeding a common discharge line.

(v) Employees who use showers shall be provided with individual clean towels.

(e) Change rooms. Whenever employees are required by a particular standard to wear protective clothing because of the possibility of contamination with toxic materials, change rooms equipped with storage facilities for street clothes and separate storage facilities for the protective clothing shall be provided.

(f) Clothes drying facilities. Where working clothes are provided by the employer and become wet or are washed between shifts, provision shall be made to insure that such clothing is dry before reuse.

(g) Consumption of food and beverages on the premises--(1) Application. This paragraph shall apply only where employees are permitted to consume food or beverages, or both, on the premises.

(2) Eating and drinking areas. No employee shall be allowed to consume food or beverages in a toilet room nor in any area exposed to a toxic material.

(3) Waste disposal containers. Receptacles constructed of smooth, corrosion resistant, easily cleanable, or disposable materials, shall be provided and used for the disposal of waste food. The number, size, and location of such receptacles shall encourage their use and not result in overfilling. They shall be emptied not less frequently than once each working day, unless unused, and shall be maintained in a clean and sanitary condition. Receptacles shall be provided with a solid tight-fitting

[[Page 455]]

cover unless sanitary conditions can be maintained without use of a cover.

(4) Sanitary storage. No food or beverages shall be stored in toilet rooms or in an area exposed to a toxic material.

(h) Food handling. All employee food service facilities and operations shall be carried out in accordance with sound hygienic principles. In all places of employment where all or part of the food service is provided, the food dispensed shall be wholesome, free from spoilage, and shall be processed, prepared, handled, and stored in such a manner as to be protected against contamination.

[39 FR 23502, June 27, 1974, as amended at 40 FR 18446, April 28, 1975;
40 FR 23073, May 28, 1975; 43 FR 49748, Oct. 24, 1978; 63 FR 33466, June
18, 1998]

EEOC Enforcement Guidance on Disability-Related Inquiries

This EEOC memo is included here because it sets forth the standard for making post-employment medical examinations and inquiries. It is important in light of the ruling of the Minnesota Supreme Court in Goins v. West Group, and the court's intimation that employers can ask their transgender employees about their surgical status in making decisions about bathroom usage. This memo suggests that such an inquiry or examination would violate the federal Americans With Disabilities Act and state statutes of similar import.

EEOC Enforcement Guidance on Disability-Related Inquiries and Medical Examinations of Employees Under the Americans with Disabilities Act

The U.S. Equal Employment Opportunity Commission

			Number
EEOC	*NOTICE*		915.002
			Date
			7/27/00

1. SUBJECT: EEOC Enforcement Guidance on Disability-Related Inquiries and Medical Examinations of Employees Under the Americans with Disabilities Act (ADA)

2. PURPOSE: This enforcement guidance explains when it is permissible for employers to make disability-related inquiries or require medical examinations of employees.

3. EFFECTIVE DATE: Upon receipt.

4. EXPIRATION DATE: As an exception to EEOC Order 205.001, Appendix B,Attachment 4, § a(5), this Notice will remain in effect until rescinded or superseded.

5. ORIGINATOR: ADA Division, Office of Legal Counsel.

6. INSTRUCTIONS: File after Section 902 of Volume II of the Compliance Manual.

ENFORCEMENT GUIDANCE:
DISABILITY-RELATED INQUIRIES AND MEDICAL EXAMINATIONS OF EMPLOYEES UNDER THE AMERICANS WITH DISABILITIES ACT (ADA)

TABLE OF CONTENTS

INDEX

INTRODUCTION

Title I of the Americans with Disabilities Act of 1990 (the "ADA")[1] limits an employer's ability to make disability-related inquiries or require medical examinations at three stages: pre-offer, post-offer, and during employment. In its guidance on preemployment disability-related inquiries and medical examinations, the Commission addressed the ADA's restrictions on disability-related inquiries and medical examinations at the pre- and post-offer stages.[2] This enforcement guidance focuses on the ADA's limitations on disability-related inquiries and medical examinations during employment.[3]

Disability-related inquiries and medical examinations of employees must be "job-related and consistent with business necessity." This guidance gives examples of the kinds of questions that are and are not "disability-related" and examples of tests and procedures that generally are and are not "medical." The guidance also defines what the term "job-related and consistent with business necessity" means and addresses situations in which an employer would meet the general standard for asking an employee a disability-related question or requiring a medical examination. Other acceptable inquiries and examinations of employees, such as inquiries and examinations required by federal law and those that are part of voluntary wellness and health screening programs, as well as invitations to voluntarily self-identify as persons with disabilities for affirmative action purposes, also are addressed.[4]

GENERAL PRINCIPLES

A. Background

Historically, many employers asked applicants and employees to provide information concerning their physical and/or mental condition.

113

This information often was used to exclude and otherwise discriminate against individuals with disabilities -- particularly nonvisible disabilities, such as diabetes, epilepsy, heart disease, cancer, and mental illness -- despite their ability to perform the job. The ADA's provisions concerning disability-related inquiries and medical examinations reflect Congress's intent to protect the rights of applicants and employees to be assessed on merit alone, while protecting the rights of employers to ensure that individuals in the workplace can efficiently perform the essential functions of their jobs.[5]

Under the ADA, an employer's ability to make disability-related inquiries or require medical examinations is analyzed in three stages: pre-offer, post-offer, and employment. At the first stage (prior to an offer of employment), the ADA prohibits all disability-related inquiries and medical examinations, *even if* they are related to the job.[6] At the second stage (after an applicant is given a conditional job offer, but before s/he starts work), an employer may make disability-related inquiries and conduct medical examinations, regardless of whether they are related to the job, as long as it does so for all entering employees in the same job category.[7] At the third stage (after employment begins), an employer may make disability-related inquiries and require medical examinations *only* if they are job-related and consistent with business necessity.[8]

The ADA requires employers to treat any medical information obtained from a disability-related inquiry or medical examination (including medical information from voluntary health or wellness programs [9]), as well as any medical information voluntarily disclosed by an employee, as a confidential medical record. Employers may share such information only in limited circumstances with supervisors, managers, first aid and safety personnel, and government officials investigating compliance with the ADA.[10]

B. Disability-Related Inquiries and Medical Examinations of Employees

The ADA states, in relevant part:

A covered entity[11] shall not require a medical examination and shall not make inquiries of an employee as to whether such employee is an individual with a disability or as to the nature and severity of the disability, unless such examination or inquiry is shown to be job-related and consistent with business necessity.[12]

This statutory language makes clear that the ADA's restrictions on inquiries and examinations apply to all employees, not just those with disabilities. Unlike other provisions of the ADA which are limited to qualified individuals with disabilities,[13] the use of the term "employee" in this provision reflects Congress's intent to cover a broader class of individuals and to prevent employers from asking questions and conducting medical examinations that serve no legitimate purpose.[14] Requiring an individual to show that s/he is a person with a disability in order to challenge a disability-related inquiry or medical examination would defeat this purpose.[15] *Any* employee, therefore, has a right to challenge a disability-related inquiry or medical examination that is not job-related and consistent with business necessity.

Only disability-related inquiries and medical examinations are subject to the ADA's restrictions. Thus, the first issue that must be addressed is whether the employer's question is a "disability-related inquiry" or whether the test or procedure it is requiring is a "medical examination." The next issue is whether the person being questioned or asked to submit to a medical examination is an "employee." If the person is an employee (rather than an applicant or a person who has received a conditional job offer), the final issue is whether the inquiry or examination is "job-related and consistent with business necessity" or is otherwise permitted by the ADA.[16]

1. What is a "disability-related inquiry"?

115

In its guidance on Preemployment Questions and Medical Examinations, the Commission explained in detail what is and is not a disability-related inquiry.[17] A "disability-related inquiry" is a question (or series of questions) that is likely to elicit information about a disability.[18] The same standards for determining whether a question is disability-related in the pre- and post-offer stages apply to the employment stage.[19]

Disability-related inquiries may include the following:
asking an employee whether s/he has (or ever had) a disability or how s/he became disabled or inquiring about the nature or severity of an employee's disability;[20]

asking an employee to provide medical documentation regarding his/her disability;

asking an employee's co-worker, family member, doctor, or another person about an employee's disability;

asking about an employee's genetic information;[21]

asking about an employee's prior workers' compensation history;[22]

asking an employee whether s/he currently is taking any prescription drugs or medications, whether s/he has taken any such drugs or medications in the past, or monitoring an employee's taking of such drugs or medications;[23] and,

asking an employee a broad question about his/her impairments that is likely to elicit information about a disability (e.g., What impairments do you have?).[24]

Questions that are not likely to elicit information about a disability are *not* disability-related inquiries and, therefore, are not prohibited under the ADA.

Questions that are permitted include the following:

asking generally about an employee's well being (e.g., How are you?),

asking an employee who looks tired or ill if s/he is feeling okay, asking an employee who is sneezing or coughing whether s/he has a cold or allergies, or asking how an employee is doing following the

death of a loved one or the end of a marriage/relationship;

asking an employee about nondisability-related impairments (e.g., how did you break your leg?)[25]

asking an employee whether s/he can perform job functions;

asking an employee whether s/he has been drinking;[26]

asking an employee about his/her current illegal use of drugs;[27]

asking a pregnant employee how she is feeling or when her baby is due;[28] and,

asking an employee to provide the name and telephone number of a person to contact in case of a medical emergency.

2. What is a "medical examination"?

A "medical examination" is a procedure or test that seeks information about an individual's physical or mental impairments or health.[29] The guidance on Preemployment Questions and Medical Examinations lists the following factors that should be considered to determine whether a test (or procedure) is a medical examination: (1) whether the test is administered by a health care professional; (2) whether the test is interpreted by a health care professional; (3) whether the test is designed to reveal an impairment or physical or mental health; (4)

117

whether the test is invasive; (5) whether the test measures an employee's performance of a task or measures his/her physiological responses to performing the task ; (6) whether the test normally is given in a medical setting; and, (7) whether medical equipment is used.[30]

In many cases, a combination of factors will be relevant in determining whether a test or procedure is a medical examination. In other cases, one factor may be enough to determine that a test or procedure is medical.

Medical examinations include, but are not limited to, the following:

vision tests conducted and analyzed by an ophthalmologist or optometrist;

blood, urine, and breath analyses to check for alcohol use;[31]

blood, urine, saliva, and hair analyses to detect disease or genetic markers (e.g., for conditions such as sickle cell trait, breast cancer, Huntington's disease);

blood pressure screening and cholesterol testing;

nerve conduction tests (i.e., tests that screen for possible nerve damage and susceptibility to injury, such as carpal tunnel syndrome);

range-of-motion tests that measure muscle strength and motor function;

pulmonary function tests (i.e., tests that measure the capacity of the lungs to hold air and to move air in and out);

psychological tests that are designed to identify a mental disorder or impairment; and,

diagnostic procedures such as x-rays, computerized axial tomography (CAT) scans, and magnetic resonance imaging (MRI).

118

There are a number of procedures and tests employers may require that generally are not considered medical examinations, including:
tests to determine the current illegal use of drugs;[32]
physical agility tests, which measure an employee's ability to perform actual or simulated job tasks, and physical fitness tests, which measure an employee's performance of physical tasks, such as running or lifting, as long as these tests do not include examinations that could be considered medical (e.g., measuring heart rate or blood pressure);
tests that evaluate an employee's ability to read labels or distinguish objects as part of a demonstration of the ability to perform actual job functions;

psychological tests that measure personality traits such as honesty, preferences, and habits; and,
polygraph examinations.[33]

3. Who is an "employee"?

The ADA defines the term "employee" as "an individual employed by an employer."[34] As a general rule, an individual is an employee if an entity controls the means and manner of his/her work performance.[35]

Where more than one entity controls the means and manner of how an individual's work is done, the individual is an employee of each entity.
Example: XYZ, a temporary employment agency, hires a computer programmer and assigns him to Business Systems, Inc. (BSI), one of its clients. XYZ determines when the programmer's assignment begins and pays him a salary based on the number of hours worked as reported by BSI. XYZ also withholds social security and taxes and provides workers' compensation coverage. BSI sets the hours of work, the duration of the job, and oversees the programmer's work. XYZ can terminate the programmer if his performance is unacceptable to BSI.
The programmer is an employee of both XYZ and BSI. Thus, XYZ and BSI may ask the programmer disability-related questions and

require a medical examination only if they are job-related and consistent with business necessity.

4. How should an employer treat an employee who applies for a new (i.e., different) job with the same employer?

An employer should treat an employee who *applies* for a new job as an applicant for the new job.[36] The employer, therefore, is prohibited from asking disability-related questions or requiring a medical examination before making the individual a conditional offer of the new position.[37] Further, where a current supervisor has medical information regarding an employee who is applying for a new job, s/he may not disclose that information to the person interviewing the employee for the new job or to the supervisor of that job.

After the employer extends an offer for the new position, it may ask the individual disability-related questions or require a medical examination as long as it does so for all entering employees in the same job category. If an employer withdraws the offer based on medical information (i.e., screens him/her out because of a disability), it must show that the reason for doing so was job-related and consistent with business necessity.

An individual is *not* an applicant where s/he is noncompetitively entitled to another position with the same employer (e.g., because of seniority or satisfactory performance in his/her current position). An individual who is temporarily assigned to another position and then returns to his/her regular job also is not an applicant. These individuals are employees and, therefore, the employer only may make a disability-related inquiry or require a medical examination that is job-related and consistent with business necessity.

Example A: Ruth, an inventory clerk for a retail store, applies for a position as a sales associate at the same store. Ruth is an applicant for the new job. Accordingly, her employer may not ask any disability-related questions or require a medical examination before extending her a conditional offer of the sales associate position. Following a

120

conditional offer of employment, the employer may ask disability-related questions and conduct medical examinations, regardless of whether they are related to the job, as long as it does so for all entering employees in the same job category.[38]

Example B: A grade 4 clerk typist has worked in the same position for one year and received a rating of outstanding on her annual performance appraisal. When she was hired, she was told that she automatically would be considered for promotion to the next grade after 12 months of satisfactory performance. Because the clerk typist is noncompetitively entitled to a promotion, she is an employee and not an applicant. The employer, therefore, only may make a disability-related inquiry or require a medical examination that is job-related and consistent with business necessity.

Example C: A newspaper reporter, who regularly works out of his employer's New York headquarters, is temporarily assigned to its bureau in South Africa to cover the political elections. Because the reporter is on a temporary assignment doing the same job, he is an employee; the employer, therefore, may make disability-related inquiries or require medical examinations only if they are job-related and consistent with business necessity.

JOB-RELATED AND CONSISTENT WITH BUSINESS NECESSITY

Once an employee is on the job, his/her actual performance is the best measure of ability to do the job. When a need arises to question the ability of an employee to do the essential functions of his/her job or to question whether the employee can do the job without posing a direct threat due to a medical condition, it may be job-related and consistent with business necessity for an employer to make disability-related inquiries or require a medical examination.

A. **In General**

5. When may a disability-related inquiry or medical examination of an employee be "job-related and consistent with business necessity"?

Generally, a disability-related inquiry or medical examination of an employee may be "job-related and consistent with business necessity" when an employer "has a reasonable belief, based on objective evidence, that: (1) an employee's ability to perform essential job functions will be impaired by a medical condition; or (2) an employee will pose a direct threat[(39)] due to a medical condition."[(40)] Disability-related inquiries and medical examinations that follow up on a request for reasonable accommodation when the disability or need for accommodation is not known or obvious also may be job-related and consistent with business necessity. In addition, periodic medical examinations and other monitoring under specific circumstances may be job-related and consistent with business necessity.[(41)]

Sometimes this standard may be met when an employer knows about a particular employee's medical condition, has observed performance problems, and reasonably can attribute the problems to the medical condition. An employer also may be given reliable information by a credible third party that an employee has a medical condition,[(42)] or the employer may observe symptoms indicating that an employee may have a medical condition that will impair his/her ability to perform essential job functions or will pose a direct threat. In these situations, it may be job-related and consistent with business necessity for an employer to make disability-related inquiries or require a medical examination.

Example A: For the past two months, Sally, a tax auditor for a federal government agency, has done a third fewer audits than the average employee in her unit. She also has made numerous mistakes in assessing whether taxpayers provided appropriate documentation for claimed deductions. When questioned about her poor performance, Sally tells her supervisor that the medication she takes for her lupus makes her lethargic and unable to concentrate.

Based on Sally's explanation for her performance problems, the agency has a reasonable belief that her ability to perform the essential functions of her job will be impaired because of a medical condition.[43] Sally's supervisor, therefore, may make disability-related inquiries (e.g.,ask her whether she is taking a new medication and how long the medication's side effects are expected to last), or the supervisor may ask Sally to provide documentation from her health care provider explaining the effects of the medication on Sally's ability to perform her job.

Example B: A crane operator works at construction sites hoisting concrete panels weighing several tons. A rigger on the ground helps him load the panels, and several other workers help him position them. During a break, the crane operator appears to become light-headed, has to sit down abruptly, and seems to have some difficulty catching his breath. In response to a question from his supervisor about whether he is feeling all right, the crane operator says that this has happened to him a few times during the past several months, but he does not know why.

The employer has a reasonable belief, based on objective evidence, that the employee will pose a direct threat and, therefore, may require the crane operator to have a medical examination to ascertain whether the symptoms he is experiencing make him unfit to perform his job. To ensure that it receives sufficient information to make this determination, the employer may want to provide the doctor who does the examination with a description of the employee's duties, including any physical qualification standards, and require that the employee provide documentation of his ability to work following the examination.[44]

Example C: Six months ago, a supervisor heard a secretary tell her co-worker that she discovered a lump in her breast and is afraid that she may have breast cancer. Since that conversation, the secretary still comes to work every day and performs her duties in her normal efficient manner.

123

In this case, the employer does not have a reasonable belief, based on objective evidence, either that the secretary's ability to perform her essential job functions will be impaired by a medical condition or that she will pose a direct threat due to a medical condition. The employer, therefore, may not make any disability-related inquiries or require the employee to submit to a medical examination.

An employer's reasonable belief that an employee's ability to perform essential job functions will be impaired by a medical condition or that s/he will pose a direct threat due to a medical condition must be based on *objective evidence* obtained, or reasonably available to the employer, prior to making a disability-related inquiry or requiring a medical examination. Such a belief requires an assessment of the employee and his/her position and cannot be based on general assumptions.

Example D: An employee who works in the produce department of a large grocery store tells her supervisor that she is HIV-positive. The employer is concerned that the employee poses a direct threat to the health and safety of others because she frequently works with sharp knives and might cut herself while preparing produce for display. The store requires any employee working with sharp knives to wear gloves and frequently observes employees to determine whether they are complying with this policy. Available scientific evidence shows that the possibility of transmitting HIV from a produce clerk to other employees or the public, assuming the store's policy is observed, is virtually nonexistent. Moreover, the Department of Health and Human Services (HHS), which has the responsibility under the ADA for preparing a list of infectious and communicable diseases that may be transmitted through food handling,[45] does not include HIV on the list.[46]

In this case, the employer does *not* have a reasonable belief, based on objective evidence, that this employee's ability to perform the essential functions of her position will be impaired or that she will pose a direct threat due to her medical condition. The employer, therefore, may not make any disability-related inquiries or require the employee to submit to a medical examination.[47]

6. May an employer make disability-related inquiries or require a medical examination of an employee based, in whole or in part, on information learned from another person?

Yes, if the information learned is reliable and would give rise to a reasonable belief that the employee's ability to perform essential job functions will be impaired by a medical condition or that s/he will pose a direct threat due to a medical condition, an employer may make disability-related inquiries or require a medical examination.

Factors that an employer might consider in assessing whether information learned from another person is sufficient to justify asking disability-related questions or requiring a medical examination of an employee include: (1) the relationship of the person providing the information to the employee about whom it is being provided; (2) the seriousness of the medical condition at issue; (3) the possible motivation of the person providing the information; (4) how the person learned the information (e.g., directly from the employee whose medical condition is in question or from someone else); and (5) other evidence that the employer has that bears on the reliability of the information provided.

Example A: Bob and Joe are close friends who work as copy editors for an advertising firm. Bob tells Joe that he is worried because he has just learned that he had a positive reaction to a tuberculin skin test and believes that he has tuberculosis. Joe encourages Bob to tell their supervisor, but Bob refuses. Joe is reluctant to breach Bob's trust but is concerned that he and the other editors may be at risk since they all work closely together in the same room. After a couple of sleepless nights, Joe tells his supervisor about Bob. The supervisor questions Joe about how he learned of Bob's alleged condition and finds Joe's explanation credible.

Because tuberculosis is a potentially life-threatening medical condition and can be passed from person to person by coughing or sneezing, the supervisor has a reasonable belief, based on objective evidence, that Bob will pose a direct threat if he in fact has active tuberculosis. Under these circumstances, the employer may make disability-related inquiries or require a medical examination to the extent necessary to determine whether Bob has tuberculosis and is contagious.[48]

Example B: Kim works for a small computer consulting firm. When her mother died suddenly, she asked her employer for three weeks off, in addition to the five days that the company customarily provides in the event of the death of a parent or spouse, to deal with family matters. During her extended absence, a rumor circulated among some employees that Kim had been given additional time off to be treated for depression. Shortly after Kim's return to work, Dave, who works on the same team with Kim, approached his manager to say that he had heard that some workers were concerned about their safety. According to Dave, people in the office claimed that Kim was talking to herself and threatening to harm them. Dave said that he had not observed the strange behavior himself but was not surprised to hear about it given Kim's alleged recent treatment for depression. Dave's manager sees Kim every day and never has observed this kind of behavior. In addition, none of the co-workers to whom the manager spoke confirmed Dave's statements.

In this case, the employer does not have a reasonable belief, based on objective evidence, that Kim's ability to perform essential functions will be impaired or that s/he will pose a direct threat because of a medical condition. The employer, therefore, would not be justified in asking Kim disability-related questions or requiring her to submit to a medical examination because the information provided by Dave is not reliable.

Example C: Several customers have complained that Richard, a customer service representative for a mail order company, has made numerous errors on their orders. They consistently have complained that Richard seems to have a problem hearing because he always asks them to repeat the item number(s), color(s), size(s), credit card number(s), etc., and frequently asks them to speak louder. They also have complained that he incorrectly reads back their addresses even when they have enunciated clearly and spelled street names.

In this case, the employer has a reasonable belief, based on objective evidence, that Richard's ability to correctly process mail orders will be impaired by a medical condition (i.e., a problem with his hearing). The employer, therefore, may make disability-related inquiries of Richard or require him to submit to a medical examination to determine whether he can perform the essential functions of his job.

7. May an employer ask an employee for documentation when s/he requests a reasonable accommodation?

Yes. The employer is entitled to know that an employee has a covered disability that requires a reasonable accommodation.[49] Thus, when the disability or the need for the accommodation is not known or obvious, it is job-related and consistent with business necessity for an employer to ask an employee for reasonable documentation about his/her disability and its functional limitations that require reasonable accommodation.[50]

8. May an employer ask all employees what prescription medications they are taking?

Generally, no. Asking all employees about their use of prescription medications is not job-related and consistent with business necessity.[51] In limited circumstances, however, certain employers may be able to demonstrate that it *is* job-related and consistent with business necessity to require employees in positions affecting public safety to report when they are taking medication that may affect their ability to perform essential functions. Under these limited circumstances, an employer must be able to demonstrate that an employee's inability or impaired ability to perform essential functions will result in a direct threat. For example, a police department could require armed officers to report when they are taking medications that may affect their ability to use a firearm or to perform other essential functions of their job. Similarly, an airline could require its pilots to report when they are taking any medications that may impair their ability to fly. A fire department, however, could not require fire department employees who perform only administrative duties to report their use of medications because it is unlikely that it could show that these employees would pose a direct threat as a result of their inability or impaired ability to perform their essential job functions.

9. What action may an employer take if an employee fails to respond to a disability-related inquiry or fails to submit to a medical examination that is job-related and consistent with business necessity?

The action the employer may take depends on its reason for making the disability-related inquiry or requiring a medical examination.

Example A: A supervisor notices that the quality of work from an ordinarily outstanding employee has deteriorated over the past several months. Specifically, the employee requires more time to complete routine reports, which frequently are submitted late and contain numerous errors. The supervisor also has observed during this period of time that the employee appears to be squinting to see her computer monitor, is holding printed material close to her face to read it, and takes frequent breaks during which she sometimes is seen rubbing her eyes. Concerned about the employee's declining performance, which appears to be due to a medical condition, the supervisor tells her to go see the company doctor, but she does not.

Any discipline that the employer decides to impose should focus on the employee's performance problems. Thus, the employer may discipline the employee for past and future performance problems in accordance with a uniformly applied policy.

Example B: An accountant with no known disability asks for an ergonomic chair because she says she is having back pain. The employer asks the employee to provide documentation from her treating physician that: (1) describes the nature, severity, and duration of her impairment, the activity or activities that the impairment limits, and the extent to which the impairment limits her ability to perform the activity or activities; and (2) substantiates why an ergonomic chair is needed.

Here, the employee's possible disability and need for reasonable accommodation are not obvious. Therefore, if the employee fails to provide the requested documentation or if the documentation does not demonstrate the existence of a disability, the employer can refuse to provide the chair.[52]

B. Scope and Manner of Disability-Related Inquiries and Medical Examinations

10. What documentation may an employer require from an employee who requests a reasonable accommodation?

An employer may require an employee to provide documentation that is sufficient to substantiate that s/he has an ADA disability and needs the reasonable accommodation requested, but cannot ask for unrelated documentation. This means that, in most circumstances, an employer cannot ask for an employee's complete medical records because they are likely to contain information unrelated to the disability at issue and the need for accommodation.[53]

Documentation is sufficient if it: (1) describes the nature, severity, and duration of the employee's impairment, the activity or activities that the impairment limits, and the extent to which the impairment limits the employee's ability to perform the activity or activities; and, (2) substantiates why the requested reasonable accommodation is needed.

Example: An employee, who has exhausted all of his available leave, telephones his supervisor on Monday morning to inform him that he had a severe pain episode on Saturday due to his sickle cell anemia, is in the hospital, and needs time off. Prior to this call, the supervisor was unaware of the employee's medical condition.

The employer can ask the employee to send in documentation from his treating physician that substantiates that the employee has a disability, confirms that his hospitalization is related to his disability, and provides information on how long he may be absent from work.[54]

11. May an employer require an employee to go to a health care professional of the employer's (rather than the employee's) choice when the employee requests a reasonable accommodation?

The ADA does not prevent an employer from requiring an employee to go to an appropriate health care professional of the employer's choice if the employee provides insufficient documentation from his/her treating physician (or other health care professional) to substantiate that s/he has an ADA disability and needs a reasonable accommodation.[55] However, if an employee provides insufficient documentation in response to the employer's initial request, the employer should explain why the documentation is insufficient and allow the employee an opportunity to provide the missing information in a timely manner.[56] The employer also should consider consulting with the employee's doctor (with the employee's consent) before requiring the employee to go to a health care professional of its choice.[57]

Documentation is insufficient if it does not specify the existence of an ADA disability and explain the need for reasonable accommodation.[58] Documentation also might be insufficient where, for example: (1) the health care professional does not have the expertise to give an opinion about the employee's medical condition and the limitations imposed by it; (2) the information does not specify the functional limitations due to the disability; or, (3) other factors indicate that the information provided is not credible or is fraudulent. If an employee provides insufficient documentation, an employer does not have to provide reasonable accommodation until sufficient documentation is provided.

Any medical examination conducted by the employer's health care professional must be job-related and consistent with business necessity. This means that the examination must be limited to determining the existence of an ADA disability and the functional limitations that require reasonable accommodation. If an employer requires an employee to go to a health care professional of the employer's choice, the employer must pay all costs associated with the visit(s).[59]

The Commission has previously stated that when an employee provides sufficient evidence of the existence of a disability and the need for reasonable accommodation, continued efforts by the employer to require that the individual provide more documentation and/or submit to a medical examination could be considered retaliation.[60] However, an employer that requests additional information or requires a medical examination based on a good faith belief that the documentation the employee submitted is insufficient would *not* be liable for retaliation.

12. May an employer require that an employee, who it reasonably believes will pose a direct threat, be examined by an appropriate health care professional of the employer's choice?

Yes. The determination that an employee poses a direct threat must be based on an individualized assessment of the employee's present ability to safely perform the essential functions of the job. This assessment must be based on a reasonable medical judgment that relies on the most current medical knowledge and/or best objective evidence.[61] To meet this burden, an employer may want to have the employee examined by a health care professional of its choice who has expertise in the employee's specific condition and can provide medical information that allows the employer to determine the effects of the condition on the employee's ability to perform his/her job. Any medical examination, however, must be limited to determining whether the employee can perform his/her job without posing a direct threat, with or without reasonable accommodation. An employer also must pay all costs associated with the employee's visit(s) to its health care professional.[62]

An employer should be cautious about relying solely on the opinion of its own health care professional that an employee poses a direct threat where that opinion is contradicted by documentation from the employee's own treating physician, who is knowledgeable about the employee's medical condition and job functions, and/or other objective evidence. In evaluating conflicting medical information, the employer may find it helpful to consider: (1) the area of expertise of each medical professional who has provided information; (2) the kind of information each person providing documentation has about the job's essential functions and the work environment in which they are performed; (3) whether a particular opinion is based on speculation or on current, objectively verifiable information about the risks associated with a particular condition; and, (4) whether the medical opinion is contradicted by information known to or observed by the employer (e.g., information about the employee's actual experience in the job in question or in previous similar jobs).

13. How much medical information can an employer obtain about an employee when it reasonably believes that an employee's ability to perform the essential functions of his/her job will be impaired by a medical condition or that s/he will pose a direct threat due to a medical condition?

An employer is entitled only to the information necessary to determine whether the employee can do the essential functions of the job or work without posing a direct threat. This means that, in most situations, an employer cannot request an employee's complete medical records because they are likely to contain information unrelated to whether the employee can perform his/her essential functions or work without posing a direct threat.

14. May an employer require an employee to provide medical certification that s/he can safely perform a physical agility or physical fitness test?

Yes. Employers that require physical agility or physical fitness tests may ask an employee to have a physician certify whether s/he can safely perform the test. [63] In this situation, however, the employer is entitled to obtain only a note simply stating that the employee can safely perform the test or, alternatively, an explanation of the reason(s) why the employee cannot perform the test. An employer may not obtain the employee's complete medical records or information about any conditions that do not affect the employee's ability to perform the physical agility or physical fitness test safely.

C. Disability-Related Inquiries and Medical Examinations Relating to Leave[64]

15. May an employer request an employee to provide a doctor's note or other explanation to substantiate his/her use of sick leave?

Yes. An employer is entitled to know why an employee is requesting sick leave. An employer, therefore, may ask an employee to justify his/her use of sick leave by providing a doctor's note or other explanation, as long as it has a policy or practice of requiring all employees, with and without disabilities, to do so.

16. May an employer require periodic updates when an employee is on extended leave because of a medical condition?

Yes. If the employee's request for leave did not specify an exact or fairly specific return date (e.g., October 4 or around the second week of November) or if the employee needs continued leave beyond what was originally granted, the employer may require the employee to provide periodic updates on his/her condition and possible date of return.[65] However, where the employer has granted a fixed period of extended leave and the employee has not requested additional leave,

133

the employer *cannot* require the employee to provide periodic updates. Employers, of course, may call employees on extended leave to check on their progress or to express concern for their health.

17. May an employer make disability-related inquiries or require a medical examination when an employee who has been on leave for a medical condition seeks to return to work?

Yes. If an employer has a reasonable belief that an employee's present ability to perform essential job functions will be impaired by a medical condition or that s/he will pose a direct threat due to a medical condition, the employer may make disability-related inquiries or require the employee to submit to a medical examination. Any inquiries or examination, however, must be limited in scope to what is needed to make an assessment of the employee's ability to work. Usually, inquiries or examinations related to the specific medical condition for which the employee took leave will be all that is warranted. The employer may not use the employee's leave as a justification for making far-ranging disability-related inquiries or requiring an unrelated medical examination.

Example A: A data entry clerk broke her leg while skiing and was out of work for four weeks, after which time she returned to work on crutches. In this case, the employer does not have a reasonable belief, based on objective evidence, either that the clerk's ability to perform her essential job functions will be impaired by a medical condition or that she will pose a direct threat due to a medical condition. The employer, therefore, may not make any disability-related inquiries or require a medical examination but generally may ask the clerk how she is doing and express concern about her injury.

Example B: As the result of problems he was having with his medication, an employee with a known psychiatric disability threatened several of his co-workers and was disciplined. Shortly thereafter, he was hospitalized for six weeks for treatment related to the condition. Two days after his release, the employee returns to work with a note from his doctor indicating only that he is "cleared to return to work." Because the employer has a reasonable belief, based on objective evidence, that the employee will pose a direct threat due to a medical condition, it may ask the employee for additional documentation regarding his medication(s) or treatment or request that he submit to a medical examination.

D. Periodic Testing and Monitoring

In most instances, an employer's need to make disability-related inquiries or require medical examinations will be triggered by evidence of current performance problems or observable evidence suggesting that a particular employee will pose a direct threat. The following questions, however, address situations in which disability-related inquiries and medical examinations of employees may be permissible absent such evidence.

18. May employers require periodic medical examinations of employees in positions affecting public safety (e.g., police officers and firefighters)?

Yes. In limited circumstances, periodic medical examinations of employees in positions affecting public safety that are narrowly tailored to address specific job-related concerns are permissible.[66]

Example A: A fire department requires employees for whom firefighting is an essential job function to have a comprehensive visual examination every two years and to have an annual electrocardiogram because it is concerned that certain visual disorders and heart problems will affect their ability to do their job without posing a direct threat. These periodic medical examinations are permitted by the ADA.

Example B: A police department may not periodically test all of its officers to determine whether they are HIV-positive because a diagnosis of that condition alone is not likely to result in an inability or impaired ability to perform essential functions that would result in a direct threat.

Example C: A private security company may require its armed security officers who are expected to pursue and detain fleeing criminal suspects to have periodic blood pressure screenings and stress tests because it is concerned about the risk of harm to the public that could result if an officer has a sudden stroke.

If an employer decides to terminate or take other adverse action against an employee with a disability based on the results of a medical examination, it must demonstrate that the employee is unable to perform his/her essential job functions or, in fact, poses a direct threat that cannot be eliminated or reduced by reasonable accommodation.[67] Therefore, when an employer discovers that an employee has a condition for which it lawfully may test as part of a periodic medical examination, it may make additional inquiries or require additional medical examinations that are necessary to determine whether the employee currently is unable to perform his/her essential job functions or poses a direct threat due to the condition.

19. May an employer subject an employee, who has been off from work in an alcohol rehabilitation program, to periodic alcohol testing when s/he returns to work?

Yes, but only if the employer has a reasonable belief, based on objective evidence, that the employee will pose a direct threat in the absence of periodic testing. Such a reasonable belief requires an individualized assessment of the employee and his/her position and cannot be based on general assumptions. Employers also may conduct periodic alcohol testing pursuant to "last chance" agreements.[68]

In determining whether to subject an employee to periodic alcohol testing (in the absence of a "last chance" agreement), the employer should consider the safety risks associated with the position the employee holds, the consequences of the employee's inability or

136

impaired ability to perform his/her job functions, and how recently the event(s) occurred that cause the employer to believe that the employee will pose a direct threat (e.g., how long the individual has been an employee, when s/he completed rehabilitation, whether s/he previously has relapsed). Further, the duration and frequency of the testing must be designed to address particular safety concerns and should not be used to harass, intimidate, or retaliate against the employee because of his/her disability. Where the employee repeatedly has tested negative for alcohol, continued testing may not be job-related and consistent with business necessity because the employer no longer may have a *reasonable* belief that the employee will pose a direct threat.

Example A: Three months after being hired, a city bus driver informed his supervisor of his alcoholism and requested leave to enroll in a rehabilitation program. The driver explained that he had not had a drink in more than 10 years until he recently started having a couple of beers before bed to deal with the recent separation from his wife. After four months of rehabilitation and counseling, the driver was cleared to return to work. Given the safety risks associated with the bus driver's position, his short period of employment, and recent completion of rehabilitation, the city can show that it would be job-related and consistent with business necessity to subject the driver to frequent periodic alcohol tests following his return to work.

Example B: An attorney has been off from work in a residential alcohol treatment program for six weeks and has been cleared to return to work. Her supervisor wants to perform periodic alcohol tests to determine whether the attorney has resumed drinking. Assuming that there is no evidence that the attorney will pose a direct threat, the employer cannot show that periodic alcohol testing would be job-related and consistent with business necessity.[69]

OTHER ACCEPTABLE DISABILITY-RELATED INQUIRIES AND MEDICAL EXAMINATIONS OF EMPLOYEES

20. May an Employee Assistance Program (EAP)[70] counselor ask an employee seeking help for personal problems about any physical or mental condition(s) s/he may have?

Yes. An EAP counselor may ask employees about their medical condition(s) if s/he: (1) does not act for or on behalf of the employer; (2) is obligated to shield any information the employee reveals from decision makers; and, (3) has no power to affect employment decisions. Many employers contract with EAP counselors so that employees can voluntarily and confidentially seek professional counseling for personal or work-related problems without having to be concerned that their employment status will be affected because they sought help.[71]

21. May an employer make disability-related inquiries and require medical examinations that are required or necessitated by another federal law or regulation?

Yes. An employer may make disability-related inquiries and require employees to submit to medical examinations that are mandated or necessitated by another federal law or regulation.[72] For example, under federal safety regulations, interstate bus and truck drivers must undergo medical examinations at least once every two years. Similarly, airline pilots and flight attendants must continually meet certain medical requirements.[73] Other federal laws that require medical examinations or medical inquiries of employees without violating the ADA include:

the Occupational Safety and Health Act;[74]
the Federal Mine Health and Safety Act;[75] and
other federal statutes that require employees exposed to toxic or hazardous substances to be medically monitored at specific intervals.[76]

22. May an employer make disability-related inquiries or conduct medical examinations that are part of its voluntary wellness program?

Yes. The ADA allows employers to conduct voluntary medical examinations and activities, including voluntary medical histories, which are part of an employee health program without having to show that they are job-related and consistent with business necessity, as long as any medical records acquired as part of the wellness program are kept confidential and separate from personnel records.[77] These programs often include blood pressure screening, cholesterol testing, glaucoma testing, and cancer detection screening. Employees may be asked disability-related questions and may be given medical examinations pursuant to such voluntary wellness programs.[78]

A wellness program is "voluntary" as long as an employer neither requires participation nor penalizes employees who do not participate.

23. May an employer ask employees to voluntarily self-identify as persons with disabilities for affirmative action purposes?

Yes. An employer may ask employees to voluntarily self-identify as individuals with disabilities when the employer is:

undertaking affirmative action because of a federal, state, or local law (including a veterans' preference law) that requires affirmative action for individuals with disabilities (i.e., the law requires some action to be taken on behalf of such individuals); or,

voluntarily using the information to benefit individuals with disabilities.[79]

If an employer invites employees to voluntarily self-identify in connection with the above-mentioned situations, the employer must indicate clearly and conspicuously on any written questionnaire used for this purpose, or state clearly (if no written questionnaire is used), that: (1) the specific information requested is intended for use solely in connection with its affirmative action obligations or its voluntary affirmative action efforts; and, (2) the specific information is being requested on a voluntary basis, that it will be kept confidential in accordance with the ADA, that refusal to provide it will not subject the employee to any adverse treatment, and that it will be used only in accordance with the ADA.[80]

In order to invite self-identification for purposes of an affirmative action program that is voluntarily undertaken or undertaken pursuant to a law that encourages (rather than requires) affirmative action, an employer must be taking some action that actually benefits individuals with disabilities. The invitation to self-identify also must be *necessary* in order to provide the benefit.

---

1. 42 U.S.C. §§ 12101-12117, 12201-12213 (1994)(codified as amended).

2. Enforcement Guidance: Preemployment Disability-Related Questions and Medical Examinations Under the Americans with Disabilities Act of 1990, 8 FEP Manual (BNA) 405:7191 (1995) [hereinafter Preemployment Questions and Medical Examinations]. This and other ADA guidances are available through the Internet at http://www.eeoc.gov.

3. Pursuant to the Rehabilitation Act Amendment of 1992, the ADA's employment standards apply to all nonaffirmative action employment discrimination claims of individuals with disabilities who are federal employees or applicants for federal employment. Pub. L. No. 102-569 §503(b), 106 Stat. 4344, 4424 (1992) (codified as amended at 29 U.S.C. §791(g)(1994)). Accordingly, the analysis in the guidance applies to federal sector complaints of nonaffirmative action employment discrimination arising under section 501 of the Rehabilitation Act of 1973. It also applies to complaints of nonaffirmative action employment discrimination arising under section 503 and to employment discrimination under section 504 of the Rehabilitation Act. Id. at §§793 (d), 794(d)(1994).

4. The purpose of this guidance is to explain when it is permissible for an employer to make a disability-related inquiry or require a medical examination of an employee. It does not focus on what actions an employer may take based on what it learns in response to such an inquiry or after it receives the result of a medical examination.

5. In the ADA legislative history, Congress stated that an employee's "actual performance on the job is, of course, the best measure of ability to do the job." S. Rep. No. 101-116, at 39 (1989); H.R. Rep. No. 101-485, pt. 2, at 75 (1990).

6. However, where an applicant has an obvious disability, and the employer has a reasonable belief that s/he will need a reasonable accommodation to perform specific job functions, the employer may ask whether the applicant needs a reasonable accommodation and, if so, what type of accommodation. These same two questions may be asked when an individual voluntarily discloses a nonvisible disability or voluntarily tells the employer that s/he will need a reasonable accommodation to perform a job. 42 U.S.C. §12112(c)(B)(1994); 29 C.F.R. §1630.13(a)(1998); see also Preemployment Questions and Medical Examinations, supra note 2, at 6-8, 8 FEP at

405:7193-94; EEOC Enforcement Guidance on the Americans with Disabilities Act and Psychiatric Disabilities at 13-15, 8 FEP Manual (BNA) 405:7461, 7467-68 (1997)[hereinafter The ADA and Psychiatric Disabilities]; Enforcement Guidance: Reasonable Accommodation and Undue Hardship Under the Americans with Disabilities Act at 20-21, 8 FEP Manual (BNA) 405:7601, 7611(1999)[hereinafter Reasonable Accommodation Under the ADA]. Under certain circumstances, an employer also may ask applicants to self-identify as individuals with disabilities for purposes of its affirmative action program. See Preemployment Questions and Medical Examinations, supra note 2, at 12-13, 8 FEP at 405:7196-97.

7. 42 U.S.C. §12112(d)(3)(1994); 29 C.F.R. §1630.14(b)(1998). However, if an individual is screened out because of a disability, the employer must show that the exclusionary criterion is job-related and consistent with business necessity. 42 U.S.C. §12112(b)(6)(1994); 29 C.F.R. §§1630.10, 1630.14(b)(3)(1998).

8. 42 U.S.C. §12112(d)(4)(A)(1994); 29 C.F.R. §1630.14(c)(1998).

9. See infra note 77.

10. 42 U.S.C. §§12112(d)(3)(B), (4)(C)(1994); 29 C.F.R. §1630.14(b)(1)(1998). The Commission also has interpreted the ADA to allow employers to disclose medical information to state workers' compensation offices, state second injury funds, workers' compensation insurance carriers, and to health care professionals when seeking advice in making reasonable accommodation determinations. 29 C.F.R. pt. 1630, app. §1630.14(b)(1998). Employers also may use medical information for insurance purposes. Id. See also Preemployment Questions and Medical Examinations, supra note 2, at 21-23, 8 FEP at 405:7201; EEOC Enforcement Guidance: Workers' Compensation and the ADA at 7, 8 FEP Manual (BNA) 405:7391, 7394 (1996)[hereinafter Workers' Compensation and the ADA].

11. "Covered entity" means an employer, employment agency, labor organization, or joint labor management committee. 29 C.F.R. §1630.2(b)(1998). For simplicity, this guidance refers to all covered entities as "employers." The definition of "employer" includes persons who are "agents" of the employer, such as managers, supervisors, or others who act for the employer (e.g., agencies used to conduct background checks on applicants and employees). 42 U.S.C. §12111(5)(1994).

12. 42 U.S.C. §12112(d)(4)(A)(1994); 29 C.F.R. §1630.14(c)(1998). See infra Question 5 and accompanying text for a discussion of what the "job-related and consistent with business necessity" standard means.

13. See e.g., 42 U.S.C. §12112(a)(1994)(no entity shall discriminate against a qualified individual with a disability because of the disability of such individual).

14. Congress was particularly concerned about questions that allowed employers to learn which employees have disabilities that are not apparent from observation. It concluded that the only way to protect employees with nonvisible disabilities is to prohibit employers from making disability-related inquiries and requiring medical examinations that are not job-related and consistent with business necessity. See S. Rep. No. 101-116 at 39-40 (1989); H.R. Rep. No. 101-485, pt. 2, at 75 (1990) ("An inquiry or medical examination that is not job-related serves no legitimate employer

purpose, but simply serves to stigmatize the person with a disability." A person with cancer "may object merely to being identified, independent of the consequences [since] being identified as [a person with a disability] often carries both blatant and subtle stigma").

15. See Roe v. Cheyenne Mountain Resort, 124 F.3d 1221, 1229, 7 AD Cas. (BNA) 779, 783 (10th Cir. 1997)("it makes little sense to require an employee to demonstrate that he has a disability to prevent his employer from inquiring as to whether or not he has a disability"). Although Roe involved only the issue of disability-related inquiries of employees, the same rationale applies to medical examinations of employees and to disability-related inquiries and medical examinations of applicants. The ADA's restrictions on disability-related inquiries and medical examinations apply to individuals both with and without disabilities at all three stages: pre-offer, post-offer, and during employment. See also Griffin v. Steeltek ,Inc., 160 F.3d 591, 595, 8 AD Cas.1249, 1252 (10th Cir. 1998), cert. denied, 119 S.Ct. 1455, 9 AD Cas. 416 (1999)(a job applicant without a disability can sue under the ADA regarding medical history questions); Gonzales v. Sandoval County, 2 F.Supp. 2d 1442, 1445, 8 AD Cas.1337, 1340 (D. N.M. 1998)(plaintiff need not establish disability to state a claim for a prohibited inquiry under the ADA); Fredenburg v. Contra Costa County Department of Health Services, 172 F.3d 1176, 9 AD Cas. 385 (9th Cir. 1999)(requiring plaintiffs to prove that they are persons with disabilities to challenge a medical examination would render §12112(d)(4)(A) of the ADA "nugatory"; thus, plaintiffs need not prove that they are qualified individuals with a disability to bring claims challenging the scope of medical examinations under the ADA).

Some courts, however, have held that to bring a claim alleging a violation of the ADA's prohibition against disability-related inquiries and medical examinations, an individual must demonstrate that s/he is a qualified individual with a disability. See e.g., Armstrong v. Turner Industries, Inc., 141 F.3d 554, 558, 8 AD Cas. (BNA) 118, 124 (5th Cir. 1998), aff'g 950 F. Supp. 162, 7 AD Cas. 875 (M.D. La. 1996) (plaintiff must be a qualified individual with a disability to challenge an illegal preemployment inquiry); Hunter v. Habegger Corp., 139 F.3d 901(7th Cir. 1998)("it seems clear that in order to assert that one has been discriminated against because of an improper inquiry, that person must also have been otherwise qualified"). For the reasons stated above, it is the Commission's position that the plain language of the statute explicitly protects individuals with and *without* disabilities from improper disability-related inquiries and medical examinations.

16. For example, employers may make disability-related inquiries and require medical examinations that are required or necessitated by another federal law or regulation. See infra Question 21 and accompanying text. Employers also may make disability-related inquiries and conduct medical examinations that are part of their voluntary wellness programs. See infra Question 22 and accompanying text.

17. Preemployment Questions and Medical Examinations, supra note 2, at 4-13, 8 FEP at 405:7191, 7192-97.

18. Id. at 4, 8 FEP at 405:7192.

19. Id. at 4-13, 8 FEP at 405:7192-97.

20. The prohibition against making disability-related inquiries applies to inquiries made directly to an employee, as well as to indirect or surreptitious inquiries such as a search through an employee's belongings to confirm an employer's suspicions about an employee's medical condition. See Doe v. Kohn Nast & Graf, P.C., 866 F. Supp. 190, 3 AD Cas. (BNA) 1322 (E.D. Pa. 1994) (employer conducted an unlawful medical inquiry when it searched the office of an employee it knew was sick and discovered a letter indicating the employee had AIDS).

21. As used in this guidance, the term "genetic information" has the same definition as "protected genetic information" in Executive Order 13145. In general, genetic information is information about an individual's genetic tests, information about the genetic tests of an individual's family members, or information about the occurrence of a disease, medical condition, or disorder in family members of the individual. See Exec. Order No. 13,145, To Prohibit Discrimination in Federal Employment Based on Genetic Information, 65 Fed. Reg. 6877 (Feb. 8, 2000).

22. See Griffin v. Steeltek, Inc., 160 F.3d 591, 594, 8 AD Cas. (BNA) 1249, 1252 (10th Cir. 1998), cert. denied, 119 S.Ct. 1455, 9 AD. Cas. 416 (1999) (on its application for employment, employer unlawfully asked: "Have you received workers' compensation or disability payments? If yes, describe.").

23. See Roe v. Cheyenne Mountain Conference Resort, Inc., 124 F.3d 1221, 7 AD Cas. (BNA) 779 (10th Cir. 1997)(employer had a policy of requiring all employees to report every drug, including legal prescription drugs); Krocka v. Bransfield, 969 F. Supp. 1073 (N.D. Ill. 1997)(police department implemented a policy of monitoring employees taking psychotropic medication).

24. Preemployment Questions and Medical Examinations, supra note 2, at 9, 8 FEP at 405:7195.

25. Preemployment Questions and Medical Examinations, supra note 2, at 9, 8 FEP at 405:7195.

26. Employers also may maintain and enforce rules prohibiting employees from being under the influence of alcohol in the workplace and may conduct alcohol testing for this purpose if they have a reasonable belief that an employee may be under the influence of alcohol at work.

27. An individual who currently uses drugs illegally is not protected under the ADA; therefore, questions about current illegal drug use are not disability-related inquiries. 42 U.S.C. §12114(a)(1994); 29 C.F.R. §1630.3(a)(1998). However, questions about past addiction to illegal drugs or questions about whether an employee ever has participated in a rehabilitation program are disability-related because past drug addiction generally is a disability. Individuals who were addicted to drugs, but are not currently using drugs illegally, are protected under the ADA. 29 C.F.R. §1630.3(b)(1),(2)(1998).

143

28. Pregnancy is not a disability for purposes of the ADA. 29 C.F.R. pt. 1630, app. §1630.2(h)(1998). However, discrimination on that basis may violate the Pregnancy Discrimination Act amendments to Title VII. 42 U.S.C. §2000e(k)(1994).

29. Preemployment Questions and Medical Examinations supra note 2, at 14, 8 FEP at 405:7197.

30. Id.

31. See supra note 26.

32. See supra note 27.

33. Under the ADA, polygraph examinations, which purportedly measure whether a person believes s/he is telling the truth in response to a particular inquiry, are not medical examinations. However, an employer cannot ask disability-related questions as part of the examination. See Preemployment Questions and Medical Examinations, supra note 2, at 17, 8 FEP at 405:7199.

34. 42 U.S.C. §12111(4)(1994); 29 C.F.R. §1630.2(f)(1998). This term has the same meaning as it does under Title VII of the Civil Rights Act of 1964. 42 U.S.C. §2000e(f)(1994).

35. In its guidance on contingent workers, the Commission lists additional factors that indicate when a worker is an employee and explains that other aspects of the relationship between the parties may affect the determination of whether an employee-employer relationship exists. See EEOC Enforcement Guidance: Application of EEO Laws to Contingent Workers Placed by Temporary Employment Agencies and Other Staffing Firms at 4-7, 8 FEP Manual (BNA) 405:7551, 7554-55 (1997).

36. An employee in this situation is an applicant with respect to rules concerning disability-related inquiries and medical examinations but *not* for employee benefits (e.g., retirement, health and life insurance, leave accrual) or other purposes.

37. Where the employer already has medical information concerning an individual at the pre-offer stage for the new position (e.g., information obtained in connection with the individual's request for reasonable accommodation in his/her current position) and this information causes the employer to have a reasonable belief that the individual will need a reasonable accommodation to perform the functions of the *new* job, the employer may ask what type of reasonable accommodation would be needed to perform the functions of the new job, before extending an offer for that job. An employer, however, may not use its knowledge of an applicant's disability to discriminate against him/her. The employer also may not use the fact that the individual will need a reasonable accommodation in the new position to deny him/her the new job unless it can show that providing the accommodation would cause an undue hardship.

38. 42 U.S.C. §12112(d)(3)(1994); 29 C.F.R. §1630.14(b)(1998).

39. "Direct threat" means a significant risk of substantial harm that cannot be eliminated or reduced by reasonable accommodation. 29 C.F.R. §1630.2(r)(1998). Direct threat determinations must be based on an individualized assessment of the individual's present ability to safely perform the essential functions of the job,

considering a reasonable medical judgment relying on the most current medical knowledge and/or best available objective evidence. Id. To determine whether an employee poses a direct threat, the following factors should be considered: (1) the duration of the risk; (2) the nature and severity of the potential harm; (3) the likelihood that potential harm will occur; and, (4) the imminence of the potential harm. Id.

40. The Commission explained this standard in its enforcement guidance on The ADA and Psychiatric Disabilities, supra note 6, at 15, 8 FEP at 405:7468-69.

41. See infra Questions 18 and 19 and accompanying text.

42. See infra Question 6 and accompanying text.

43. See Yin v. State of California, 95 F.3d 864, 868, 5 AD Cas. (BNA) 1487, 1489 (9th Cir. 1996)(where employee missed an inordinate number of days and her performance declined, employer's request that she submit to a medical examination was job-related and consistent with business necessity).

44. See also infra Question 12.

45. 42 U.S.C. §12113 (d)(1994).

46. The most current list was published by HHS, Centers for Disease Control and Prevention (CDC), in 1998. 63 Fed.Reg. 49359 (Sept. 15, 1998).

47. But see EEOC v. Prevo's Family Market, Inc., 135 F.3d 1089, 1097, 8 AD Cas. (BNA) 401, 408 (6th Cir. 1998) (employer did not violate the ADA when it required a produce clerk, who claimed to be HIV-positive, to submit to a medical examination to determine whether he posed a direct threat). The Commission believes that Prevo's was wrongly decided because the employer did not base its belief that the employee posed a direct threat on reasonably available objective evidence and, therefore, its request that the employee submit to a medical examination was not job-related and consistent with business necessity. A number of sources, such as the Centers for Disease Control (www.cdc.gov), a physician or health care provider knowledgeable about HIV and other infectious diseases, a state or local health department, a public or university library, or a state or county medical association can provide information about the likelihood of an employee transmitting HIV or other infectious diseases to co-workers or the public.

48. This guidance does not affect the obligation of a physician, under any state law, to report cases of active tuberculosis to appropriate public health authorities.

49. See Reasonable Accommodation Under the ADA, supra note 6, at 14-15, 8 FEP at 405:7608 for examples of other situations where employers may ask for documentation; see also id. at 16-17, 8 FEP at 405: 7609 for examples of situations in which an employer cannot ask for documentation in response to a request for reasonable accommodation.

50. 29 C.F.R. pt. 1630 app. §1630.9 (1998); see also Preemployment Questions and Medical Examinations, supra note 2, at 6, 8 FEP at 405: 7193; ADA and Psychiatric Disabilities, supra note 6, at 22-23, 8 FEP at 405:7472-73; Reasonable Accommodation Under the ADA, supra note 6, at 12-13, 8 FEP at 405: 7607. See also Templeton v. Neodata Services, Inc., 162 F.3d 617, 618, 8 AD Cas. (BNA)

1615, 1616 (10th Cir. 1998)(employer's request for updated medical information was reasonable in light of treating physician's letter indicating doubt as to employee's ability to return to work as scheduled, and employer needed the requested information to determine appropriate reasonable accommodation for employee in event she was able to return to work).

51. See Roe v. Cheyenne Mountain Conference Resort, 124 F.3d 1221, 1229, 7 AD Cas. (BNA) 779, 784 (10th Cir. 1997) (employer, who implemented a drug and alcohol policy that included many permissible inquiries but also asked employees to inform the employer of every drug they were taking, including legal prescription drugs, violated the ADA by failing to demonstrate that this inquiry was job-related and consistent with business necessity).

52. See Reasonable Accommodation Under the ADA, supra note 6, at 15, 8 FEP at 405:7608.

53. See id. at 13, 8 FEP at 405:7607. (An "employer may require only the documentation that is needed to establish that a person has an ADA disability, and that the disability necessitates a reasonable accommodation." If an employee has more than one disability, an employer can request information pertaining only to the disability for which the employee is requesting an accommodation.)

54. See Reasonable Accommodation Under the ADA, supra note 6, at 14-15, 16-17, 8 FEP at 405:7607-09. If the employee subsequently should request another reasonable accommodation related to his sickle cell anemia, the employer may ask for reasonable documentation relating to the new request (if the need is not obvious). The employer, however, cannot ask again for documentation that the employee has an ADA disability where the medical information the employee provided in support of his first reasonable accommodation request established the existence of a long-term impairment that substantially limits a major life activity. Id. at 16-17, 8 FEP at 405: 7609.

55. See Reasonable Accommodation Under the ADA, supra note 6, at 15-16, 8 FEP at 405:7698; The ADA and Psychiatric Disabilities, supra note 6, at 23, 8 FEP at 405:7473.

56. See Reasonable Accommodation Under the ADA, supra note 6, at 15, 8 FEP at 405:7608.

57. Since a doctor cannot disclose information about a patient without his/her permission, an employer must obtain a release from the employee that will permit the doctor to answer questions. The release should be clear as to what information will be requested. See Reasonable Accommodation Under the ADA, supra note 6, at 13-14, 8 FEP at 405:7607.

58. Id. at 15, 8 FEP at 405:7608-09.

59. Id. at 16, 8 FEP at 405:7609; The ADA and Psychiatric Disabilities, supra note 6, at 23, 8 FEP at 405:7473.

60. See Reasonable Accommodation Under the ADA, supra note 6, at 15 (n.30), 8 FEP at 405:7609.

61. 29 C.F.R. §1630.2(r)(1998).

62. See Reasonable Accommodation Under the ADA, supra note 6, at 16, 8 FEP at 405:7609; The ADA and Psychiatric Disabilities, supra note 6, at 23, 8 FEP at 405:7473.

63. See Preemployment Questions and Medical Examinations, supra note 2, at 16, 8 FEP at 405:7198.

64. The questions and answers in this section address situations in which an employee has used sick, annual, or some other kind of leave because of a medical condition, but has not taken leave under the Family and Medical Leave Act (FMLA). 29 U.S.C. §2601(1994). Where an employee has been on leave under the FMLA, the employer must comply with the requirements of that statute. For example, the FMLA generally does not authorize an employer to make its own determination of whether an employee is fit to return to work but, rather, states that the employer must rely on the evaluation done by the employee's own health care provider. Id. at §2613(b).

65. See Reasonable Accommodation Under the ADA, supra note 6, at 57, 8 FEP at 405:7632.

66. See The ADA and Psychiatric Disabilities, supra note 6, at 16 (n.41), 8 FEP at 405:7469.

67. See supra note 39.

68. Some employers, including some federal government agencies, commonly use "last chance agreements" in disciplinary actions involving employee use of alcohol. Such agreements typically provide that, as a condition of continued employment, employees must enter into a rehabilitation program and submit to periodic alcohol testing.

69. The employer, however, may require the attorney to submit to an alcohol test if it has objective evidence that she is violating a workplace policy prohibiting all employees from being under the influence of alcohol on the job. See supra note 26.

70. Generally, EAPs are confidential programs designed to assist employees in coping with personal issues (e.g., substance abuse, grief) that may interfere with their job performance.

71. See Vardiman v. Ford Motor Co., 981 F. Supp. 1279, 1283, 7 AD Cas. (BNA) 1068, 1072 (E.D. Mo. 1997)(EAP representative had no power to affect employment decisions and, in fact, was obligated to shield the decision makers from an employee's personal or substance abuse problems).

72. 29 C.F.R. 1630.15(e)(1998)("it may be a defense to a charge of discrimination . . . that a challenged action is required or necessitated by another Federal law or regulation . . . .").

73. See e.g., 14 C.F.R. pt. 67(1999)(Federal Aviation Administration (FAA) and Department of Transportation (DOT) medical certifications); 14 C.F.R. pt. 121, app. I (1999)(FAA and DOT drug testing program); 49 C.F.R. pt. 40 and app. (1999)(procedures for transportation workplace drug testing programs); 49 C.F.R. 240.207(1996)(Federal Railroad Administration and DOT procedures for making determination on hearing and visual acuity); 49 C.F.R. pt. 391(1999)(Federal Highway Administration and DOT medical certification requirements); 49 C.F.R. pt.

653(1999)(Federal Transit Administration (FTA) procedures for prevention of prohibited drug use in transit operations); 49 C.F.R. pt. 654(1999)(FTA procedures for prevention of alcohol abuse in transit operations).

74. 29 U.S.C. §§651-678 (1994).

75. 30 U.S.C. §§801-962 (1994).

76. See e.g., The Comprehensive Environmental Response, Compensation and Liability Act, 42 U.S.C. §9601(1994).

77. See H.R. Rep. No. 101-485, pt. 2, at 75 (1990) ("As long as the programs are voluntary and the medical records are maintained in a confidential manner and not used for the purpose of limiting health insurance eligibility or preventing occupational advancement, these activities would fall within the purview of accepted activities.").

78. If a program simply promotes a healthier life style but does not ask any disability-related questions or require medical examinations (e.g., a smoking cessation program that is available to anyone who smokes and only asks participants to disclose how much they smoke), it is not subject to the ADA's requirements concerning disability-related inquiries and medical examinations.

79. See Preemployment Questions and Medical Examinations, supra note 2, at 12, 8 FEP at 405:7196-97.

80. Id.

Guidelines Regarding "Gender Identity" Discrimination, A Form of Gender Discrimination Prohibited by The New York City Human Rights Law

(Title 8 of the NYC Administrative Code)

New York City Commission on Human Rights
40 Rector Street New York, NY 10006
www.nyc.gov/cchr

CONTENTS

I. PURPOSE

In April 2002, the New York City Human Rights Law, located in Title 8 of the Administrative Code of the City of New York, was amended to make it clear that an individual's gender identity is an area of protection under the Law.

It is the law and policy of the City of New York to eliminate discrimination based upon an individual's "actual or perceived gender."

"Gender" is defined in the City's Human Rights Law to include:

• actual or perceived sex;
• gender identity;
• self-image;
• appearance; and,
• behavior or expression,

whether or not that gender identity, selfimage, appearance, behavior or expression is different from that traditionally associated with the legal sex assigned to an individual at birth.

The Human Rights Commission developed these guidelines:

• To educate the public about the prohibition of gender discrimination, particularly as it protects transgender and gender-variant people in New York City;
• To inform individuals of their rights under the Law; and,
• To assist employers, housing providers, businesses, organizations, service providers (including government) and other entities in understanding their responsibilities under the Law.

These guidelines do not constitute legal advice and do not cover every aspect of the Law. For specific questions regarding the coverage of the Human Rights Law, see the Administrative Code of the City of New York, contact the New York City Commission on Human Rights, or seek legal counsel.

II. DEFINITIONS

A. Gender Identity/Gender Expression
Gender identity is an individual's sense of being either male or female, man or woman, or something other or in-between. Gender expression describes the external characteristics and behaviors that are socially defined as either masculine or feminine, such as dress, mannerisms, speech patterns and social interactions.

B. Transgender
"Transgender" is an umbrella term that includes anyone whose gender identity and/or gender expression does not match society's expectations of how an individual who was assigned a particular sex at birth should behave in relation to their gender. The term includes, but is not limited to:

• pre-operative, post-operative and non-operative transsexuals who may or may not use hormones;
• intersex individuals;
• persons exhibiting gender characteristics
and identities that are perceived to be
inconsistent with their gender at birth;
• persons perceived to be androgynous;
• transvestites;
• cross-dressers; or,
• drag queens or kings.

1. Transsexuals
Transsexuals are individuals whose gender expression or identity is perceived to conflict with the sex assigned to them at birth, and who may or may not begin or continue the process of hormone replacement therapy and/or gender confirmation surgery. Transsexuals are often described as female-to-male (FTM) or male-to-female (MTF).

2. Gender Variant, Gender Non-conforming or Gender Different
Gender variant, gender non-conforming, or gender different individuals have a gender identity and/or gender expression that is not completely male or female. This includes individuals who do not conform to expectations of a specific gender role and individuals who express both masculine and

feminine qualities. These individuals are sometimes referred to as "androgynous."

C. Intersex Individuals

Intersex individuals are born with chromosomes, external genitalia, and/or an internal reproductive system that varies from what is considered "standard" for either males or females.

III. AREAS OF APPLICATION

A. Employment

(Administrative Code: Section 8-107(1)) It is an unlawful discriminatory practice for an employer, or an employee or agent thereof, to discriminate against any employee or applicant for employment based upon actual or perceived gender (including the individual's actual or perceived sex, gender identity, self-image, appearance, behavior or expression, whether or not that gender identity, self-image, appearance, behavior or expression is different from that traditionally associated with the legal sex assigned to an individual at birth) with regard to recruitment, hiring, firing, promotions, wages, job assignments, training, benefits, and other terms and conditions of employment.

B. Public Accommodations

(Administrative Code: Section 8-107(4)) "Public accommodations" refer to providers of goods and/or services to the public. Restaurants, hospitals, stores, theaters, and service providers (including government) are some examples of public accommodations. It is an unlawful discriminatory practice for a place or provider of public accommodation directly or indirectly to refuse, withhold from, or deny a person any of the accommodations, advantages, facilities, services or privileges of an accommodation based upon the person's actual or perceived gender (including the individual's actual or perceived sex, gender identity, self-image, appearance, behavior or expression, whether or not that gender identity, self-image, appearance, behavior or expression is different from that traditionally associated with the legal sex assigned to an individual at birth).

C. Housing & Lending Institutions

(Administrative Code: Section 8-107(5)) The housing discrimination provisions apply to the owner, lessor, managing agent or other person having the right to sell, rent or lease or approve the sale, rental or lease of a housing accommodation.

It is an unlawful discriminatory practice for such persons to refuse to sell, rent, lease, approve the sale, rental or lease or otherwise deny to or withhold a housing accommodation or an interest therein from, or otherwise discriminate against any person on the basis of actual or perceived gender (including the individual's actual or perceived sex, gender identity, self-image, appearance, behavior or expression, whether or not that gender identity, self-image, appearance, behavior or expression is different from that traditionally associated with the legal sex assigned to an individual at birth).

Real estate brokers, real estate sales persons, employees or agents thereof may not discriminate on the basis of actual or perceived gender (including the individual's actual or perceived sex, gender identity, self image, appearance, behavior or expression, whether or not that gender identity, self image, appearance, behavior or expression is different from that traditionally associated with the legal sex assigned to an individual at birth) in the rental or sale of property based upon an individual's actual or perceived gender. The prohibited behavior includes all aspects of real property transactions, such as the refusal to show, rent, or sell real property that is available for sale or lease, the addition of different or additional terms or conditions in a lease or mortgage, and the refusal to provide services or make repairs or improvements for any tenant or lessee.

Banks and other lending institutions may not discriminate against an applicant for credit on the basis of actual or perceived gender (including the individual's actual or perceived sex, gender identity, self-image, appearance, behavior or expression, whether or not that gender identity, self-image, appearance, behavior or expression is different from that traditionally associated with the legal sex assigned to an individual at birth).

D. Civil Action for Discriminatory Harassment or Violence
(Administrative Code: Section 8-602)
It is illegal to interfere by force or threat of force, or knowingly injure, intimidate or interfere with, oppress, or threaten any other person in the free exercise or enjoyment of any right or privilege secured to him or her by the constitution or laws of this state or by the constitution or laws of the United States or local law of the city when such injury, intimidation, interference,

oppression or threat is motivated in whole or in part by the victim's actual or perceived gender (including the individual's actual or perceived sex, gender identity, self-image, appearance, behavior or expression, whether or not that gender identity, self-image, appearance, behavior or expression is different from that traditionally associated with the legal sex assigned to an individual at birth). It is also illegal to knowingly deface, damage or destroy the real or personal property of any person for the purpose of intimidating or interfering with the free exercise or enjoyment of any right or privilege secured to the other person by the constitution or laws of this state or by the constitution or laws of the United States or by local law of the city when such defacement, damage or destruction of real or personal property is motivated in whole or in part by the victim's actual or perceived gender (including the individual's actual or perceived sex, gender identity, self-image, appearance, behavior or expression, whether or not that gender identity, self-image, appearance, behavior or expression is different from that traditionally associated with the legal sex assigned to an individual at birth).

In addition to coming to the New York City Commission on Human Rights, victims of bias-related harassment or violence are encouraged to report the incident immediately to the police and/or the County District Attorney's Offices.

E. Retaliation
It is against the law for an employer, housing provider, lending institution, or provider of a public accommodation to retaliate against an individual because the individual opposed an unlawful discriminatory practice or made a charge, or because the individual testified, assisted or participated in an investigation, proceeding or hearing.

IV. AVOIDING DISCRIMINATORY PRACTICES

A. Preventing Discrimination
Discrimination on the basis of actual or perceived gender (including the individual's actual or perceived sex, gender identity, self image, appearance, behavior or expression, whether or not that gender identity, self image, appearance, behavior or expression is different from that traditionally associated with the legal sex assigned to an individual at birth) is a violation of the Human Rights Law. Discrimination may take the form of unwelcome

verbal or physical conduct, including, but not limited to, derogatory comments, jokes, graffiti, drawings or photographs, touching or gestures.

To avoid the appearance of discrimination, individuals should be addressed with names, titles, pronouns, and other terms appropriate to their gender identity. The refusal to address individuals in a manner appropriate to their gender identity is a factor that the Commission will consider when determining if discrimination exists. • In general, individuals in New York may change their names without having to go through a formal legal process, as long as the new name is used consistently and without intent to defraud others. Prefixes such as "Ms." and "Mr." and suffixes such as "Jr." and "Sr." do not have legal significance. • When an individual is uncertain about which name, pronoun (he/she; him/her) or title (Ms./Miss/Mrs./Mr.) to use in addressing or referring to another individual, it is generally appropriate to ask the individual. Requesting proof of an individual's gender, except when legally required, challenging an individual's gender, or asking inappropriate questions about intimate details of an individual's anatomy, are factors that the Commission will consider when determining if discrimination exists.

B. Ensuring that Dress Codes Allow for Expression of Individuals' Gender Identity
When developing and enforcing dress codes that are gender-specific, employers should permit employees to comply with the gender specific provisions in the codes in an appropriate manner that is consistent with their gender identity and gender expression.

C. Providing Access to Restrooms and Other Sex-Segregated Facilities
Nothing in the Human Rights Law prohibits restrooms from being designated by gender. With respect to facilities that are restricted on the basis of sex, the following are some of the factors that suggest that discriminatory conduct related to gender identity has occurred:

• Not allowing individuals to use a restroom or other sex-segregated facility consistent with their gender identity or gender expression; or

• Requiring individuals to provide identification as a means of identifying their gender before allowing them to use the restroom or other sex-segregated facility.

Policies and practices aimed at preventing or addressing lewd behavior or conduct that violates the privacy of others should apply to and protect all individuals. The Commission recommends that, where single occupancy restrooms are available, they be designated as "gender neutral." The Commission also encourages covered entities to provide accommodations to individuals who have concerns about use of public restrooms because of gender identity or gender expression. Such accommodations could include, for example, offering the use of a private restroom to a member of the public. If an individual feels uncomfortable using a particular restroom because of another individual's presence in the restroom, he or she may be encouraged to wait until that individual has left, or to use another restroom.

D. Public Accommodations Where Nudity is Unavoidable (e.g., health clubs, dressing or changing rooms, etc.)

Public accommodations should provide access to appropriate facilities for all individuals. The Human Rights Commission recommends that public accommodation facilities, such as locker rooms which are designated for use based on sex, take steps to create private spaces within them (for example, by installing curtains or cubicles). Factors that suggest discriminatory conduct has occurred will include not allowing individuals to use a dressing or changing room consistent with their gender identity or gender expression.

E. Policy/Training
The Commission recommends that employers, housing providers, providers of public accommodations, and banks/lending institutions implement anti-discrimination policies that address gender identity and gender expression issues, as well as all other areas covered by the Human Rights Law, and institute training for employees and agents on an ongoing basis.

V. ENFORCEMENT AND PENALTIES
The City Human Rights Law is enforced in a number of ways:
• The Commission on Human Rights provides opportunities for mediation of complaints and also investigates and prosecutes violations of the Law. If the Commission, after a hearing, finds that violation of the Law has occurred, it may award damages and order other affirmative relief such as, for example, hiring, reinstating, or upgrading an employee and requiring admission to an organization. In addition, the Commission may order civil penalties up to $100,000. A person who fails to comply with an order issued by the

156

Commission may also be liable for a civil penalty of not more than $50,000 and an additional civil penalty of not more than $100 per day for each day the violation continues.

• A private cause of action may be brought under the City's Human Rights Law. Upon finding that a violation of the Law has occurred, a court may award damages, injunctive relief, and attorney's fees.

• The New York City Corporation Counsel may bring a civil action when there is reasonable cause to believe that a person or group is engaging in a pattern or practice that denies to any person the full enjoyment of rights under the City Human Rights Law. In this instance, the court may award damages, injunctive relief, and attorney's fees, and may also award civil penalties of not more than $250,000. • In a case involving discriminatory harassment or violence, where a person has been found to have interfered or attempted to interfere by threats, intimidation or coercion with rights protected under law, and the interference or attempted interference was motivated in whole or in part by the victim's actual or perceived gender, the New York City Corporation Counsel may ask a court to award civil penalties of not more than $100,000.

ACKNOWLEDGEMENTS

The Commission on Human Rights thanks the following individuals for their assistance in the creation of these guidelines:
- Randolph Wills
- Matt Foreman
- Michael Silverman
- Carrie Davis
- Pauline Park
- Melissa Sklarz
- Dean Spade
- Moonhawk Stone

District of Columbia Regulations

CHAPTER 8 COMPLIANCE RULES AND REGULATIONS REGARDING GENDER IDENTITY OR EXPRESSION

800 Purpose

800.1 In order to meet the obligations to prohibit discrimination based on gender identity or expression as set forth in the Act, the Office and the Commission adopt this chapter for the following purposes:

(a) To implement the provisions of the Act regarding discrimination based on gender identity or expression in employment, housing, public accommodations, or educational institutions, including all agencies of the District of Columbia government and its contractors;

(b) To provide guidance with regard to the requirements of the law to all employers, housing providers, businesses, organizations, educational institutions, and District government agencies and contractors in seeking compliance with the law;

(c) To educate the public on the behaviors, conduct, and actions that constitute unlawful discrimination based on gender identity or expression;

(d) To ensure that transgender people are treated in a manner that is consistent with their identity or expression, rather than according to their presumed or assigned sex or gender; and

(e) To guide the internal processing of complaints filed with the Office or cases heard by the Commission.

801 GENERAL PROHIBITIONS OF GENDER IDENTITY OR EXPRESSION DISCRIMINATION

801.1 It shall be unlawful for any person or entity, including agencies of the District of Columbia government and its contractors, to discriminate against a person in employment, housing, public accommodations, or educational institutions on the basis of that person's actual or perceived gender identity or expression. Such unlawful discriminatory practices shall include but not be limited to the following in:

(a) EMPLOYMENT: failing to hire or promote; engaging in disparate treatment; engaging in unlawful termination and transfers; engaging in verbal or physical harassment; creation of a hostile environment; failing to make a reasonable accommodation when requested by the employee in accordance with 4 DCMR § 804 (1995); and denying access to restrooms and other gender specific facilities that are consistent with the employee's gender identity or expression.

(b) HOUSING AND COMMERCIAL SPACE: refusing to show, rent, or sell real property that is available for lease or sale; discriminating in financial transactions related to real property; engaging in disparate treatment by adding or using different terms or conditions in a lease; refusing to make or provide services, repairs, or improvements for any tenant or lessee; denying access to restrooms or gender specific facilities in common areas that are consistent with an individual's gender identity or expression; creating a hostile environment; and failing to stop or prevent harassment by co-tenants, landlords, or property managers.

(c) PUBLIC ACCOMMODATIONS: refusing to provide goods or services of any kind; engaging in disparate treatment in the provision of goods and services; engaging in verbal or physical harassment; creating a hostile environment; and denying access to restrooms and other gender specific facilities that are consistent with a customer's or client's gender identity or expression.

(d) EDUCATIONAL INSTITUTIONS: refusing or limiting educational opportunities in admission, matriculation, or access to extracurricular activities; engaging in disparate treatment of a student; engaging in or failing to prevent verbal or physical harassment;

160

creating a hostile environment; and denying access to restrooms and other gender specific facilities that are consistent with a student's gender identity or expression.

(e) DISTRICT OF COLUMBIA GOVERNMENT: refusing to provide any facility, service, program, or benefit of the District of Columbia government; engaging in verbal or physical harassment; creating a hostile environment; and denying access to restroom facilities and other gender specific facilities that are consistent with a person's gender identity or expression. 801.2 All entities covered under the Act shall clearly and explicitly communicate the District of Columbia's laws regarding gender identity or expression and other protected categories to all management, employees, and volunteers as required by D.C. Official Code § 2-1402.51.

802 RESTROOMS AND OTHER GENDER SPECIFIC FACILITIES

802.1 All entities covered under the Act, as amended, shall allow individuals the right to use gender-specific restrooms and other gender-specific facilities such as dressing rooms, homeless shelters, and group homes that are consistent with their gender identity or expression. 802.2 All entities covered under the Act with single-occupancy restroom facilities shall use gender-neutral signage for those facilities (for example, by replacing signs that indicate "Men" and "Women" with signs that say "Restroom").

803 ACCOMMODATIONS FOR HEALTH CARE NEEDS
803.1 When requested by the employee, an employer shall make reasonable accommodations (including medical leave) for transgender-related health care needs that are consistent with such accommodations that are provided for other medical needs. Such needs include but are not limited to medical or counseling appointments, surgery, recovery from surgery, and any other transgender-related procedures.

804 DRESS AND GROOMING STANDARDS

804.1 No employer, housing provider, public accommodation, educational institution, or any agency of the District of Columbia government or its contractors shall require individuals to dress or groom themselves in a manner inconsistent with their sex or their gender identity or expression.

804.2 Employers, housing providers, public accommodations, educational institutions, and agencies of the District of Columbia government and its contractors may prescribe standards of dress which shall serve a reasonable business purpose, as long as such standards do not discriminate or have a discriminatory impact on the basis of an individual's sex or the individual's gender identity or expression.

804.3 Except as otherwise provided in this chapter, the Office and Commission adopt and incorporate by reference the provisions of 4 DCMR § 512 (1995).

805 GENDER-SPECIFIC FACILITIES WHERE NUDITY IN THE PRESENCE OF OTHERS IS CUSTOMARY

805.1 All entities covered under the Act shall provide access to and the safe use of facilities that are segregated by gender.

805.2 In gender-specific facilities where nudity in the presence of other people is customary, entities covered by the Act shall make reasonable accommodations to allow an individual access to and the use of the facility that is consistent with that individual's gender identity or expression, regardless of whether the individual has provided identification or other documentation of their gender identity or expression.

805.3 Requiring documentation or other proof of an individual's gender is prohibited, except in situations where all persons are asked to provide documentation or other proof of their gender for a reasonable business or medical purpose.

806 RECORDING OF GENDER AND NAME

806.1 An entity covered under the Act shall not require an applicant to state whether the individual is transgender.

806.2 If an application form asks for the applicant to identify as male or female, designation by the applicant of a sex that is inconsistent with the applicant's assigned or presumed gender shall not be considered, without more, to be fraudulent or to be a misrepresentation for the purpose of adverse action on the application.

806.3 An applicant's giving of a name publicly and consistently used by the applicant, even when the name given is not the applicant's legal name, shall not be grounds for adverse action, if the name given is consistent with the applicant's gender identity or expression. However, where use of a person's legal name is required by law or for a reasonable business purpose, the applicant may be required to disclose it.

806.4 An applicant's failure to disclose a change of gender or name (unless specifically required as part of an application process for a reasonable business purpose) shall not be considered grounds for an adverse action.

807 BACKGROUND CHECKS

807.1 If an entity covered under the Act learns through a background check or other means that a person is transgender, the entity shall not, without more, take an adverse action against the individual on the basis of the learned information and shall take reasonable measures to preserve the confidentiality of that information.

808 HARASSMENT AND HOSTILE ENVIRONMENT

808.1 All harassment and actions that create a hostile environment based on gender identity or expression shall be prohibited.

808.2 The following behaviors may constitute evidence of unlawful harassment and hostile environment: (a) Deliberately misusing an individual's preferred name form of address or gender-related pronoun; (b) Asking personal questions about an individual's body, gender identity or expression, or gender transition; (c) Causing distress to an individual by disclosing to others that the individual is transgender; and (d) Posting offensive pictures, or sending offensive electronic or other communications.

In determining whether there is unlawful harassment or a hostile environment, the totality of the circumstances surrounding the alleged violation of the Act must be considered, including the nature, frequency, and severity of the behavior, whether it is physically threatening or humiliating, or a mere offensive utterance; and whether it unreasonably interferes with the alleged victim. Ultimately the standard is an objective one, focusing on whether the behavior was sufficiently severe or pervasive to alter the conditions of the victim's employment, housing, education, or access to or use of public accommodations, or relations with a District of Columbia agency or contractor, and to create an abusive environment.

899 DEFINITIONS

899.1 When used in this chapter, the following terms and phrases shall have the meanings ascribed: "Act" - the Human Rights Act of 1977, effective December 13, 1977 (D.C. Law 2-38; D.C. Official Code § 2-1401.01 *et seq.*). "Commission" – the Commission on Human Rights, established by section 401 of the Act (D.C. Official Code § 2-1404.01). "Entities" - include all employers, housing providers, public accommodations, educational institutions, and government agencies and their contractors that come within the jurisdictional reach of the

Act. "Gender identity or expression" - a gender-related identity, appearance, expression, or behavior of an individual, regardless of the individual's assigned sex at birth. "Office" – the Office of Human Rights, established by section 202 of the Fiscal Year 2000 Service Improvement and Budget Support Act of 1999, effective October 20, 1999 (D.C. Law 13-38; D.C. Official Code § 2- 1411.01). "Transgender" - an adjective that refers to any individual whose identity or behavior differs from stereotypical or traditional gender expectations, including transsexual individuals, cross-dressers, androgynous individuals, and others whose appearance or characteristic are perceived to be gender atypical.

San Francisco Compliance Rules and Regulations Regarding Gender Identity Discrimination

San Francisco Administrative Code Chapter 12A, 12B, 12C

San Francisco Police Code Article 33

City and County of San Francisco
Human Rights Commission
25 Van Ness Ave., Suite 800
San Francisco, CA 94102-6033

December 10, 2003

Introduction and History of Gender Identity Protection in San Francisco

In 1995 San Francisco included "gender identity" as a protected class to its nondiscrimination ordinances in response to a 1994 public hearing held by the Human Rights Commission. At that hearing, Supervisors and other City officials learned that there are transgender people in every race, class and culture, and of every age, ability, gender, and sexual orientation. The Supervisors and other City officials also learned that transgender people are subjected to severe discrimination in employment, housing and public accommodations and that no local, state or federal law provided protection and no recourse existed when discriminatory actions occurred.

Therefore, the San Francisco Administrative Codes and Police Codes were amended to prohibit discrimination based on gender identity. Since the law was changed, the Human Rights Commission has continued to receive complaints from people who are not hired, not promoted, are fired, denied housing, denied services, and denied access to facilities, and are discriminated against because of their gender identity. These guidelines are intended to assist City Departments, agencies, businesses, and organizations in complying with the law.

In this introduction, we would like to emphasize that a person's gender identity is that person's sense of self regarding characteristics labeled as masculine, feminine, both or neither. An individual determines their own gender identity and the sole proof of a person's gender identity is that person's statement or expression of their self identification.

While any given individual's gender identity or expression may make other people uncomfortable, refusing to treat transgender or gender-variant people in the same manner as other people is a violation of San Francisco laws. The Human Rights Commission is charged with investigating complaints of discrimination based on gender identity. It has been the experience of the Human Rights Commission that most situations in which people experience discomfort or have a fear of confrontation can be addressed so that all individuals are treated with dignity and the law is not violated.

In addition to these Regulations, the staff of the Human Rights Commission is available to provide training and education, and to help create flexible implementation plans for agencies, business establishments and organizations seeking to comply with the law. For more information, visit the Human Rights Commission website at www.sfgov.org or call (415)252–2500.

TABLE OF CONTENTS

1. PURPOSE:

It is the law and policy of the City and County of San Francisco to eliminate discrimination based on gender identity in San Francisco and in City & County of San Francisco contracting. These guidelines supercede prior gender identity guidelines approved December 10, 1998 and are effective as of December 10, 2003.

The Human Rights Commission developed these guidelines for several purposes:

- To implement the provisions of San Francisco Administrative Code Chapters 12A, 12B, 12C and San Francisco Police Code Article 33 regarding discrimination based on gender identity;

- To provide guidance to employers, businesses, organizations, City departments, and entities contracting with the City and County of San Francisco seeking to comply with the law.

169

- To educate the public about gender identity law and policy so as to prevent and address discrimination.

2. DEFINITION OF GENDER IDENTITY

Chapters 12A, 12B, and 12C of the San Francisco Administrative Code and Article 33 of the San Francisco Police Code define "Gender Identity" as "a person's various individual attributes as they are understood to be masculine and/or feminine." * Gender Identity therefore includes discrimination based upon an individual's self-asserted gender identity and/or gender expression whether or not different from that traditionally associated with the person's actual or perceived sex as assigned at birth.

[*12A.3(a); 12B.1(c); 12C.2; 33]

3. REGULATIONS

It is unlawful to discriminate against a person in employment, housing, or public accommodations, on the basis of that person's actual or perceived gender identity, or to discriminate against a person who associates with persons in this protected category, or to retaliate against any person objecting to, or supporting enforcement of legal protections against gender identity discrimination in employment, housing, and public accommodations

4. EXAMPLES OF UNLAWFUL GENDER IDENTITY DISCRIMINATION

A. EMPLOYMENT: Includes but is not limited to failure to hire, failure to promote, disparate treatment, unlawful termination, verbal and/or physical harassment, deliberate misuse of appropriate forms of address and pronouns, failure to make a reasonable accommodation when requested by the employee, and/or denial of access to bathroom that is appropriate to the employee's gender identity.

B. HOUSING: Includes but is not limited refusal to show, rent, or sell real property that is available for lease or sale, addition of different or additional terms or conditions in a lease, and refusal to provide services or make repairs or improvements for any tenant or lessee, deliberate misuse of appropriate forms of address and pronouns by the landlord or property manager, tolerating harassment by co-tenants, landlords, or property managers.

C. PUBLIC ACCOMMODATIONS: Includes but is not limited to refusal to provide goods or services, disparate treatment, verbal and/or physical harassment, intentional and deliberate misuse of appropriate forms of address and/or pronouns, and/or denial of access to bathroom/restroom that is consistent with and appropriate to the customer's or client's gender identity.

5. GUIDELINES

A. BATHROOMS/RESTROOMS: Individuals have the right to use the bathroom/restroom that is consistent with and appropriate to their gender identity. The Commission wants to ensure that people of all genders have safe bathroom access. Therefore, the Commission strongly urges that all single-use bathrooms be designated gender neutral (unisex) and that all places of public accommodation and employment provide a gender neutral bathroom option.

B. VERIFICATION OF GENDER: Requiring proof of an individual's gender is prohibited, except in situations where all persons are asked to verify their gender.

C. EMPLOYMENT: When requested by the employee, an employer must make reasonable accommodations for an employee's health care needs, including but not limited to health care provider or counseling appointments, time off to recover from surgery or from a transition-related complication.

D. DRESS CODES: Employees have the right to comply with the gender-specific dress code that is appropriate to their gender identity when employers implement employee dress codes that are gender-specific.

E. ONGOING TRAINING AND POLICY COMMUNICATION: To ensure that employers understand their obligations to maintain a discrimination-free workplace, the Commission recommends that employers require all management, employees, and volunteers to receive training regarding gender identity issues. All agencies, businesses, organizations, City contractors, and City departments are required to clearly and explicitly communicate San Francisco's laws regarding gender identity and other protected categories to all management, employees, and volunteers. In addition, all businesses within the City and County of San Francisco are required to conspicuously post the San Francisco Human Rights Commission employment non-discrimination poster in a place accessible to all employees.

F. SEX-SPECIFIC FACILTIES WITH UNAVOIDABLE NUDITY:

A. All people have an equal and binding right to the access and safe use of those facilities that are segregated by sex. In sex-specific facilities, where nudity in the presence of other people is unavoidable, agencies, businesses, organizations, City contractors, and City departments shall make reasonable accommodations to allow an individual access and use of the facility that is consistent with that individual's gender identity which is publicly and exclusively asserted.

B. Access and use of a sex-specific facility may not be denied to any individual with an identification that designates the gender they are asserting. If an individual does not voluntarily show identification designating their gender identity, reasonable accommodations shall be made to integrate the individual into the facility that corresponds with the gender identity that the individual publicly and exclusively asserts or intends to assert over a period of time.

The Human Rights Commission recommends that alternative forms of gender identification be accepted, such as a letter from a City department, community-based organization, healthcare provider, or counselor.

Litigation

Smith v. City of Salem is a court opinion from the U.S. Sixth Circuit Court of Appeals, covering Kentucky, Michigan, Ohio and Tennessee. It holds that Title VII "sex discrimination" protects transgender employees from discrimination. Several other district courts have issued similar rulings. The Seventh, Eighth and Ninth Circuit Courts of Appeals have issued opposing rulings.

Smith v. City of Salem

JIMMIE L.SMITH, *Plaintiff-Appellant*

v.

CITY OF SALEM,OHIO, THOMAS EASTEK,WALTER GREENAMYER, BROOKE ZELLERS, LARRY D. DE JANE, JAMES A. A RMENI, JOSEPH JULIAN, and HARRY DUGAN, *Defendants-Appellees.*

R. GUY COLE, JR., Circuit Judge.

Plaintiff-Appellant Jimmie L. Smith appeals from a judgment of the United States District Court for the Northern District of Ohio dismissing his claims against his employer, Defendant- Appellant City of Salem, Ohio, and various City officials, and granting judgment on the pleadings to Defendants, pursuant to Federal Rule of Civil Procedure 12(c). Smith, who considers himself a transsexual and has been diagnosed with Gender Identity Disorder, alleged that Defendants discriminated against him in his employment on the basis of sex. He asserted claims pursuant to Title VII of the Civil Rights Act of 1964, 42 U.S.C. § 2000e *et seq.*, and 42 U.S.C. § 1983. The district court dismissed those claims pursuant to Rule 12(c). Smith also asserted state law claims for invasion of privacy and civil conspiracy; the district court dismissed those claims as well, having declined to exercise supplemental jurisdiction over them.

For the following reasons, we reverse the judgment of the district court and remand the case for further proceedings consistent with this opinion.

I. BACKGROUND

In reviewing a motion for judgment on the pleadings pursuant to Rule 12(c), we construe the complaint in the light most favorable to the plaintiff and accept the complaint's factual inferences as true. *Ziegler v. IBP Hog Market, Inc.*, 249 F.3d 509, 511-12 (6th Cir. 2001). The following facts are drawn from Smith's complaint.

Smith is – and has been, at all times relevant to this action employed by the city of Salem, Ohio, as a lieutenant in the Salem Fire Department (the "Fire Department"). Prior to the events surrounding this action, Smith worked for the Fire Department for seven years without any negative incidents.

Smith – biologically and by birth a male – is a transsexual and has been diagnosed with Gender Identity Disorder ("GID"), which the American Psychiatric Association characterizes as a disjunction between an individual's sexual organs and sexual identity.

AMERICAN PSYCHIATRIC ASSOCIATION, DIAGNOSTIC AND STAT ISTICAL MANUAL OF MENTAL DISORDERS 576-582 (4th ed. 2000). After being diagnosed with GID, Smith began "expressing a more feminine appearance on a full-time basis" – including at work – in accordance with international medical protocols for treating GID. Soon thereafter, Smith's co-workers began questioning him about his appearance and commenting that his appearance and mannerisms were not "masculine enough." As a result, Smith notified his immediate supervisor, Defendant Thomas Eastek, about his GID diagnosis and treatment. He also informed Eastek of the likelihood that his treatment would eventually include complete physical transformation from male to female. Smith had approached Eastek in order to answer any questions Eastek might have concerning his appearance and manner and so that Eastek could address Smith's co-workers' comments and inquiries. Smith specifically asked Eastek, and Eastek promised, not to divulge the substance of their conversation to any of his superiors, particularly to Defendant Walter Greenamyer, Chief of the Fire Department. In short order, however, Eastek told Greenamyer about Smith's behavior and his GID. Greenamyer then met with Defendant C. Brooke Zellers, the Law Director for the City of Salem, with the intention of using Smith's transsexualism and its manifestations as a basis for terminating his employment. On April 18, 2001, Greenamyer and Zellers arranged a meeting of the City's executive body to discuss Smith and devise a plan for terminating his employment. The executive body included Defendants Larry D. DeJane, Salem's mayor; James A. Armeni, Salem's auditor; and Joseph S. Julian, Salem's service director. Also present was Salem Safety Director Henry L. Willard, now deceased, who was never a named defendant in this action.

Although Ohio Revised Code § 121.22(G) – which sets forth the state procedures pursuant to which Ohio municipal officials may meet to take employment action against a municipal employee – provides that officials "may hold an executive session to consider the appointment, employment, dismissal, discipline, promotion, demotion, or compensation of a public employee only after a majority of a quorum of the public body determines, by a roll call vote, to hold an executive session and only at a regular or special meeting for the sole purpose of [considering such matters]," the City did not abide by these procedures at the April 18, 2001 meeting.

During the meeting, Greenamyer, DeJane, and Zellers agreed to arrange for the Salem Civil Service Commission to require Smith to undergo three separate psychological evaluations with physicians of the City's choosing. They hoped that Smith would either resign or refuse to comply. If he refused to comply, Defendants reasoned, they could terminate Smith's employment on the ground of insubordination. Willard, who remained silent during the meeting, telephoned Smith afterwards to inform him of the plan, calling Defendants' scheme a "witch hunt."

Two days after the meeting, on April 20, 2001, Smith's counsel telephoned DeJane to advise him of Smith's legal representation and the potential legal ramifications for the City if it followed through on the plan devised by Defendants during the April 18 meeting. On April 22, 2001, Smith received his "right to sue" letter from the U.S. Equal Employment Opportunity Commission ("EEOC"). Four days after that, on April 26, 2001, Greenamyer suspended Smith for one twenty-four hour shift, based on his alleged infraction of a City and/or Fire Department policy.

At a subsequent hearing before the Salem Civil Service Commission (the "Commission") regarding his suspension, Smith contended that the suspension was a result of selective enforcement in retaliation for his having obtained legal representation in response to Defendants' plan to terminate his employment because of his transsexualism and its manifestations. At the hearing, Smith sought to elicit testimony from witnesses regarding the meeting of April 18, 2001, but the City objected and the Commission's chairman, Defendant Harry Dugan, refused to allow any testimony regarding the meeting, despite the fact that Ohio Administrative Code § 124-9-11 permitted Smith to introduce evidence of disparate treatment and selective enforcement in his hearing before the Commission.

The Commission ultimately upheld Smith's suspension. Smith appealed to the Columbiana County Court of Common Pleas, which reversed the suspension, finding that "[b]ecause the regulation [that Smith was alleged to have violated] was not effective[,] [Smith] could not be charged with violation of it."

Smith then filed suit in the federal district court. In his complaint, he asserted Title VII claims of sex discrimination and retaliation, along with claims pursuant to 42 U.S.C.§ 1983 and state law claims of invasion of privacy and civil conspiracy. In a Memorandum Opinion and Order dated February 26, 2003, the district court dismissed the federal claims and granted judgment on the pleadings to Defendants pursuant to Federal Rule of Civil Procedure 12(c). The district judge also dismissed the state law claims without prejudice, having declined to exercise supplemental jurisdiction over them pursuant to 28 U.S.C. § 1367(c)(3).

II. ANALYSIS

On appeal, Smith contends that the district court erred in holding that: (1) he failed to state a claim of sex stereotyping; (2) Title VII protection is unavailable to transsexuals; (3) even if he had stated a claim of sex stereotyping, he failed to demonstrate that he suffered an adverse employment action; and (4) he failed to state a claim based on the deprivation of a constitutional or federal statutory right, pursuant to 42 U.S.C. § 1983.

We review *de novo* the dismissal of a complaint pursuant to Rule 12(c). *Grindstaff v. Green*, 133 F.3d 416, 421 (6th Cir. 1998). A motion for judgment on the pleadings shall be granted only where, construing the complaint in the light most favorable to the plaintiff, and accepting all of its factual allegations as true, the plaintiff can prove no set of facts in support of the claims that would entitle him to relief. *Id.*(citation omitted).

A. *Title VII*

The parties disagree over two issues pertaining to Smith's Title VII claims: (1) whether Smith properly alleged a claim of sex stereotyping, in violation of the Supreme Court's pronouncements in *Price Waterhouse v. Hopkins*, 490 U.S. 228 (1989); and (2) whether Smith alleged that he suffered an adverse employment action.

Defendants do not challenge Smith's complaint with respect to any of the other elements necessary to establish discrimination and retaliation claims pursuant to Title VII. In any event, we affirmatively find that Smith has made out a *prima facie* case for both claims. To establish a *prima facie* case of employment discrimination pursuant to Title VII, a plaintiff must show that: (1) he is a member of a protected group; (2) he suffered an adverse employment action; (3) he was qualified for the position in question; and (4) he was treated differently from similarly situated members of the protected class. *Gettings v. Bldg. Laborers Local 310 FringeBenefits Fund,* 349 F.3d 300, 305 (6th Cir. 2003). Smith is a member of a protected class. His complaint asserts that he is a male with Gender Identity Disorder, and Title VII's prohibition of discrimination "because of . . . sex" protects men as well as women. *Newport News Shipbuilding and Dry Dock Co. v. E.E.O.C.,* 462 U.S. 669, 682 (1983). The complaint also alleges both that Smith was qualified for the position in question – he had been a lieutenant in the Fire Department for seven years without any negative incidents – and that he was treated differently from other males in the department because of his non-masculine behavior and GID.

To establish a *prima facie* case of retaliation pursuant to Title VII, a plaintiff must show that: (1) he engaged in an activity protected by Title VII; (2) the defendant knew he engaged in this protected activity; (3) thereafter, the defendant took an employment action adverse to him; and (4) there was a causal connection between the protected activity and the adverse employment action. *DiCarlo v. Potter,* 358 F.3d 408, 420 (6th Cir. 2004) (citation omitted). Smith's complaint satisfies the first two requirements by explaining how he sought legal counsel after learning of the Salem executive body's April 18, 2001 meeting concerning his employment; how his attorney contacted Defendant DeJane to advise Defendants of Smith's representation; and how Smith filed a complaint with the EEOC concerning Defendants' meeting and intended actions. With respect to the fourth requirement, a causal connection between the protected activity and the adverse employment action, "[a]lthough no one factor is dispositive in establishing a causal connection, evidence . . . that the adverse action was taken shortly after the plaintiff's exercise of protected rights is relevant to causation." *Nguyen v. City of Cleveland*, 229 F.3d 559, 563 (6th Cir. 2000); *see also Oliver v. Digital Equip. Corp.*, 846 F.2d 103, 110 (1st Cir. 1988) (employee's discharge "soon after" engaging in protected activity "is indirect proof of a causal connection between the firing and the activity because it is strongly suggestive of retaliation."); *Miller v. Fairchild Indus., Inc.*, 797 F.2d 727, 731 (9th Cir. 1986) ("Causation sufficient to establish a prima facie case of unlawful retaliation may be inferred from the proximity in time between the protected action and the allegedly retaliatory discharge."). Here, Smith was suspended on April 26, 2001, just days after he engaged in protected activity by receiving his "right to sue" letter from the EEOC, which occurred four days before the suspension, and by his attorney's contacting Mayor DeJane, which occurred six days before the suspension. The temporal proximity between the events is significant enough to constitute direct evidence of a causal connection for the purpose of satisfying Smith's burden of demonstrating a *prima facie* case.

We turn now to examining whether Smith properly alleged a claim of sex stereotyping, in violation of the Supreme Court's pronouncements in *Price Waterhouse v. Hopkins*, 490 U.S. 228 (1989), and whether Smith alleged that he suffered an adverse employment action.

1. Sex Stereotyping

Title VII of the Civil Rights Act of 1964 provides, in relevant part, that "[i]t shall be an unlawful employment practice for an employer . . . to discriminate against any individual with respect to his compensation, terms, conditions, or privileges of employment because of such individual's race, color, religion, sex, or national origin." 42 U.S.C. § 2000e-2(a).

In his complaint, Smith asserts Title VII claims of retaliation and employment discrimination "because of sex." The district court dismissed Smith's Title VII claims on the ground that he failed to state a claim for sex stereotyping pursuant to *Price Waterhouse v. Hopkins*, 490 U.S. 228 (1989). The district court implied that Smith's claim was disingenuous, stating that he merely "invokes the term-of-art created by *Price Waterhouse*, that is, 'sex-stereotyping,'" as an end run around his "real" claim, which, the district court stated, was "based upon his transsexuality." The district court then held that "Title VII does not prohibit discrimination based on an individual's transsexualism."

Relying on *Price Waterhouse* – which held that Title VII's prohibition of discrimination "because of . . . sex" bars gender discrimination, including discrimination based on sex stereotypes – Smith contends on appeal that he was a victim of discrimination "because of . . . sex" both because of his gender non-conforming conduct and, more generally, because of his identification as a transsexual. We find both bases of discrimination actionable pursuant to Title VII. We first address whether Smith has stated a claim for relief, pursuant to *Price Waterhouse*'s prohibition of sex stereotyping, based on his gender non-conforming behavior and appearance. In *Price Waterhouse*, the plaintiff, a female senior manager in an accounting firm, was denied partnership in the firm, in part, because she was considered "macho." 490 U.S. at 235. She was advised that she could improve her chances for partnership if she were to take "a course at charm school," "walk more femininely, talk more femininely, dress more femininely, wear make-up, have her hair styled, and wear jewelry." *Id.* (internal quotation marks omitted). Six members of the Court agreed that such comments bespoke gender discrimination, holding that Title VII barred not just discrimination because Hopkins was a woman, but also sex stereotyping – that is, discrimination because she failed to *act* like a woman. *Id.* at 250-51 (plurality opinion of four Justices); *id.* at 258-61 (White, J., concurring); *id.* at 272-73 (O'Connor, J., concurring) (accepting plurality's sex stereotyping analysis and characterizing the "failure to conform to [gender] stereotypes" as a discriminatory criterion; concurring separately to clarify the separate issues of causation and allocation of the burden of proof). As Judge Posner has pointed out, the term "gender" is one "borrowed from grammar to designate the sexes as viewed as social rather than biological classes."

181

RICHARD A. POSNER, SEX AND REASON , 24-25 (1992). The Supreme Court made clear that in the context of Title VII, discrimination because of "sex" includes gender discrimination: "In the context of sex stereotyping, an employer who acts on the basis of a belief that a woman cannot be aggressive, or that she must not be, has acted on the basis of gender." *Price Waterhouse*, 490 U.S. at 250. The Court emphasized that "we are beyond the day when an employer could evaluate employees by assuming or insisting that they matched the stereotype associated with their group." *Id.* at 251.

Smith contends that the same theory of sex stereotyping applies here. His complaint sets forth the conduct and mannerisms which, he alleges, did not conform with his employers' and co-workers' sex stereotypes of how a man should look and behave. Smith's complaint states that, after being diagnosed with GID, he began to express a more feminine appearance and manner on a regular basis, including at work. The complaint states that his co-workers began commenting on his appearance and mannerisms as not being masculine enough; and that his supervisors at the Fire Department and other municipal agents knew about this allegedly unmasculine conduct and appearance. The complaint then describes a high-level meeting among Smith's supervisors and other municipal officials regarding his employment. Defendants allegedly schemed to compel Smith's resignation by forcing him to undergo multiple psychological evaluations of his gender non-conforming behavior. The complaint makes clear that these meetings took place soon after Smith assumed a more feminine appearance and manner and after his conversation about this with Eastek. In addition, the complaint alleges that Smith was suspended for twenty-four hours for allegedly violating an unenacted municipal policy, and that the suspension was ordered in retaliation for his pursuing legal remedies after he had been informed about Defendants' plan to intimidate him into resigning. In short, Smith claims that the discrimination he experienced was based on his failure to conform to sex stereotypes by expressing less masculine, and more feminine mannerisms and appearance.

Having alleged that his failure to conform to sex stereotypes concerning how a man should look and behave was the driving force behind Defendants' actions, Smith has sufficiently pleaded claims of sex stereotyping and gender discrimination.

In so holding, we find that the district court erred in relying on a series of pre-*Price Waterhouse* cases from other federal appellate courts holding that transsexuals, as a class, are not entitled to Title VII protection because "Congress had a narrow view of sex in mind" and "never considered nor intended that [Title VII] apply to anything other than the traditional concept of sex." *Ulane v. Eastern Airlines, Inc.*, 742 F.2d 1081, 1085, 1086 (7th Cir. 1984); *see also Holloway v. Arthur Andersen & Co.*, 566 F.2d 659, 661-63 (9th Cir. 1977) (refusing to extend protection of Title VII to transsexuals because discrimination against transsexuals is based on "gender" rather than "sex"). It is true that, in the past, federal appellate courts regarded Title VII as barring discrimination based only on "sex" (referring to an individual's anatomical and biological characteristics), but not on "gender" (referring to socially-constructed norms associated with a person's sex). *See, e.g., Ulane*, 742 F.2d at 1084 (construing "sex" in Title VII narrowly to mean only anatomical sex rather than gender); *Sommers v. Budget Mktg., Inc.*, 667 F.2d 748, 750 (8th Cir. 1982) (holding that transsexuals are not protected by Title VII because the "plain meaning" must be ascribed to the term "sex" in the absence of clear congressional intent to do otherwise); *Holloway*, 566 F.2d at 661-63 (refusing to extend protection of Title VII to transsexuals because discrimination against transsexualism is based on "gender" rather than "sex;" and "sex" given its traditional definition based on the anatomical characteristics dividing "organisms" and "living beings" into male and female). In this earlier jurisprudence, male-to-female transsexuals (who were the plaintiffs in *Ulane, Sommers,* and *Holloway*) – as biological males whose outward behavior and emotional identity did not conform to socially-prescribed expectations of masculinity – were denied Title VII protection by courts because they were considered victims of "gender" rather than "sex" discrimination.

However, the approach in *Holloway, Sommers,* and *Ulane* – and by the district court in this case – has been eviscerated by *Price Waterhouse.* *See Schwenk v. Hartford,* 204 F.3d 1187, 1201 (9th Cir. 2000) ("The initial judicial approach taken in cases such as *Holloway* [and *Ulane*] has been overruled by the logic and language of *Price Wterhouse.*").

By holding that Title VII protected a woman who failed to conform to social expectations concerning how a woman should look and behave, the Supreme Court established that Title VII's reference to "sex" encompasses both the biological differences between men and women, and gender discrimination, that is, discrimination based on a failure to conform to stereotypical gender norms. *See Price Waterhouse,* 490 U.S. at 251; *see also Schwenk,* 204 F.3d at 1202 (stating that Title VII encompasses instances in which "the perpetrator's actions stem from the fact that he believed that the victim was a man who 'failed to act like' one" and that "sex" under Title VII encompasses both the anatomical differences between men and women, and gender); *Rene v.MGM Grand Hotel, Inc.,* 305 F.3d 1061, 1068 (9th Cir. 2002) (en banc) (Pregerson, J., concurring) (noting that the Ninth Circuit had previously found that "same-sex gender stereotyping of the sort suffered by Rene – i.e. gender stereotyping of a male gay employee by his male co-workers" constituted actionable harassment under Title VII and concluding that "[t]he repeated testimony that his co-workers treated Rene, in a variety of ways, 'like a woman' constitutes ample evidence of gender stereotyping"); *Bibby v. Philadelphia Coca Cola Bottling Co.,* 260 F.3d 257, 262-63 (3d Cir. 2001) (stating that a plaintiff may be able to prove a claim of sex discrimination by showing that the "harasser's conduct was motivated by a belief that the victim did not conform to the stereotypes of his or her gender"); *Nichols v. Azteca Rest. Enters., Inc.,* 256 F.3d 864, 874-75 (9th Cir.2001) (holding that harassment "based upon the perception that [the plaintiff] is effeminate" is discrimination because of sex, in violation of Title VII), *overruling DeSantis v. Pac. Tel. & Tel. Co., Inc.,* 608 F.2d 327 (9th Cir. 1979); *Doe v. Belleville,* 119 F.3d 563, 580-81 (7th Cir. 1997) (holding that "Title VII does not permit an employee to be treated adversely because his or her appearance or conduct does not conform to stereotypical gender roles" and explaining that "a man who is harassed because his voice is soft, his physique is slight, his hair long, or because in some other respect he exhibits his masculinity in a way that does not meet his coworkers' idea of how men are to appear and behave, is harassed 'because of his sex'"), *vacated and remanded on other grounds*, 523 U.S. 1001 (1998).

After *Price Waterhouse*, an employer who discriminates against women because, for instance, they do not wear dresses or makeup, is engaging in sex discrimination because the discrimination would not occur but for the victim's sex. It follows that employers who discriminate against men because they *do* wear dresses and makeup, or otherwise act femininely, are also engaging in sex discrimination, because the discrimination would not occur but for the victim's sex. *See, e.g., Nichols,* 256 F.3d 864 (Title VII sex discrimination and hostile work environment claim upheld where plaintiff's male co-workers and supervisors repeatedly referred to him as "she" and "her" and where co-workers mocked him for walking and carrying his serving tray "like a woman"); *Higgins v. New Balance Athletic Shoe, Inc.,* 194 F.3d 252, 261 n.4 (1st Cir. 1999) ("[J]ust as a woman can ground an action on a claim that men discriminated against her because she did not meet stereotyped expectations of femininity, a man can ground a claim on evidence that other men discriminated against him because he did not meet stereotypical expectations of masculinity." (internal citation omitted)); *see also Rosa v. Park West Bank & Trust Co.,* 214 F.3d 213 (1st Cir. 2000) (applying *Price Waterhouse* and Title VII jurisprudence to an Equal Credit Opportunity Act claim and reinstating claim on behalf of biologically male plaintiff who alleged that he was denied an opportunity to apply for a loan because was dressed in "traditionally feminine attire").

Yet some courts have held that this latter form of discrimination is of a different and somehow more permissible kind. For instance, the man who acts in ways typically associated with women is not described as engaging in the same activity as a woman who acts in ways typically associated with women, but is instead described as engaging in the different activity of being a transsexual (or in some instances, a homosexual or transvestite). Discrimination against the transsexual is then found not to be discrimination "because of . . . sex," but rather, discrimination against the plaintiff's unprotected status or mode of self-identification.

In other words, these courts superimpose classifications such as "transsexual" on a plaintiff, and then legitimize discrimination based on the plaintiff's gender non-conformity by formalizing the non-conformity into an ostensibly unprotected classification. *See, e.g., Dillon v. Frank*, No. 90-2290, 1992 WL 5436 (6th Cir. Jan. 15, 1992).

Such was the case here: despite the fact that Smith alleges that Defendants' discrimination was motivated by his appearance and mannerisms, which Defendants felt were inappropriate for a male, the district court expressly declined to discuss the applicability of *Price Waterhouse*. The district court therefore gave insufficient consideration to Smith's well-pleaded claims concerning his contra-gender behavior, but rather accounted for that behavior only insofar as it confirmed for the court Smith's status as a transsexual, which the district court held precluded Smith from Title VII protection.

Such analyses cannot be reconciled with *Price Waterhouse*, which does not make Title VII protection against sex stereotyping conditional or provide any reason to exclude Title VII coverage for non sex-stereotypical behavior simply because the person is a transsexual. As such, discrimination against a plaintiff who is a transsexual – and therefore fails to act like and/or identify with the gender norms associated with his or her sex – is no different from the discrimination directed against Ann Hopkins in *Price Waterhouse*, who, in sex-stereotypical terms, did not act like a woman. Sex stereotyping based on a person's gender non-conforming behavior is impermissible discrimination, irrespective of the cause of that behavior; a label, such as "transsexual," is not fatal to a sex discrimination claim where the victim has suffered discrimination because of his or her gender nonconformity. Accordingly, we hold that Smith has stated a claim for relief pursuant to Title VII's prohibition of sex discrimination.

Even if Smith had alleged discrimination based only on his self-identification as a transsexual – as opposed to his specific appearance and behavior – this claim too is actionable pursuant to Title VII. By definition, transsexuals are individuals who fail to conform to stereotypes about how those assigned a particular sex at birth should act, dress, and self-identify. *Ergo*, identification as a transsexual is the statement or admission that one wishes to be the opposite sex or does not relate to one's birth sex. Such an admission – for instance the admission by a man that he self-identifies as a woman and/or that he wishes to be a woman – itself violates the prevalent sex stereotype that a man should perceive himself as a man. Discrimination based on transsexualism is rooted in the insistence that sex (organs) and gender (social classification of a person as belonging to one sex or the other) coincide. This is the very essence of sex stereotyping. Accordingly, to the extent that Smith also alleges discrimination based solely on his identification as a transsexual, he has alleged a claim of sex stereotyping pursuant to Title VII. As noted above, Smith's birth sex is male and this is the basis for his protected class status under Title VII even under this formulation of his claim.

Finally, we note that, in its opinion, the district court repeatedly places the term "sex stereotyping" in quotation marks and refers to it as a "term of art" used by Smith to disingenuously plead discrimination because of transsexualism. Similarly, Defendants refer to sex stereotyping as "the *Price Waterhouse* loophole." (Appellees' Brief at 6.) These characterizations are almost identical to the treatment that Price Waterhouse itself gave sex stereotyping in its briefs to the U.S. Supreme Court. As we do now, the Supreme Court noted the practice with disfavor, stating: In the specific context of sex stereotyping, an employer who acts on the basis of a belief that a woman cannot be aggressive, or that she must not be, has acted on the basis of gender. Although the parties do not overtly dispute this last proposition, the placement by Price Waterhouse of "sex stereotyping" in quotation marks throughout its brief seems to us an insinuation either that such stereotyping was not present in this case or that it lacks legal relevance. We reject both possibilities. *Price Waterhouse*, 490 U.S. at 250.

2. *Adverse Employment Action*

Despite having dismissed Smith's Title VII claim for failure to state a claim of sex stereotyping – a finding we have just rejected – the district court nevertheless addressed the merits of Smith's Title VII claims *arguendo*. Relying on *White v. Burlington Northern & Sante Fe Ry. Co.*, 310 F.3d 443 (6th Cir. 2002), the district court held that Smith's suspension was not an adverse employment action because the Court of Common Pleas, rendering the "ultimate employment decision," reversed the suspension, and that accordingly, Smith's Title VII claim could not lie. Because Smith's com plaint does not state whether he was suspended with or without pay. Because we must construe the complaint in the light most favorable to the plaintiff, Ziegler, 249 F.3d at 512, and given the liberal pleading standard s of Federal Rule of Civil Procedure 8, we do not find this failure dispositive. A "materially adverse change" in employment conditions often involves a material loss of pay or benefits, but that is not this Circuit has since vacated and overruled White, 364 F.3d 789 (6th Cir. 2004) (en banc), and joined the majority of other circuits in rejecting the "ultimate employment decision" standard, we hold that the district court erred in its analysis and that Smith has successfully pleaded an adverse employment action in support of his employment discrimination and retaliation claims pursuant to Title VII. Common to both the employment discrimination and retaliation claims is a showing of an adverse employment action, which is defined as a "materially adverse change in the terms and conditions of [plaintiff's] employment." *Hollins v. Atlantic Co.*, 188 F.3d 652, 662 (6th Cir. 1999). A "bruised ego," a "mere inconvenience or an alteration of job responsibilities" is not enough to constitute an adverse employment action. *White,* 364 F.3d at 797 (quoting *Kocsis v. Multi-Care Mgmt. Inc.,* 97 F.3d 876, 886 (6th Cir. 1996)).

Examples of adverse employment actions include firing, failing to promote, reassignment with significantly different responsibilities, a material loss of benefits, suspensions, and other indices unique to a particular situation. *Burlington Indus., Inc. v. Ellerth*, 524 U.S. 742, 761 (1998); *White*, 364 F.3d at 798. Here, the Fire Department suspended Smith for twenty-four hours. Because Smith works in twenty-four hour shifts, that twenty-four hour suspension was the equivalent of three eight-hour days for the average worker, or, approximately 60% of a forty-hour work week. Pursuant to the liberal notice pleading requirements set forth in Fed. R. Civ. P. 8, this allegation, at this phase of the litigation, is sufficient to satisfy the adverse employment requirement of both an employment discrimination and retaliation claim pursuant to Title VII. always the case, and "other indices that might be unique to a particular situation" can constitute a "materially adverse change" as well. *Ho llins,* 188 F.3d at 662 . Because no discovery has been conducted yet, we do not know the full contours of the suspension. For now, however, for the reasons just stated, we find that Smith has sufficiently alleged an adverse employment action.

It is irrelevant that Smith's suspension was ultimately reversed by the Court of Common Pleas after he challenged the suspension's legality. In *White*, this Court recently joined the majority of other circuits in rejecting the "ultimate employment decision" standard whereby a negative employment action is not considered an "adverse employment action" for Title VII purposes when the decision is subsequently reversed by the employer, putting the plaintiff in the position he would have been in absent the negative action. *White*, 364 F.3d 789 (holding that the suspension of a railroad employee without pay, followed thirty-seven days later by reinstatement with back pay, was an "adverse employment action" for Title VII purposes). Even if the "ultimate employment decision" standard were still viable, the district court erred in concluding that, because the Court of Common Pleas overturned the suspension, it was not an adverse employment action. There is no legal authority for the proposition that reversal by a *judicial* body – as opposed to the employer – declassifies a suspension as an adverse employment action.

Accordingly, Smith has stated an adverse employment action and, therefore, satisfied all of the elements necessary to allege a *prima facie* case of employment discrimination and retaliation pursuant to Title VII. We therefore reverse the district court's grant of judgment on the pleadings to Defendants with respect to those claims.

B. *42 U.S.C. § 1983 Claims* The district court also dismissed Smith's claims pursuant to 42 U.S.C. § 1983 on the ground that he failed to state a claim based on the deprivation of a constitutional or federal statutory right. 42 U.S.C. § 1983 provides a civil cause of action for individuals who are deprived of any rights, privileges, or immunities secured by the Constitution or federal laws by those acting under color of state law. Smith has stated a claim for relief pursuant to § 1983 in connection with his sex-based claim of employment discrimination. Individuals have a right, protected by the Equal Protection clause of the Fourteenth Amendment, to be free from discrimination on the basis of sex in public employment. *Davis v. Passman*, 442 U.S. 228, 234-35 (1979). To make out such a claim, a plaintiff must prove that he suffered purposeful or intentional discrimination on the basis of gender. *Vill. of Arlington Heights v. Metro. Hous. Dev. Corp.*, 429 U.S. 252, 264-65 (1977). As this Court has noted several times, "the showing a plaintiff must make to recover on a disparate treatment claim under Title VII mirrors that which must be made to recover on an equal protection claim under section § 1983." *Gutzwiller v. Fenik*, 860 F.2d 1317, 1325 (6th Cir. 1988) (citing *Kitchen v. Chippewa Valley Schs.*, 825 F.2d 1004, 1011 (6th Cir. 1987); *Daniels v. Bd. of Educ.*, 805 F.2d 203, 207 (6th Cir. 1986); *Grano v. Dep't of Dev.*, 637 F.2d 1073, 1081-82 (6th Cir. 1980); *Lautermilch v. Findlay City Schs.*, 314 F.3d 271, 275 (6th Cir. 2003) ("To prove a violation of the equal protection clause under § 1983, [a plaintiff] must prove the same elements as are required to establish a disparate treatment claim under Title VII.") (quotation and citation omitted). The facts Smith has alleged to support his claims of gender discrimination pursuant to Title

190

VII easily constitute a claim of sex discrimination grounded in the Equal Protection Clause of the Constitution, pursuant to § 1983. *See Back v. Hastings on Hudson Union Free Sch. Dist.*, — F.3d —, No. 03-7058, 2004 WL 739846, at * 5-7 (2d Cir. Apr. 7, 2004) (holding that claims premised on *Price Waterhouse* sex stereotyping theory sufficiently constitute claim of sex discrimination pursuant to § 1983).

Defendants urge us to hold otherwise, on the ground that Smith's complaint fails to refer specifically to the Equal Protection Clause of the U.S. Constitution. But the Federal Rules of Civil Procedure provide for a liberal system of notice pleading. Fed. R. Civ. P. 8(a). A plaintiff need only provide "a short and plain statement of the claim showing that the pleader is entitled to relief." Fed. R. Civ. P. 8(a)(2). "Such a statement must simply 'give the defendant fair notice of what the plaintiff's claim is and the grounds upon which it rests.'" *Swierkiewicz v. Soremna N.A.*, 534 U.S. 506, 512 (2002) (quoting *Conley v. Gibson*, 355 U.S. 41, 47 (1957)). Claims made pursuant to 42 U.S.C. § 1983 are not subject to heightened pleading standards. *Leatherman v. Tarrant County Narcotics Intelligence and Coordination Unit*, 507 U.S. 163, 165-66 (1993) (rejecting heightened pleading standard for § 1983 claims); *Jones v. Duncan*, 840 F.2d 359 (6th Cir. 1988) (holding that § 1983 claims need not set forth in detail all the particularities of a plaintiff's claim against a defendant). Moreover, legal theories of recovery need not be spelled out as long as the relevant issues are sufficiently implicated in the pleadings; in considering motions pursuant to Fed. R. Civ. P. 12(c), we ask not whether a complaint points to a specific statute, but whether relief is possible under any set of facts that could be established consistent with the allegation. Because Smith's sex discrimination claim so thoroughly and obviously sounds in a constitutional claim of equal protection, Defendants had fair notice of his claim and the ground upon which it rests. As such, we hold that Smith has satisfied the liberal notice pleading requirements set forth in Fed. R. Civ. P. 8 with respect to his claim of sex discrimination, grounded in an alleged equal protection violation, and we therefore reverse the district court's grant of judgment on the pleadings dismissing Smith's § 1983 claim.

In his appellate brief, Smith also contends that his complaint alleges a violation of his constitutional right to due process, based on the City's failure to comply with the state statutory and administrative procedures that an Ohio municipality must follow when taking official employment action against a public employee. His complaint outlines the statutory procedures, governed by O.R.C. § 121.22(G), pursuant to which members of an Ohio municipality may meet for purposes of taking official employment action against a public employee, and it alleges that those procedures were not followed. The complaint also discusses O.A.C. § 124-9-11, which would have permitted Smith to call witnesses at his post-suspension hearing in front of the Salem Civil Service Commission; and the complaint alleges that he was barred from calling witnesses. Smith contends that these allegations implicate his right to due process pursuant to the Fourteenth Amendment of the U.S. Constitution.

However, it is well-settled that state law does not ordinarily define the parameters of due process for Fourteenth Amendment purposes, and that state law, by itself, cannot be the basis for a federal constitutional violation. *See Purisch v. Tennessee Technological Univ.*, 76 F.3d 1414, 1423 (6th Cir. 1996) ("Violation of a state's formal [employment grievance] procedure . . . does not in itself implicate constitutional due process concerns."). Neither Smith's complaint nor his brief specifies what deprivation of property or liberty allegedly stemmed from the City's failure to comply with state procedural and administrative rules concerning his employment.

Accordingly, he has failed to state a federal due process violation pursuant to § 1983. In sum, we hold that Smith has failed to state a § 1983 claim based on violations of his right to due process.

However, he has stated a § 1983 claim of sex discrimination, grounded in an alleged equal protection violation, and, for that reason, we reverse the district court's grant of judgment on the pleadings dismissing Smith's § 1983 claim.

192

III. CONCLUSION

Because Smith has successfully stated claims for relief pursuant to both Title VII and 42 U.S.C. § 1983, the judgment of the district court is REVERSED and this case is REMANDED to the district court for further proceedings consistent with this opinion.

Enriquez v. West Jersey Health Systems

Enriquez v. West Jersey Health Systems is a court opinion that discusses in detail the view of transgender identity as protected under state disability statutes. While New Jersey now has a statute explicitly including gender identity or expression among the state's civil rights protections, the opinion is instructive regarding the relationship between transgender identity and disability laws.

SUPERIOR COURT OF NEW JERSEY

APPELLATE DIVISION

DOCKET NO. A-2017-99T5 AND A-5581-99T5

Argued May 31, 2001 - Decided July 3, 2001
Before Judges King, Lefelt and Axelrad.

On appeal from the Superior Court of
New Jersey, Law Division, Camden
County, Docket Nos. L-9328-98 and
L-7543-99.

Arthur B. Jarrett, of the Pennsylvania
bar, admitted pro hac vice, argued the
cause for appellant (James & Jarrett,
attorneys; Mr. Jarrett and Walter D.
Schirrmacker, also of the Pennsylvania
bar and also admitted pro hac vice, and
Brem Moldovsky, on the brief).
William M. Honan argued the cause
for respondents West Jersey Health

Systems, West Jersey Center for
Behavior, Learning & Attention,

West Jersey Clinical Assoc., John
Cossa, M.D., Richard Miller, Maureen
Miller, Ellen Feinstein, Greg
Maddison, Ed Dunn, Kevin Manley and
Tony Chigounis (Fox, Rothschild,
O'Brien & Frankel, attorneys; Mr.
Honan, of counsel; Mr. Honan and
Kathryn D. Portner, on the brief).
Darren H. Goldstein argued the cause
for respondents Family Guidance
Center, Les Pascal & James Varrell,
M.D. (Speziali, Greenwald, Goldstein
& Hawkins, attorneys; Mr. Goldstein,
on the brief).

The opinion of the court was delivered by

LEFELT, J.A.D.

These consolidated appeals arise from the summary judgment
dismissal of two complaints filed by plaintiff Carla Enriquez, a male-
to-female transsexual, for wrongful termination of her employment as
medical director of a learning behavior center owned and managed by
the various corporate and individual defendants. Most significantly,
this appeal raises the novel issues of whether gender dysphoria or
transsexualism is a handicap under the New Jersey Law Against
Discrimination, N.J.S.A. 10:5-1 through -49 ("LAD"), and whether the
LAD precludes an employer from discriminating on the basis of
someone's sexual identity or gender. We answer both questions in the
affirmative and reverse and remand for further proceedings.

We recount only those portions of the procedural history and facts
necessary to explain our resolution of the issues raised in these

consolidated appeals. Plaintiff was born a biological male and, until February 1998, was legally known as "Carlos." Plaintiff is a licensed New Jersey physician who was in the private practice of general and developmental pediatrics from 1974 to 1995.

On November 20, 1995, defendant West Jersey Health Systems ("West Jersey") hired plaintiff as medical director of defendant outpatient treatment facility, West Jersey Center for Behavior, Learning and Attention ("Center"). Plaintiff and West Jersey entered into a written Professional Services Agreement that could be terminated by either party upon ninety days' written notice.

In September 1996, less than a year after plaintiff's employment with West Jersey commenced, she began the external transformation from male to female. Plaintiff shaved her beard and eventually removed all vestiges of facial hair. She sculpted and waxed her eyebrows, pierced her ears, started wearing emerald stone earrings, and began growing breasts.

In the early months of 1997, plaintiff was confronted by defendants John Cossa, Maureen Miller, and Ellen Feinstein regarding their discomfort over her transformation. Cossa was West Jersey's vice president and president and chief executive officer of defendant West Jersey Clinical Association, also known as defendant West Jersey Physicians' Associates ("Physicians' Associates"), the entity which assumed control of the Center's professional staff in September 1997. Miller was vice president of outpatient services at West Jersey and Feinstein was her assistant.

By February 1997, plaintiff began manicuring and polishing her nails, growing long hair, and wearing a ponytail. On February 13, 1997, Cossa expressly questioned plaintiff about her appearance. According to plaintiff, Cossa asked if plaintiff would be willing to go back to her prior appearance if West Jersey asked her to. Cossa told plaintiff, "stop all this and go back to your previous appearance!"

In June 1997, plaintiff was diagnosed with gender dysphoria, which is a gender identity disorder listed in the <u>Diagnostic and Statistical Manual of Mental Disorders</u>, (fourth edition, 1994)("<u>DSM-IV</u>"), published by the American Psychiatric Association. This disorder is also known as transsexualism.

On July 22, 1997, plaintiff received a letter from Miller stating that the hospital, pursuant to the professional services agreement, was terminating the agreement, without cause, effective in ninety days, on October 22, 1997. According to this letter, the Center's program was being assumed by Physicians' Associates as of the end of October. Plaintiff was advised that she would be contacted by Cossa to discuss a new contract with that entity.

From July 22 to September 29, 1997, plaintiff repeatedly tried to discuss a new contract with Cossa, without any success. Plaintiff claimed that as of September 1997, all of the other professional staff employed at the Center had become employees of Physicians' Associates.

On September 29, 1997, when plaintiff finally met with Cossa regarding a new contract for plaintiff, Cossa advised plaintiff that "[N]o one's going to sign this contract unless you stop this business that you're doing."

When Cossa and plaintiff next met, on October 13, plaintiff presented Cossa with a letter she had drafted to her family and patients, explaining her gender identity disorder and the treatment she was following. She had not yet sent the letter to anyone. Cossa asked plaintiff not to say anything yet and to let Cossa try to work things out.

On October 22, 1997, Cossa handed plaintiff a termination letter. According to this letter, Cossa and plaintiff had discussed the possibility of moving plaintiff to Physicians' Associates. However, defendants decided not to pursue that option and had made arrangements for other doctors to be available immediately to provide care to the Center's patients.

Cossa told plaintiff that the hospital would not allow plaintiff to send her proposed letter to the patients, and that the hospital had drafted a different letter. Plaintiff was also told not to return to the office for the rest of that day and that her patients had been canceled for the next three months.

In February 1998, plaintiff legally changed her name to Carla. In July 1998, approximately nine months after she was terminated, plaintiff underwent the surgical procedure to become a female. Plaintiff stated that while she was a man, she was not gay and was not sexually attracted to other men. No one at West Jersey ever accused plaintiff of being gay. Since her surgery, plaintiff has continued to live as a "spouse" with Monica, to whom plaintiff was married while she was a man. Plaintiff believes, according to her deposition testimony, that Monica is a lesbian. Plaintiff believes that the course of treatment she began, that ended with sex reassignment surgery, cured her gender dysphoria.

In December 1998, plaintiff filed her first complaint against defendants for disability discrimination under the LAD, gender or sexual orientation-affection discrimination under the LAD, breach of contract, and trade libel. The West Jersey defendants filed a motion for partial summary judgment, seeking dismissal of plaintiff's claim for disability discrimination. The motion judge granted defendant's motion, noting that other courts had concluded that transsexualism was not a recognized mental or physical disability under statutes very similar to ours.

Thereafter, all defendants moved for summary judgment seeking dismissal of the remainder of plaintiff's claims. Before these motions could be heard, plaintiff filed a separately docketed complaint on October 21, 1999, naming the same defendants and reciting the same factual allegations. This complaint, however, alleged causes of action for intentional interference with a contractual relationship, conspiracy, wrongful refusal to continue a business, and unjust enrichment.

In dealing with the summary judgment motions made by all defendants regarding the remaining counts of plaintiff's first complaint, the motion judge found that plaintiff could not bring a claim for sexual orientation discrimination because plaintiff admitted that, while she was a male, she was not gay and was never accused of being gay. The judge did not believe that the Legislature has provided any remedy for persons who elected to change their sex.

The judge dismissed the breach of contract claim on the ground that plaintiff's employment contract contained a ninety- day termination provision. With regard to the trade libel claim, the judge noted that plaintiff had refused to identify those patients she claimed had been told by defendants that something was wrong with plaintiff and that plaintiff was no longer practicing medicine. The judge acknowledged that plaintiff had submitted two affidavits in opposition to summary judgment, but did not comment on whether these affidavits would alter his decision.

The affidavits that plaintiff had submitted in opposition to the summary judgment motion were from the parents of two patients. According to one parent, after plaintiff's termination, West Jersey told her that they had no idea where plaintiff was. The parent was also told that plaintiff might have stopped practicing medicine and that the parent should look for a new doctor for her child.

The affidavit from the other parent was similar. In addition to telling this parent that they had no idea where plaintiff went, defendants also said that plaintiff was going through some personal issues and would probably not be practicing medicine anymore.

In February 2000, all defendants moved for a summary judgment dismissal of plaintiff's second complaint. In granting these motions, a different motion judge concluded that the second complaint was a "repackaging" of the first complaint, which had been dismissed by the first motion judge.

Plaintiff appealed from the summary judgments dismissing the two complaints, and we consolidated the two appeals. In addition to contesting the dismissal of the entire first complaint, only two of the causes of action alleged by plaintiff in the second complaint, interference with economic opportunity and unjust enrichment, are being challenged in the appeal.

II.

We first detail what the record discloses concerning plaintiff's gender dysphoria or transsexualism. Essentially, plaintiff claimed that she felt like a woman trapped in a man's body from a very early age, and that she was called upon to act manly even though she did not feel masculine. This is consistent with general clinical findings regarding other transsexuals. "Transsexuals do not alternate between gender roles; rather, they assume a fixed role of attitudes, feelings, fantasies, and choices consonant with those of the opposite sex, all of which clearly date back to early development." Current Medical Diagnosis & Treatment 928 (Lawrence M. Tierney, Jr. et al. eds., 35th ed. 1996).

Though plaintiff is a physician, she did not diagnose herself. Dr. William Stayton from the University of Pennsylvania formally diagnosed plaintiff's condition. Plaintiff claims Dr. Stayton is an "internationally renowned expert in gender and sexual medicine." According to the letter plaintiff wanted to send her patients explaining her situation, there are "internationally accepted norms for treatment of this condition." These encompass the steps that plaintiff went through including "extensive psychological counseling, extended planning for 'transition,' the use of contrahormonal therapy, hair removal, living in the putative gender role full time (the so called 'Real Life Test') and finally, in some cases, sex reassignment surgery."

Also in the letter she planned to send her patients, plaintiff further explained gender dysphoria in this fashion:

Current research tells us that early in fetal development, the infant's brain undergoes masculinization or feminization unrelated to chromosomal complement. Later, as we grow up, we identify with the 'cortical' or brain gender we were endowed with. Happily, for the majority of the population, the genetic (or chromosomal gender) and the cortical (or brain gender) are congruent. Later in development, we develop sexual preferences, sexual orientation, gender attribution, and gender function. Again, in the majority of the population, all of these are congruent and society and the individual are happy.

But some people do not have this harmony. We call these feelings 'dysphoria' in medicine. Literally, this means 'unhappy,' but doctors have expanded its meaning to describe conditions that significantly effect the individual. Gender Dysphoria describes a condition in which there is not this harmony. The physical and the inner selves are at odds.

Plaintiff argues that the court erred in dismissing her claim of discrimination based on either gender or sexual orientation/affection. The LAD provides in pertinent part that it is unlawful for an employer to terminate someone's employment based on that person's "affectional or sexual orientation, genetic information, sex or atypical hereditary cellular or blood trait," N.J.S.A. 10:5-12(a). The part of the LAD dealing with "affectional or sexual orientation" was added by the Legislature in 1992. L. 1991, c. 519, § 8, effective January 19, 1992.

"'Affectional or sexual orientation' means male or female heterosexuality, homosexuality or bisexuality by inclination, practice, identity or expression, having a history thereof or being perceived, presumed or identified by others as having such an orientation." N.J.S.A. 10:5-5(hh). "Heterosexuality" is defined as affectional, emotional or physical attraction or behavior primarily directed towards persons of the other gender, "homosexuality" is directed towards

202

persons of the same gender, and "bisexuality" is directed towards persons of either gender. N.J.S.A. 10:5-5(ii)-(kk).

We conclude that plaintiff failed to establish a prima facie case for discrimination based on her affectional or sexual orientation because she was not a homosexual or bisexual or perceived to be homosexual or bisexual. This portion of the statute refers to one's relations with others and not to his or her own sexual identity, and plaintiff presented no evidence that she was discriminated against because of her "affectional, emotional or physical attraction" to others.

Plaintiff's complaint, however, also included a claim for gender discrimination. Plaintiff specifically charged that her "sexual affectation and/or orientation and/or gender, real or as perceived by the defendants was and is a determining factor in connection with defendants ongoing discriminatory, retaliatory and harassing treatment of Plaintiff." Thus, we proceed to consider whether plaintiff has set forth a viable LAD cause of action based on her gender.

We note preliminarily that the LAD bars discrimination on the basis of "sex" and gender is not specifically mentioned in the law. "Sex" is generally understood to mean "whether a person is anatomically male or female." Taylor Flynn, Transforming the Debate: Why We Need to Include Transgender Rights in the Struggles for Sex and Sexual Orientation Equality, 101 Colum. L. Rev. 392, 394 (2001). Gender is "whether a person has qualities that society considers masculine or feminine." Ibid.

Title VII of the Civil Rights Act of 1964, 42 U.S.C.A. § 2000e-2(a)(1), does not contain language barring discrimination based on one's affectional or sexual orientation. Moreover, the federal courts construing Title VII have unanimously concluded that discrimination on the basis of gender dysphoria is not sex discrimination. Basically, the federal courts conclude that discrimination on the basis of sex outlaws discrimination against women because they are women, and against men because they are men. E.g., Ulane v. E. Airlines, Inc., 742

F.2d 1081, 1085 (7th Cir. 1984), cert. denied, 471 U.S. 1017, 105 S. Ct. 2023, 85 L. Ed.2d 304 (1985); Sommers v. Budget Mktg., Inc., 667 F.2d 748, 750 (8th Cir. 1982); Holloway v. Arthur Andersen & Co., 566 F.2d 659, 662-63 (9th Cir. 1977); Grossman v. Bernards Tp. Bd. of Educ., 11 Fair Empl. Prac. Cas. (BNA) 1196 (D.N.J. 1975), aff'd, 538 F.2d 319 (3d Cir.), cert. denied, 429 U.S. 897, 97 S. Ct. 261, 50 L. Ed.2d 181 (1976).

In 1989, however, the United States Supreme Court signaled a possible change in the federal approach to gender dysphoria. In Price Waterhouse v. Hopkins, 490 U.S. 228, 109 S. Ct. 1775, 104 L. Ed.2d 268 (1989), the Court held that Title VII barred discrimination of a woman who failed to "act like a woman" or to conform to socially-constructed gender expectations. This approach would seem to indicate that the word "sex" in Title VII encompasses both gender and sex, and forbids discrimination because of one's failure to act in a way expected of a man or a woman. Schwenk v. Hartford, 204 F.3d 1187, 1201-02 (9th Cir. 2000). The United States Supreme Court has stated that Congress, in barring discrimination based on sex, "intended to strike at the entire spectrum of disparate treatment of men and women resulting from sex stereotypes." Price Waterhouse v. Hopkins, supra, 490 U.S. at 251, 109 S. Ct. at 1791, 104 L. Ed. 2d at 288 (citation omitted). Again, as further evidence of this change in approach, Rosa v. Park West Bank & Trust Co., 214 F.3d 213 (1st Cir. 2000), found under the Equal Credit Opportunity Act, 15 U.S.C. §1691 (1994), that discrimination against a man because he was wearing a dress could constitute sex discrimination. Id. at 214.

The states are split on this issue. For example, in Sommers v. Iowa Civil Rights Comm'n, 337 N.W.2d 470, 474 (Iowa 1983), the Iowa Supreme Court concluded that the word "sex" in Iowa's Civil Rights Act did not include transsexuals and that sexual discrimination was intended to prohibit conduct which, had the victim been a member of the opposite sex, would not have otherwise occurred.

Similarly, in <u>James v. Ranch Mart Hardware, Inc.</u>, 881 F. Supp. 478, 481, n.4 (D. Kan. 1995) (applying Kansas law), the federal court held that under the Kansas Act Against Discrimination, a male-to-female transsexual could not sue for discrimination. Moreover, because male employees constituted the "majority," the plaintiff had to prove a case of "reverse" discrimination, that is, that her employer was the rare employer who discriminated against the majority. <u>Id.</u> at 481.

In <u>Underwood v. Archer Mgmt. Servs., Inc.</u>, 857 F. Supp. 96, 98 (D.D.C. 1994), the court, applying local federal law, held that "sex" in the District of Columbia's Human Rights Act did not include transsexuality because the District's Commission on Human Rights had defined the term to mean the state of being male or female and the conditions associated therewith. Moreover, although the statute also included a prohibition against sexual orientation discrimination, transsexuality was not the same thing as homosexuality, and the complaint had been devoid of any reference to plaintiff's sexual orientation. <u>Ibid.</u>

We disagree with the rationale of these decisions. A person who is discriminated against because he changes his gender from male to female is being discriminated against because he or she is a member of a very small minority whose condition remains incomprehensible to most individuals. The view of sex discrimination reflected in these decisions is too constricted.

Rather, we believe that the New York case <u>Maffei v. Kolaeton Indus., Inc.</u>, 626 N.Y.S.2d 391 (Sup. Ct. 1995), is better reasoned. In <u>Maffei</u>, a state law prohibited sex discrimination and a city law also prohibited sexual orientation discrimination. <u>Id.</u> at 392. The court agreed with the reasoning of <u>Underwood</u> that sexual orientation discrimination did not apply to a transsexual because such discrimination dealt only with the sex of the person's sexual partner. <u>Id.</u> at 393.

However, in concluding that discrimination against a transsexual constituted sex discrimination, the New York court held that the contrary holdings of the federal courts under Title VII were unduly restrictive and should not be followed in interpreting state and local statutes. Id. at 394-95. Although the city statute used the term "gender" whereas the state statute used the term "sex," the court held that harassment based on the fact an employee changed his sexual status also constituted sex discrimination. Id. at 395-96. Such behavior was similar to harassment based on one's secondary sexual characteristics. Id. at 396.

The Minnesota Human Rights Act is unique because it is one of the only state statutes to include in its definition of sexual orientation, "having or being perceived as having . . . a self- image or identity not traditionally associated with one's biological maleness or femaleness." Minn. Stat. §363.01, subd. 45 (added by L. 1993, c. 22, §§ 1, 2). In Goins v. West Group, 619 N.W.2d 424, 428 (Minn. Ct. App. 2000), this statute was held to include within its protected class an individual who was born male, who changed her legal name to that of a female, and who took female hormones to identify herself as a female, even though she elected not to undergo sexual reassignment surgery. Id. at 426, 428.

We conclude that the reasoning reflected in Goins, Maffei, as well as Price Waterhouse, Schwenk, and Rosa is more closely connected to our own state's historic policy of liberally construing the LAD. Fraser v. Robin Dee Day Camp, 44 N.J. 480, 486 (1965). There is also some New Jersey support for the position that precluding discrimination on the basis of sex also precludes gender discrimination.

In Zalewski v. Overlook Hosp., 300 N.J. Super. 202 (Law Div. 1996), Judge Menza decided that the LAD applied to sexual harassment of a heterosexual male by other heterosexual males when the harassment was based on gender stereotyping. In Zalewski, the plaintiff's coworkers harassed him because they thought he was a virgin. They never suggested his sexual orientation was anything other than heterosexual and there was no evidence that he was homosexual or bisexual. Id. at 203-04. Nevertheless, Judge Menza found a violation and noted that we should not "condone severe sexual harassment of a person because he is perceived or presumed to be less than someone's definition of masculine." Id. at 211.

A generation ago, when Justice Handler served in the Appellate Division, he found that "[t]he evidence and authority which we have examined, however, show that a person's sex or sexuality embraces an individual's gender, that is, one's self- image, the deep psychological or emotional sense of sexual identity and character." M.T. v. J.T., 140 N.J. Super. 77, 86 (App. Div.), certif. denied, 71 N.J. 345 (1976). We agree with Justice Handler that "sex" embraces an "individual's gender," and is broader than anatomical sex. "[S]ex is comprised of more than a person's genitalia at birth." Flynn, supra, 101 Colum. L. Rev. at 415. The word "sex" as used in the LAD should be interpreted to include gender, protecting from discrimination on the basis of sex or gender.

It is incomprehensible to us that our Legislature would ban discrimination against heterosexual men and women; against homosexual men and women; against bisexual men and women; against men and women who are perceived, presumed or identified by others as not conforming to the stereotypical notions of how men and women behave, but would condone discrimination against men or women who seek to change their anatomical sex because they suffer from a gender identity disorder. We conclude that sex discrimination under the LAD includes gender discrimination so as to protect plaintiff from gender stereotyping and discrimination for transforming herself from a man to a woman.

III.

Plaintiff also contends that gender dysphoria is a handicap and a recognized disability under the LAD. It is unlawful to discriminate against an employee because of a handicap "unless the nature and

207

extent of the handicap reasonably precludes the performance of the particular employment." N.J.S.A. 10:5-4.1. The LAD has defined "handicapped" as:

> suffering from physical disability, infirmity, malformation or disfigurement which is caused by bodily injury, birth defect or illness, . . . or from any mental, psychological or developmental disability resulting from anatomical, psychological, physiological or neurological conditions which prevents the normal exercise of any bodily or mental functions or is demonstrable, medically or psychologically, by accepted clinical or laboratory diagnostic techniques. . . .

> [N.J.S.A. 10:5-5(q).]

In this case we are not dealing with any "physical disability, infirmity, malformation or disfigurement which is caused by bodily injury, birth defect or illness." We are dealing with the portion of the statute that provides that a person can be handicapped if they suffer from a "mental, psychological or developmental disability resulting from anatomical, psychological, physiological or neurological conditions which prevents the normal exercise of any bodily or mental functions or is demonstrable, medically or psychologically, by accepted clinical or laboratory diagnostic techniques."

Plaintiff is, however, relying exclusively on the clinical or laboratory diagnostic portion of the definition. She does not argue that transsexualism prevented the normal exercise of any bodily or mental functions. And, according to plaintiff, her condition did not interfere with the adequate performance of her work at the Center. Termination of a "handicapped" employee, whose condition does not prevent the employee from doing her job, is actionable under the LAD. Gimello v. Agency Rent-A-Car Sys., Inc., 250 N.J. Super. 338, 365 (App. Div. 1991).

Therefore, in this case plaintiff asks us to determine whether gender dysphoria is a handicap and protected by the LAD because it is a "mental, psychological or developmental disability resulting from anatomical, psychological, physiological or neurological conditions which . . . is demonstrable, medically or psychologically, by accepted clinical or laboratory diagnostic techniques."

As remedial social legislation, the LAD is deserving of a liberal construction, especially with regard to handicaps. Clowes v. Terminix Int'l, Inc., 109 N.J. 575, 590 (1988); Andersen v. Exxon Co., U.S.A., 89 N.J. 483, 495 (1982). The statutory definition of handicapped under N.J.S.A. 10:5-5(q) is very broad in its scope, Clowes v. Terminix, supra, 109 N.J. at 593, and is not limited to "severe" disabilities. Andersen v. Exxon, supra, 89 N.J. at 494-95. Rather, it prohibits discrimination against those suffering from any disability. Id. at 495.

The parties agree that gender dysphoria is listed in the DSM-IV as a disorder. Defendants argue correctly, however, that this listing is not dispositive for classification as a disability under the LAD. Merely because a condition is a disorder listed in the DSM-IV does not mean it is also a handicap under the LAD. A.B.C. v. XYZ Corp., 282 N.J. Super. 494, 508 (App. Div. 1995) (Petrella, J.A.D., concurring).

A disorder is not necessarily the equivalent of a disease, disability, illness, or defect, especially where these terms carry legal significance. Id. at 507-08 (Petrella, J.A.D., concurring). Moreover, the LAD itself does not preclude discrimination based on conduct. N.J.S.A. 10:5-2.1. In addition, the DSM-IV also cautions that categorization of conditions contained in the manual "may not be wholly relevant to legal judgments, for example, that take into account such issues as individual responsibility, disability determination, and competency." DSM-IV, supra, Cautionary Statement at xxvii.

The Americans with Disabilities Act (ADA) expressly excludes "transvestism, transsexualism, pedophilia, exhibitionism, voyeurism, gender identity disorders not resulting from physical impairments, other sexual behavior disorders." 42 U.S.C.A. §12211(b)(1). That statute also contains a requirement that the impairment be one which substantially limits a major life activity. 42 U.S.C.A. §12102(2)(A). Our own statute does not contain such a restriction. Moreover, our own Legislature has not considered or addressed similar exclusions. A.B.C. v. XYZ, supra, 282 N.J. Super. at 508 n.3 (Petrella, J.A.D., concurring).

Other state courts, however, appear to be split on this issue when construing their own statutes. For example, a Pennsylvania court has concluded that transsexualism is not a disability under the Pennsylvania Human Relations Act because that statute requires that the disability substantially limit a major life activity and because petitioner did not contend that transsexualism affected any bodily function. Holt v. Northwest Pa. Training P'ship Consortium, Inc., 694 A.2d 1134, 1139 (Pa. Commw. Ct. 1997).

A Washington state court, however, has construed gender dysphoria as a handicap under the Washington Law Against Discrimination, finding that it is a medically cognizable and diagnosable condition, that those who suffer from it endure great mental and emotional agony, and that it has a prescribed course of treatment. Doe v. Boeing Co., 846 P.2d 531, 535-36 (Wash. 1993).

An Iowa court reached the contrary conclusion construing its statute which also contains a "major life activity" restriction. Sommers v. Iowa Civil Rights Comm'n, supra, 337 N.W. 2d at 475. The court noted that a person who is anatomically of one sex but psychologically and emotionally of the other sex has a problem that does not necessarily constitute the kind of mental condition that the Legislature intended to be treated as a substantial handicap. Id. at 476. Transsexualism should not ordinarily affect a person's capacity to engage in major life activities. Ibid.

Our problem with the out-of-state cases concluding that gender dysphoria is not a disability is that our statute is very broad and does not require that a disability restrict any major life activities to any degree. In Olson v. Gen. Elec. Astrospace, 966 F. Supp. 312 (D.N.J. 1997), for example, the federal court found that plaintiff's conditions of depression and multiple personality disorder were recognized disabilities under the LAD because they were demonstrable, medically or psychologically, by accepted clinical or laboratory diagnostic techniques, because these ailments were generally understood by the medical profession as diseases, and because the plaintiff had sought legitimate treatment for them. Id. at 315.

Our courts have held that the LAD recognizes as disabilities such conditions as alcoholism, Clowes v. Terminix, supra, 109 N.J. at 593-94; obesity, Gimello v. Agency Rent-A-Car, supra, 250 N.J. Super. at 361-62; and substance abuse, In re Cahill, 245 N.J. Super. 397, 400 (App. Div. 1991). The LAD has thus been broadly and liberally construed to include what otherwise might be termed emotional or mental disorders, in order to eradicate the evil of discrimination in New Jersey. "Employment discrimination due to sex or any other invidious classification is peculiarly repugnant in a society which prides itself on judging each individual by his or her merits." Peper v. Princeton Univ. Bd. of Trs., 77 N.J. 55, 80 (1978).

Gender dysphoria is regarded medically as a "mental disorder occurring in an estimated frequency of 1:50,000 individuals." Cole, Emory, Huang, Meyer, Treatment of Gender Dysphoria, 90 Tex. Med. 68 (1994). Moreover, treatment for the disorder can now "be regarded as accepted medical practice." Ibid. See also Farmer v. Brennan, 511 U.S. 825, 829, 114 S. Ct. 1970, 1975, 128 L. Ed.2d 811, 820 (1994) (transsexualism is a rare psychiatric disorder in which a person feels persistently uncomfortable about his or her anatomical sex and seeks medical treatment including hormonal therapy and surgery to bring about permanent sex change) (citations omitted).

The disorder is recognized within DSM-IV, thus confirming that the condition can be diagnosed by accepted clinical techniques. In fact, the DSM-IV lists four criteria necessary for diagnosing a gender identity

211

disorder. Furthermore, gender dysphoria does not cause violations of the law as does exhibitionism, which was the DSM-IV disorder Judge Petrella struggled with in A.B.C. v. XYZ, supra, 282 N.J. Super. at 506- 09; N.J.S.A. 2C:14-4.

The DSM-IV also notes that each recognized disorder contained within the manual "is associated with present distress (e.g., a painful symptom) or disability (i.e., impairment in one or more important areas of functioning) or with a significantly increased risk of suffering death, pain, disability, or an important loss of freedom." DSM-IV, supra, at xxi. With regard to gender dysphoria specifically, the manual notes that the "disturbance causes clinically significant distress or impairment in social, occupational, or other important areas of functioning." DSM-IV, supra, §302.85 at 537-38. Transsexualism can be accompanied by a profound sense of loathing for an individual's primary and secondary sexual characteristics, which is overwhelming and unalterable. Dr. L. Gooren, An Appraisal of endocrine theories of homosexuality and gender dysphoria. In: Handbook of Sexology vol. 6, 410-24 (Sitsen JMA, Amsterdam, Elsevier Science Publishers 1988). Thus, gender dysphoria is a recognized mental or psychological disability that can be demonstrated psychologically by accepted clinical diagnostic techniques and qualifies as a handicap under the LAD. N.J.S.A. 10:5-5(q).

To establish the first element of a discriminatory discharge case under the LAD, however, an employee must submit proof that he or she was handicapped. Maher v. N.J. Transit Rail Operations, Inc., 125 N.J. 455, 480-81 (1991); Clowes v. Terminix Int'l, Inc., supra, 109 N.J. at 596. Here, the dismissal of plaintiff's complaint was based solely on the motion judge's conclusion that gender dysphoria was not a handicap under the LAD. While we have concluded that gender dysphoria can constitute a handicap, we have problems with the proofs submitted by plaintiff during the summary judgment proceedings.

We note that plaintiff's proofs are not clear regarding the quality and quantity of impairment plaintiff may have suffered from this disorder. While the LAD does not require proof that some major life activity was impaired, plaintiff must suffer a disability. There is some evidence that before the surgery plaintiff's stress increased and her "moods worsened." There is also evidence that before her surgery plaintiff was argumentative and had difficulty controlling her temper. Since the surgery, plaintiff acknowledged experiencing greater "humanity," with her patients noting "how much more open and able to talk to me they are, particularly the adolescents."

In addition, we recognize that as part of her treatment protocol, plaintiff underwent sexual reassignment surgery, a process that most persons would not undertake unless necessary to eliminate great stress or extreme discomfort. Solely from the circumstances of plaintiff's course of treatment, we can infer sufficient impairment of plaintiff's emotional and mental well being to constitute a disability under the LAD. Plaintiff's proofs were adequate to at least raise a factual issue for summary judgment purposes establishing that her condition was a disability under the LAD. Brill v. Guardian Life Ins. Co. of Am., 142 N.J. 520, 540 (1995).

To constitute a handicap, however, the disability must also result "from anatomical, psychological, physiological or neurological conditions which . . . is demonstrable . . . psychologically, by accepted clinical . . . diagnostic techniques. N.J.S.A. 10:5-5(q). The record is completely silent on this issue.

There is an absence of evidence from Dr. Stayton confirming that he diagnosed gender dysphoria in plaintiff, explaining the condition as it manifested itself in plaintiff, and detailing the methods the doctor utilized to diagnose plaintiff. While "[n]othing . . . prevents a medical doctor from testifying as an expert in [her] own case," Carey v. Lovett, 132 N.J. 44, 64 (1993), evidence of her specific disorder and its diagnosis appear to be beyond plaintiff's training and specialty.

While the DSM-IV does detail the elements necessary to diagnose a gender disorder, there has been some criticism of these elements. Dr.

213

Herbert Bower contends, for example, that the classification "neglects a number of diagnostically significant symptoms and characteristics of classical transsexualism." The doctor argues that:

The initially mentioned four criteria omit the overwhelming desire to have the genitalia altered. The symptomatology does not include important features such as masturbation with fantasy of intercourse with a person of the same anatomical gender, occasional arousal during cross-dressing in the initial phase, lack of sexual interest during adolescence, stressful puberty and an essentially normal child rearing process.

[Herbert Bower, The gender identity disorder in the DSMIV classification - a critical evaluation, at http://www.pfc.org.uk/ congress/abstract/abs-005.html.]

Thus, to establish that she is handicapped under the LAD, plaintiff must prove that she had gender dysphoria and that the disorder was diagnosed by "accepted clinical or laboratory diagnostic techniques." N.J.S.A. 10:5-5(q). The record is silent regarding whether the diagnostic technique utilized by Dr. Stayton was "accepted."

The motion judge rejected plaintiff's complaint solely because he believed that gender dysphoria could not be a handicap under the LAD. We disagree with this assessment and reverse on that basis. Because the case must be remanded for trial on plaintiff's gender discrimination claim, we leave plaintiff to her proofs on whether she had gender dysphoria and whether her condition was diagnosed in a fashion sufficient to qualify as a handicap under the LAD.

IV.

Because the matter must be remanded, we briefly consider the other claims raised by this appeal.

A.

Summary judgment was granted the Center for Family Guidance ("CFG") defendants, and plaintiff's complaint was dismissed as to them. According to plaintiff's complaint, defendant CFG was the successor to the Center and was owned by defendant James Varrell, M.D. Defendant Les Pascal was the chief financial officer of CFG. There is nothing in the summary judgment record to support plaintiff's allegation that the CFG defendants refused to hire plaintiff for her gender or any other discriminatory reasons. None of the CFG defendants ever worked with plaintiff, employed plaintiff or were parties to her employment contract. In addition, there is nothing in this record establishing that these defendants uttered any false or defamatory statements about her. Indeed, plaintiff was never involved in any business relationship or transaction with the CFG defendants. Consequently, all of plaintiff's claims against these defendants were properly dismissed.

B.

Plaintiff argues that the court erred in dismissing her claim for breach of contract. Plaintiff acknowledges that her contract permitted West Jersey to terminate her services on ninety-days notice for any reason or no reason. She nevertheless contends that the contract contained a good faith provision, and her written notice of termination also advised that she would be contacted by Cossa to discuss a new contract with Physicians' Associates, the entity which would be assuming control over the Center's program. Thus, plaintiff contends that she reasonably relied on defendants to negotiate with her in good faith leading to a new contract. This is not the kind of good faith breach that is actionable. Noye v. Hoffmann-LaRoche, Inc., 238 N.J. Super. 430, 433 (App. Div.), certif. denied, 122 N.J. 146, 147 (1990). There is no breach of any kind in this case. Nothing in plaintiff's contract required defendants to re-hire her once they chose to terminate her. Also, this claim is nothing more than her LAD claim restated as a common-law contract claim.

215

Plaintiff also argued that there were other provisions of her contract, such as educational leave, equipment requirements and billing procedures that were breached by defendants. As pointed out by defendants, however, plaintiff is unable to demonstrate any compensable loss to her relating to defendants' alleged "breach" of these provisions. Most, if not all, of these alleged "breaches" relate to plaintiff's displeasure regarding the manner in which the Center operated. Consequently, plaintiff's breach of contract claim was correctly dismissed.

C.

Plaintiff argues that the court erred in dismissing her claim for trade libel. Trade libel consists of communications made to a third person of false statements concerning the plaintiff, or plaintiff's property or business. Henry V. Vaccaro Constr. Co. v. A.J. DePace, Inc., 137 N.J. Super. 512, 514 (Law Div. 1975). The communication must be made to a third person, and it must be false and play a material part in inducing others not to deal with plaintiff. Prosser & Keeton on Torts § 128 at 967 (5th ed. 1984). It can include a false statement that plaintiff has gone out of business. Id. at 963. It is also essential that the plaintiff establish damages. Id. at 965.

In such an action brought against a former employer for publishing defamatory information about the employee to prospective new employers, a qualified privilege extends to the defendant who responds in good faith to specific inquiries about the employee's qualifications. Kass v. Great Coastal Express, Inc., 152 N.J. 353, 355-56 (1998). This privilege will be abused if the defendant knows the statement is false or acts in reckless disregard of its truth or falsity, if the publication serves a purpose contrary to the interests of the qualified privilege, or if the statement is excessively published. Id. at 356.

Here, plaintiff's trade libel claim was dismissed on summary judgment, despite the fact that in opposition, plaintiff submitted two affidavits from parents of two patients who alleged that defendants had lied to them about the status of plaintiff's medical license and practice following her termination.

If plaintiff's allegations are true, she has established a prima facie case of trade libel. Whether plaintiff can ultimately prevail on this claim will depend on the proofs plaintiff can marshal regarding defendants' conduct and on whether defendants can validly assert a qualified privilege.

Defendants also argue, however, that plaintiff failed to prove that any patient chose to go elsewhere as a result of what defendants said about her. While plaintiff's damages for this tort appear, at this time, to be nebulous, we believe that plaintiff submitted sufficient opposition to withstand summary judgment. Brill v. Guardian Life Ins. Co. of Am., supra, 142 N.J. at 535.

The affidavits together with plaintiff's deposition testimony lead to a reasonable inference that plaintiff may have suffered some damage from defendants' alleged conduct. Plaintiff's deposition indicated that of the approximate fifty patients who communicated with her after her termination by West Jersey, she retained about half as patients. Thus, plaintiff should be given an opportunity to establish her damages, if any, through further discovery or trial, and we reinstate plaintiff's trade libel claim.

D.

Plaintiff claims that the court erred in dismissing her claims for malicious interference with economic relations and unjust enrichment. These claims were asserted in plaintiff's second complaint, the one she filed right before the court ruled on defendants' motions for summary judgment regarding her first complaint. These claims are based on the same set of facts as plaintiff's trade libel claim.

The West Jersey defendants assert that plaintiff's employment contract provided that all patients treated at the Center and all of their

217

medical records were solely those of West Jersey. Defendants claim that the contract negates any finding that they were unjustly enriched or maliciously interfered with plaintiff's relationships with her patients because none of the patients belonged to plaintiff.

Even if the patients did not "belong" to plaintiff, the contract between West Jersey and plaintiff cannot prevent the patients from seeing any medical professional they choose. If patients who wished to continue their relationships with plaintiff were dissuaded solely because of defendants' malicious or unjust behavior, plaintiff may have valid causes of action.

These claims were rejected by the motion judge because he believed them to be "a repetition, a repackaging of the first complaint" including the trade libel claim, which had been previously dismissed. We are reinstating plaintiff's trade libel claim, and note that alternative or even inconsistent pleading of viable claims is permissible. R. 4:5-6.

We conclude that plaintiff should have the opportunity to seek to amend her first complaint to add counts for unjust enrichment and interference with economic advantage. Assuming that after remand plaintiff moves to amend the complaint, the trial court shall decide whether or not to permit plaintiff to add these claims.

V.

In conclusion, the LAD "was first enacted in 1945. Its purpose is 'nothing less than the eradication' of the cancer of discrimination." Lehmann v. Toys 'R' Us, Inc., 132 N.J. 587, 600 (1993) (citing Fuchilla v. Layman, 109 N.J. 319, 334 (quoting Jackson v. Concord Co., 54 N.J. 113, 124 (1969), cert. denied sub nom., Univ. of Med. & Dentistry of N.J. v. Fuchilla, 488 U.S. 826, 109 S. Ct. 75, 102 L. Ed.2d 51, (1988)). The Legislature's goal is that only "legitimate distinctions between citizens" be made. N.J.S.A. 10:5-3. Distinctions must be made on the basis of merit, rather than skin color, age, sex or gender, or any other measure that obscures a person's individual humanity and worth. This case represents another step toward achieving what has thus far been an elusive goal.

With respect to the West Jersey defendants, we reverse the dismissal of plaintiff's claims for sex discrimination and trade libel and affirm the dismissal of plaintiff's breach of contract claim. We reinstate the sex discrimination and trade libel claims and remand the case for further proceedings. With regard to plaintiff's claim for handicap discrimination, we reverse the dismissal of plaintiff's claim and conclude that gender dysphoria can be a handicap under the LAD. We remand the handicap discrimination claim so plaintiff can attempt, if she wishes, to establish her cause of action in accordance with the guidance we have provided. On remand, plaintiff may seek to amend her complaint to add claims for malicious interference and unjust enrichment, and the trial court shall decide whether to grant or deny this motion. We take no position on the merits of such a motion.

We affirm the dismissal of all claims brought against the CFG defendants.

Affirmed in part, reversed in part and remanded

Julienne Goins v. West Group

Goins v. West Group is a court opinion that discusses the bathroom usage issue. While there are many criticisms of the court's reasoning, any discussion of transgender usage of bathrooms, dressing rooms, locker rooms or shower rooms must take the Goins opinion into account. It should be noted that state or city statutes may also be important to a consideration of these issues.

STATE OF MINNESOTA
IN SUPREME COURT
CX-00-706

SYLLABUS

An employer's designation of employee restroom use based on biological gender is not sexual orientation discrimination in violation of the Minnesota Human Rights Act. Summary judgment of dismissal was properly entered upon the determination that respondent failed to make a prima facie case of impermissible discrimination.

Reversed and judgment reinstated.

Heard, considered and decided by the court en banc.

OPINION

ANDERSON, Russell A., Justice.

West Group (West) has obtained review of a decision of the court of appeals reversing summary judgment entered in its favor and remanding for trial respondent Julienne Goins' claims of discrimination. Goins claims that West discriminated against her based upon her sexual orientation by designating restrooms and restroom use on the basis of biological gender, in violation of the Minnesota Human Rights Act (MHRA), Minn. Stat. § 363.03, subd. 1(2) (2000). Goins also claims that such discrimination created a hostile work environment. We hold that an employer's designation of employee restroom use based on biological gender is not sexual orientation discrimination in violation of the MHRA. We also conclude that Goins has not established a factual basis for the hostile work environment claim. We reverse the court of appeals and reinstate the judgment entered by the district court dismissing Goins' claims.

Respondent Julienne Goins was designated male at birth and given the name Justin Travis Goins, but Goins was confused about that sexual identity throughout much of childhood and adolescence. Since 1994, Goins has taken female hormones and, with the exception of one occasion, has presented publicly as female since 1995. In October 1995, a Texas court granted Goins' petition for a name change as well as a request for a gender change "from genetic male to reassigned female." Goins identifies as transgender or "trans-identified."[1]

In May 1997, Goins began full-time work with West in its Rochester, New York, office. Goins transferred to West's Minnesota facility in Eagan in October 1997. Prior to the actual relocation, Goins visited the Eagan facility and used the employee women's restrooms. A few of West's female employees observed Goins' use of the women's restrooms and, believing Goins to be biologically male, expressed concern to West supervisors about sharing a restroom with a male. This concern was brought to the attention of West's director of human resources who, in turn, discussed the concern with other human resources personnel and legal counsel. West's director of human resources considered the female employees' restroom use complaint as a hostile work environment concern and decided to enforce the policy of restroom use according to biological gender. After considering the options, the director decided that it would be more appropriate for Goins to use either a single-occupancy restroom in the building where she worked but on a different floor or another single-occupancy restroom in another building.

The decision on restroom use was conveyed to Goins by the director of human resources in the morning of her first day of work at the Eagan facility. The director explained that West was attempting to accommodate the conflicting concerns of Goins and the female employees who expressed uneasiness about sharing their restroom with a male. Goins objected, proposing instead education and training regarding transgender individuals so as to allay female coworker concerns. She also refused to comply with the restroom use policy, in protest in part, and continued to use the employee women's restroom closest to her workstation. In November 1997, Goins was threatened with disciplinary action if she continued to disregard the restroom use policy. In January 1998, Goins tendered her resignation, declining West's offer of a promotion and substantial salary increase, and accepted a job offer elsewhere. In her letter of resignation, Goins stated that West's human resources department had treated her in a manner that had caused undue stress and hostility.

Goins subsequently commenced an action in district court, alleging that West had engaged in discrimination based on sexual orientation in the enforcement of a policy that denied her access to the employee women's restroom. Goins further asserted that West's discriminatory treatment, as well as conduct of West employees, created a hostile work environment. The district court granted West's motion for summary judgment, concluding that Goins had failed to make a prima facie case on either claim. On appeal, the court of appeals reversed, concluding that Goins had established a prima facie showing of sexual orientation discrimination and that there were factual allegations with regard to the hostile work environment claim sufficient to raise genuine issues of material fact precluding summary judgment. *Goins v. West Group*, 619 N.W.2d 424, 429-30 (Minn. App. 2000).

Summary judgment is appropriate when the evidence, viewed in the light most favorable to the nonmoving party, shows that there is no genuine issue of material fact and the moving party is entitled to judgment as a matter of law. *Funchess v. Cecil Newman Corp.*, 632 N.W.2d 666, 672 (Minn. 2001); *Rathbun v. W. T. Grant Co.*, 300 Minn. 223, 229, 219 N.W.2d 641, 646 (1974). On appeal from a summary judgment, the reviewing court determines whether there are any genuine issues of material fact and whether the district court erred in its application of the law. *Funchess*, 632 N.W.2d at 672.

I.

The MHRA prohibits sexual orientation discrimination in the workplace. Minn. Stat. § 363.03, subd. 1(2)(c) (2000). The definition of "sexual orientation" includes "having or being perceived as having a self-image or identity not traditionally associated with one's biological maleness or femaleness." Minn. Stat. § 363.01, subd. 41a (2000). The parties agree that Goins consistently presents herself as a woman. Her discrimination claim is predicated on her self-image as a woman that is or is perceived to be inconsistent with her biological gender. Accordingly, for purposes of Goins' discrimination claim, her self-image is inconsistent with her biological gender. *Cf. Winslow v. IDS Life Ins. Co.*, 29 F. Supp. 2d 557, 560 (D. Minn. 1998) (insurance applicant perceived as being disabled has a disability for purposes of the Americans with Disabilities Act).

Employment discrimination may be established under either a disparate impact or disparate treatment theory. *Sigurdson v. Isanti County*, 386 N.W.2d 715, 719 n.1 (Minn. 1986). Goins alleged disparate treatment. When a plaintiff alleges disparate treatment, liability "'depends on whether the protected trait * * * actually motivated the employer's decision.'" *Reeves v. Sanderson Plumbing Prods., Inc.*, 530 U.S. 133, 141 (2000) (quoting *Hazen Paper Co. v. Biggins*, 507 U.S. 604, 610 (1993)). The plaintiff's protected trait must have "'actually played a role in the [employer's decisionmaking] process.'" *Id.* Proof of discriminatory motive is critical in a disparate treatment claim. *International Bhd. of Teamsters v. United States*, 431 U.S. 324, 335 n.15 (1977). Of course, proof of a discriminatory motive may be established by direct evidence. *Hardin v. Stynchcomb*, 691 F.2d 1364, 1369 n.16 (11th Cir. 1982).

Direct evidence of an employer's discriminatory motive shows that the employer's discrimination was purposeful, intentional or overt. *Hardin*, 691 F.2d at 1369 n.16; *Ramirez v. Sloss*, 615 F.2d 163, 168 (5th Cir. 1980) (distinguishing between discrimination which is "relatively open and easy to recognize" and discrimination which must be demonstrated by inference). Courts have found direct evidence of discriminatory motive where a statement or a policy is discriminatory on its face. *See, e.g., Trans World Airlines, Inc. v. Thurston*, 469 U.S. 111, 121 (1985) (finding that a collective bargaining agreement constituted direct evidence of discrimination because the agreement allowed airline captains displaced for any reason other than age to bump a less senior flight engineer); *Febres v. Challenger Caribbean Corp.*, 214 F.3d 57, 61 (1st Cir. 2000) (finding direct evidence of discriminatory motive where manager admitted that age was one of three criteria used to determine which employees would be retained and which would not); *Hardin*, 691 F.2d at 1369 n.16 (finding direct evidence of discrimination where a sheriff stated that he would not consider hiring women for seven open deputy positions). *Cf. Cengr v. Fusibond Piping Systems, Inc.*, 135 F.3d 445, 451-52 (7th Cir. 1998) (finding no direct evidence of discriminatory motive where the employer did not state that termination was based on age and where employer's statements did not relate to his motivation as the decisionmaker in terminating employee).

The court of appeals concluded that Goins "made a prima facie case of direct discrimination under the MHRA by showing that she was denied the use of a workplace facility based on the inconsistency between her self-image and her anatomy." *Goins*, 619 N.W.2d at 429. The evidence, however, was that West's policy of restroom designation and use was based on gender. In that Goins sought and was denied access only to those restrooms designated for women, West's enforcement of that policy was likewise grounded on gender.

Goins does not argue that an employer engages in impermissible discrimination by designating the use of restrooms according to gender. Rather, her claim is that the MHRA prohibits West's policy of designating restroom use according to biological gender, and requires instead that such designation be based on self-image of gender. Goins alleges that West engaged in impermissible discrimination by denying her access to a restroom consistent with her self-image of gender. We do not believe the MHRA can be read so broadly. As the district court observed, where financially feasible, the traditional and accepted practice in the employment setting is to provide restroom facilities that reflect the cultural preference for restroom designation based on biological gender. To conclude that the MHRA contemplates restrictions on an employer's ability to designate restroom facilities based on biological gender would likely restrain employer discretion in the gender designation of workplace shower and locker room facilities, a result not likely intended by the legislature. We believe, as does the Department of Human Rights, that the MHRA neither requires nor prohibits restroom designation according to self-image of gender or according to biological gender. *See Cruzan v. Special Sch. Dist. No. 1,* No. 31706 (Dep't of Human Rights Aug. 26, 1999). While an employer may elect to offer education and training as proposed by Goins, it is not for us to condone or condemn the manner in which West enforced the disputed employment policy. Bearing in mind that the obligation of the judiciary in construing legislation is to give meaning to words accorded by common experience and understanding, to go beyond the parameters of a legislative enactment would amount to an intrusion upon the policy-making function of the legislature. Accordingly, absent more express guidance from the legislature, we conclude that an employer's designation of employee restroom use based on biological gender is not sexual orientation discrimination in violation of the MHRA. [2]

Even though West's restroom policy is permissible under the MHRA, Goins could still establish discriminatory motive by circumstantial evidence. *See Feges v. Perkins Restaurants*, 483 N.W.2d 701, 710 (Minn. 1992); *Sigurdson*, 386 N.W.2d at 720. Disparate treatment claims based on circumstantial evidence are governed by the burden-shifting framework established in *McDonnell Douglas Corp. v. Green*, 411 U.S. 792 (1973).[3] The *McDonnell Douglas* scheme allocates the burden of producing evidence between the parties and establishes the order of presentation of proof. *Reeves*, 530 U.S. at 142. A plaintiff must establish a prima facie case of discriminatory motive. If the plaintiff makes this showing, the burden of production then shifts to the employer to articulate a legitimate, nondiscriminatory reason for its adverse employment action. If the employer articulates such a reason, the plaintiff must then put forward sufficient evidence to demonstrate that the employer's proffered explanation was a pretext for discrimination. *Reeves*, 530 U.S. at 143. The burden of persuasion, however, remains with the plaintiff at all stages. *Id.*

In the context of a discriminatory discharge claim, to establish a prima facie case as that term is used in *McDonnell Douglas*, a plaintiff typically must demonstrate that she "'(1) is a member of [a] protected class; (2) was qualified for the position from which she was discharged; and (3) was replaced by a non-member of the protected class.'" *Hoover v. Norwest Private Mortgage Banking*, 632 N.W.2d 534, 542 (Minn. 2001) (quoting *Feges*, 483 N.W.2d at 711). The *McDonnell Douglas* elements "vary with the circumstances of the alleged discrimination." *Jones v. Frank*, 973 F.2d 673, 676 (8th Cir. 1992) (citing *McDonnell Douglas*, 411 U.S. at 802 n.13).

Under the circumstances presented here, Goins must demonstrate that (1) she is a member of a protected class; (2) she is qualified – which, in the context of the issues presented in this case, means that she must establish that she is eligible to use the restrooms designated for her biological gender; and (3) West denied her access to such a restroom. Under the *McDonnell Douglas* framework, if Goins

227

fails to establish any one of the elements of the prima facie case, no additional analysis is required and West is entitled to dismissal of her claim as a matter of law.

The MHRA prohibits an employer, because of sex or sexual orientation, from discriminating against a person "with respect to * * * conditions, facilities, or privileges of employment."[4] Minn. Stat. § 363.03, subd. 1(2)(c). The MHRA defines "sexual orientation" as including "having or being perceived as having a self-image or identity not traditionally associated with one's biological maleness or femaleness." *Id.* § 363.01, subd. 41a. Goins alleges that she has such a self-image and West does not contend that she is not a member of the class protected by this statutory provision. Accordingly, Goins has successfully made out the first element of her prima facie case.

Having established that she is a member of the class protected by the MHRA, Goins next bears the burden of establishing that she is qualified. As discussed above, West's designation of restroom facilities based solely on biological gender does not violate the MHRA. Thus, to meet that burden, Goins must establish that she was eligible to use the restrooms that West designated for use according to biological gender.[5] On the record before us, she has not done so. As a result, she has failed to make out the second element of her prima facie case under *McDonnell Douglas*. Having failed to establish that she was qualified, no further inquiry is necessary. Goins' disparate treatment sexual orientation discrimination claim fails as a matter of law.

II.

Goins also claims that West created a hostile work environment based on her sexual orientation. To prevail on a hostile work environment claim, a plaintiff must establish that (1) she is a member of a protected group; (2) she was subject to unwelcome harassment; (3) the harassment was based on membership in a protected group; (4) the harassment affected a term, condition or privilege of her employment; and (5) the employer knew of or should have known of the harassment and failed to take appropriate remedial action. *Carter v. Chrysler Corp.*, 173 F.3d 693, 700 (8th Cir. 1999). Even if a plaintiff demonstrates discriminatory harassment, such conduct is not actionable unless it is "so severe or pervasive" as to "'alter the conditions of the [plaintiff's] employment and create an abusive working environment.'" *Meritor Sav. Bank, FSB v. Vinson*, 477 U.S. 57, 67 (1986) (quoting *Henson v. City of Dundee*, 682 F.2d 897, 904 (11th Cir. 1982)). The objectionable environment "must be both objectively and subjectively offensive, one that a reasonable person would find hostile or abusive, and one that the victim did in fact perceive to be so." *Faragher v. City of Boca Raton*, 524 U.S. 775, 787 (1998) (citing *Harris v. Forklift Systems, Inc.*,510 U.S. 17, 21-22 (1993)). In ascertaining whether an environment is sufficiently hostile or abusive to support a claim, courts look at the totality of the circumstances, including the "'frequency of the discriminatory conduct; its severity; whether it is physically threatening or humiliating, or a mere offensive utterance; and whether it unreasonably interferes with an employee's work performance.'" *Faragher*, 524 U.S. at 787-88 (quoting *Harris*, 510 U.S. at 23).

Assuming that the MHRA contemplates a hostile work environment claim based on sexual orientation and that Goins otherwise carried her burden,[6] we find that summary judgment was appropriate. Goins' hostile work environment claim was predicated on allegations that she was the subject of scrutiny, gossip, stares, glares and restrictions on the use of the restroom near her workstation because of her sexual orientation. The restroom policy, as we have concluded, was not based on sexual orientation. As for the remaining allegations, we agree with the district court's conclusion that Goins' claim fails because the alleged conduct of coworkers, however inappropriate, was not of the type of severe or pervasive harassment required to sustain an actionable hostile work environment claim. *See Mendoza v. Borden, Inc.*, 195 F.3d 1238, 1249 (11th Cir. 1999) (supervisor's constant following and staring not sufficiently severe or pervasive); *Gonzales v. Sea-Mar, Inc.*, 99 F. Supp. 2d 753, 755 (E.D. La. 2000) (coworkers' offensive and boorish comments together with glaring insufficient); *Bishop v. Nat'l R.R. Passenger Corp.*, 66 F. Supp. 2d 650, 663-66 (W.D. Pa. 1999) (staring, leering and offensive comments insufficient).

We therefore reverse the court of appeals decision and reinstate judgment for West on all claims.

Reversed and judgment reinstated.

SPECIAL CONCURRENCE

PAGE, Justice (concurring specially).

I concur in the result reached by the court. I write separately to clarify one point with respect to the court's conclusion that Goins has failed to establish that "she is eligible to use the restrooms designated for her biological gender." *Supra* pp. 10-11. To satisfy this element, Goins must establish that she is biologically female. Because she has failed to do so, her disparate treatment discrimination claim fails as a matter of law.

ANDERSON, PAUL H., Justice (concurring specially).

I join in the special concurrence of Justice Page.

---

[1]   Transgender people seek to live as a gender other than that attributed to them at birth but without surgery. Susan Etta Keller, *Operations of Legal Rhetoric: Examining Transsexual and Judicial Identity*, 34 Harv. C.R.-C.L. L. Rev. 329, 332 (1999). Because Goins refers to herself as female, we will refer to her in this opinion using feminine pronouns.

[2]   Nonetheless, in concluding that the MHRA does not cover workplace restroom designation and use according to biological gender or according to the employee's self-image of gender, we by no means imply that workplace restrooms are, in other respects, beyond the coverage of the Act. Typically, workplace restroom discrimination claims have more to do with an employer's obligation to provide appropriate and sanitary facilities. *See, e.g., DeClue v. Central Illinois*

Light Co., 223 F.3d 434 (7th Cir. 2000); *Lynch v. Freeman*, 817 F.2d 380 (6th Cir. 1987). While the MHRA does not go so far as to protect Goins' choice of restroom use, it does protect her right to be provided an adequate and sanitary restroom.

[3]   We adopted the *McDonnell Douglas* framework in *Danz v. Jones*, 263 N.W.2d 395 (Minn. 1978) to analyze disparate treatment claims brought under the MHRA. We often have applied principles developed in Title VII adjudications because of substantial similarities between Title VII and the MHRA. *See, e.g., Sigurdson*, 386 N.W.2d at 719.

[4]   Here, the issue is Goins' use of West's restroom facilities. It is hardly open to debate that the use of employee restrooms qualifies as a condition, facility, or privilege of employment.

[5]   The record is not clear whether Goins was ever denied access to the men's restroom.

[6]   While the MHRA does not explicitly provide for a hostile work environment claim based upon sexual orientation discrimination, a hostile work environment claim may be based upon sexual harassment. Minn. Stat. § 363.01, subd. 41(3). We have recognized that sexual harassment is a form of sex discrimination, *Continental Can Co., Inc. v. State*, 297 N.W.2d 241, 248-49 (Minn. 1980), but we have not recognized sexual harassment as a form of sexual orientation discrimination. The MHRA is to be construed liberally, however, with reference to federal law. Title VII, while not including claims based on sexual orientation discrimination, does include a hostile work environment claim for "discriminatory harassment so severe or pervasive as to alter the conditions of employment and create a hostile working environment." *Carter v. Chrysler Corp*, 173 F.3d 693, 700

(8th Cir. 1999). Goins did not separately plead a hostile work environment claim, but she did allege in her sexual orientation discrimination claim that West created a hostile work environment.

Opilla v. Lucent Technologies

This court opinion specifically discusses the issue of transgender usage of dressing rooms in the context of a sexual harassment claim against a transgender employee and the employer. It suggests that there is not much to fear from lawsuits by female employees for sexual harassment based simply on the presence of transgender employees in a dressing room.

Superior Court of New Jersey,
Appellate Division.

Carolyn OPILLA, Plaintiff-Appellant,
v.
Karen PARKER, Lucent Technologies, Defendants-Respondents,
and
Robert Austin and Corporate Health Fitness Center, [FN1] Defendants.

FN1. Plaintiff is not appealing from the dismissal of her claims against Robert Austin and Corporate Health Fitness Center.

Submitted Sept. 18, 2006.
Decided Sept. 29, 2006.

SYNOPSIS
On appeal from the Superior Court of New Jersey, Law Division, Union County, L-3749-03.
Fernando Iamurri, attorney for appellant.
Epstein, Becker & Green, attorneys for respondents (Maxine H. Neuhauser, of counsel and on the brief; Peter F. Berk, on the brief).

Before Judges LINTNER and S.L. REISNER.

PER CURIAM.

Plaintiff, Carolyn Opilla, appeals from the dismissal on summary judgment of her complaint for sexual harassment and hostile work environment, related common law tort claims, and equal pay discrimination. We affirm.

I

Plaintiff's entire sexual harassment claim, as well as her related claims for hostile work environment, emotional distress and invasion of privacy, stem from one incident. According to plaintiff's proofs, on September 3, 2003, she was using the locker room of an on-premises health center provided by her employer, Lucent Technologies, but operated by a separate corporate entity, Corporate Health Fitness Center. According to plaintiff, one of her co-workers who was a transgendered female entered the women's locker room and stared at plaintiff, who was then dressed only in her underwear. [FN2]

FN2. At the time the incident occurred, this employee had not yet undergone sex reassignment surgery, although she had been taking hormone therapy, identified herself as a woman, and dressed as a woman. She had sex reassignment surgery in October 2003. In *Enriquez v. W. Jersey Health Sys.,* 342 *N.J.Super.* 501 (App .Div.), *certif. denied,* 170 *N.J.* 211 (2001), we discussed at length the condition known as "gender dysphoria" and concluded that discrimination against transgendered persons is a form of prohibited sex discrimination and, depending on the proofs, may also constitute handicap discrimination. *Id.* at 526-27. Plaintiff's proofs in this case do not require us to address any right of the transgendered employee to use the women's locker room.

When asked how long the incident lasted, plaintiff testified that "[i]t could have been a minute. It felt like a long time." The transgendered co-worker left after another employee entered the locker room and told her to go change on the "other side."

Plaintiff immediately complained to the manager of the Health Center, who told her that he "didn't know what to do about the situation. He didn't know how to direct which locker room [the co-worker] should go into." But he promised plaintiff that he would check with Human Resources and "ask them what he should do."

After plaintiff complained about this episode to the Health Center manager, there were no further incidents. Plaintiff did not report the incident to her supervisor at Lucent or to Lucent's Human Resources department. She testified that she did tell a Lucent manager, Matt Olenowski, who was not her supervisor, that she "was embarrassed and upset and felt sick over the whole situation." He suggested that she go home early, which she did, although she did not tell her female supervisor why she was leaving early.

Plaintiff did not follow up with the Health Center manager to find out what Human Resources had advised him to do in the future. Plaintiff continued to use the Health Center, and never saw the co-worker there again.

Plaintiff's equal pay claim is based on her contentions that in 2001 she became a Lab Planner, and in that capacity she took over the job functions of a male employee, Dennis Matera, and a female employee, Pat Valdez, but was not given a pay raise or a promotion to a management position. She contended that since she was performing job functions previously performed by Matera, who was a manager, she should have been given a job title and pay equivalent to his. However, at her deposition, plaintiff admitted that she did not know Matera's educational background, job title, salary, salary grade, or work history at Lucent. She did not "recall" whether she assumed all of Matera's job duties or only some of them. She also did not know Valdez's salary. She further admitted that when she was being considered for the Lab Planner position, she told her supervisor that "I didn't know how to do the job and I didn't know the technical side of it." [FN3]

FN3. We infer from the record that plaintiff did not depose Matera or obtain any discovery from Lucent concerning his salary or job duties.

237

In support of her equal pay claim, plaintiff submitted a certification from Olenowski. In the certification, Olenowski claimed to have "interfaced with" plaintiff in his capacity as a manager, although he did not claim that he supervised her. He claimed to know that she took over Matera's job and that she did not receive equal pay although she was performing the same duties as Matera. At her deposition, plaintiff admitted that she did not "recall" ever working for Olenowski, that he never performed a review of her work performance, that he never worked with Matera and that he never supervised anyone holding Matera's job title. She testified that Olenowski was laid off from Lucent shortly before she was.

Plaintiff's complaint included a claim of retaliatory discharge, but at her deposition she indicated that she and other employees were "laid off" from Lucent and that she was not suing Lucent "for anything" related to her discharge. Plaintiff has not pursued the claim on appeal.

Relying on *Lehmann v. Toys 'R' Us, Inc.,* 132 *N.J.* 587 (1993), the motion judge concluded that the one incident in the Health Center was not "severe or ... pervasive enough to make a reasonable female believe that the conditions of employment were altered and the working environment was hostile or abusive." Hence, she dismissed the discrimination complaint against Lucent. Citing *Tyson v. Cigna Corp.,* 918 *F.Supp.* 836 (D.N.J.1996), *aff'd,* 149 *F.*3d 1165 (3d Cir.1998), the judge also concluded that since the transgendered employee was not a supervisor, plaintiff could not maintain a hostile work environment claim against her under the Law Against Discrimination (LAD), *N.J.S.A.* 10:5- 12. The judge also concluded that plaintiff's common law tort claims against her employer Lucent, and against her co-worker, were barred by the Worker's Compensation Act.

With respect to the equal pay claim, the judge granted summary judgment based on plaintiff's failure to establish what Matera's salary was, compared to plaintiff's salary, and her failure to establish what his job duties were so as to prove that she was performing the same duties at a lower rate of pay. [FN4]

FN4. We have been able to glean the judge's findings from the record and we agree with her conclusions. But we note for future reference that

hearing the attorneys' arguments first and then setting forth findings and conclusions produces a clearer record, as opposed to interspersing judicial conclusions among questions to the attorneys and their responses and arguments.

II

On this appeal, plaintiff raises the following issues:

POINT I: SINCE THE TRIAL COURT MISAPPLIED THE STANDARD OF REVIEW ON THE MOTION FOR SUMMARY JUDGMENT THE ORDER GRANTING SUMMARY JUDGMENT SHOULD BE REVERSED.

POINT II: SINCE THE COURT FOUND ERRONEOUSLY THAT THE PLAINTIFF'S COMMON LAW CAUSES OF ACTION AGAINST LUCENT SHOULD BE DISMISSED BASED UPON THE WORKERS' COMPENSATION REMEDY THE ORDER SHOULD BE REVERSED.

POINT III: SINCE A GENUINE ISSUE OF MATERIAL FACT EXISTS CONCERNING WHETHER PLAINTIFF RECEIVED DISPARATE PAY AND WAS OTHERWISE DISCRIMINATED AGAINST BECAUSE OF HER GENDER THE ORDER GRANTING SUMMARY JUDGMENT MUST BE DENIED.

Having reviewed the entire record, we conclude that plaintiff's appellate contentions are completely without merit and do not warrant discussion in a written opinion. *R.* 2:11-3(e)(1)(E). We add only the following comments.

Our review of a trial court's grant of summary judgment is de novo, employing the *Brill* standard. *Prudential Prop. & Cas. Ins. Co. v. Boylan,* 307 *N.J.Super.* 162, 167 (App.Div.), *certif. denied,* 154 *N.J.*

608 (1998); *Brill v. Guardian Life Ins. Co. of Am.,* 142 *N.J.* 520, 540 (1995).

Employing this standard, we agree with the motion judge that the one brief and isolated incident on which plaintiff rests her LAD complaint was not enough to create a hostile work environment. Plaintiff's proofs fall far short of establishing conduct "that a reasonable woman would consider sufficiently severe or pervasive to alter the conditions of employment and create an intimidating, hostile, or offensive working environment." *Lehmann, supra,* 132 *N.J.* at 603. In light of plaintiff's patently insubstantial claim, we need not address the issues of whether the incident would not have occurred "but for" plaintiff's gender, *ibid.* (emphasis omitted), or whether the transgendered employee had a right to use the women's changing room prior to having sex reassignment surgery.

We also agree with the motion judge that the exclusive remedy provision of the Workers' Compensation Act, *N.J.S.A.* 34:15-8, bars plaintiff's common law tort claims. The facts as plaintiff presented them do not fall within the "intentional wrong" exception to the Act. *Ibid; see Laidlow v. Hariton Mach. Co., Inc .,* 170 *N.J.* 602, 623-24 (2002).

Finally, we conclude that plaintiff's equal pay claim was properly dismissed. She failed to present the most basic evidence needed to compare her salary, qualifications and job responsibilities to those of the male employee to whom she compared herself. *See Bitsko v. Main Pharmacy, Inc.,* 289 *N.J.Super.* 267, 272 (App.Div.1996).

Affirmed.

About the Author

Dr. Weiss has a J.D. and a Ph.D. in Law, Policy & Society. Currently Associate Professor of Law and Society at Ramapo College of New Jersey, she has conducted research involving hundreds of companies and public agencies that have adopted "gender identity" policies. She publishes a popular blog on the subject of Transgender Workplace Diversity, and has published several articles on the subject of gender identity, which may be found at her Ramapo College website.

Dr. Weiss is also Principal Consultant for Jillian T. Weiss & Associates, a consulting firm that works with organizations on transgender workplace diversity issues. She consults with corporations, law firms, diversity trainers and governmental organizations regarding training, policy development and communications strategies in the area of gender transition. Dr. Weiss has worked successfully with Fortune 500 companies and large public agencies during the past few years. Her work has been featured in news stories by the Associated Press, the Society for Human Resource Management, Workforce Management Magazine, and HR Executive Magazine.